Giovanni Pierluigi da Palestrina

The Style of Palestrina and the Dissonance

By
Knud Jeppesen

With an Introduction by
Edward J. Dent

Dover Publications, Inc.
Mineola, New York

Bibliographical Note

This Dover edition, first published in 1970 and reprinted in 2005, is an unabridged republication, with corrections, of the second revised and enlarged edition originally published in 1946 by Oxford University Press.

International Standard Book Number

ISBN-13: 978-0-486-44268-6
ISBN-10: 0-486-44268-3

Manufactured in the United States by Courier Corporation
44268302   2013
www.doverpublications.com

Introduction

Palestrina is a composer who has suffered much from indiscriminate admiration. His name is surrounded by a thick mass of tradition and legend which scientific research has only recently begun to clear away. Ecclesiastical interest has exalted his music to a plane on which the listener is expected not to criticize but to adore. For two hundred years pedagogues have invoked his name as the model of pure counterpoint, but it is seldom that they have taken the trouble to make a careful study of his works in order to see whether their conventional rules were in accordance with the master's actual practice.

This book of Dr. Jeppesen's approaches Palestrina in a strictly scientific spirit. It is not a life of Palestrina, nor even a comprehensive study of his works; it sets out merely to investigate Palestrina's treatment of dissonance. But the study of dissonance in Palestrina involves the study of almost every element that contributes to his general style, and that study further involves a consideration of his predecessors and a consideration of the psychological principles underlying all musical composition. English readers are as a rule repelled rather than attracted by books which display immense erudition. But Dr. Jeppesen's vast learning is no empty show. His overflowing footnotes are not the results of mere ant-like industry. Every one of them suggests a train of new thought; every reference points to some book or article which one ought to read, some principle which one ought to follow up in the hopes of getting a step or two nearer to the solution of the ultimate mystery of musical expression. From Dr. Jeppesen's casual illustrations and comments the student of musical history will derive a far more illuminating view of mediaeval music than is to be found in many professed studies of that remote and difficult subject. The practical musician who wishes to perform some work of Palestrina may learn much that is new as regards its interpretation.

Teachers and students of counterpoint and composition will do well to read this book and devote careful study to its arguments. It is gratifying to find that Dr. Jeppesen regards Mr. R. O. Morris's "Contrapuntal Technique in the XVIth Century" as by far the best book which has been written on the subject. He is not always in agreement with Mr. Morris, and it may shock the English reader to be told that the English composers of Palestrina's period, like others in Northern countries, were considerably behind their times. Nevertheless, Dr. Jeppesen does full justice to the earlier English influences on mediaeval music; and the more carefully one reads his book, the more deeply one is convinced of his sympathetic insight into the human and expressive aspects of the composers whom he anatomizes.

Edward J. Dent.

Author's Note to the 2nd Edition

I have but little to say of this new edition, since I have not found occasion to alter my original exposition on any essential point. But since the first publication there have of course appeared various kinds of literature, both practical and theoretical, which I have been glad to use and embody in my exposition. Further I have completely revised the book with the result that I have made several small emendations, alterations or additions. Finally I have added at last some observations on the treatment in Palestrina of hidden consecutives which seem to me to be psychologically related to dissonances, and consequently will form a suitable supplement to this exposition.

Unfortunately the original translator of the book, Mrs. Margaret Hamerik, died some years ago, but I owe thanks to Miss Annie I. Fausbøll whose assistance I have had for the linguistic alterations and additions.

Finally I should like to express my thanks to the publisher, and to the Rask Ørsted Foundation with whose financial support I have been honoured for the publication of this new edition.

Table of Contents

Table of Abbreviations

M. f. M. = Monatshefte für Musikgeschichte, publ. by the "Gesellschaft für Musikforschung", edited by Robt. Eitner. 37th annual series, 1869—1905, Berlin, Trautwein; Leipzig, Breitkopf & Härtel.

Obr. I—V. = Werke van Jacob Obrecht, uitgegeven door Prof. Dr. Johannes Wolf, Amsterdam, Johannes Müller; Leipzig, Breitkopf & Härtel 1908. — Missen.

Obr. VI. = Motetten.

Obr. VII. = Wereldlijke Werke.

Oldh = Old Hall Manuscript, transcribed and edited by A. Ramsbotham. Vol. I—III. The Plainsong & Mediaeval Music Society, London 1933—38.

P. = "Pierluigi da Palestrinas Werke", Leipzig, Breitkopf & Härtel 1862—1903, 33 volumes.

Pal. m. = Paléographie musicale. Solesmes and Tournai, 1889—

Ph. St. = Philosophische Studien, publ. by W. Wundt, Leipzig, Engelmann, 1883—1902.

Ps. St. = Psychologische Studien, publ. by W. Wundt, Leipzig and Berlin, Engelmann, 1905—17.

R. M. = Hugo Riemann: Geschichte der Musiktheori, Leipzig, Hesse, 2. Aufl. 1920.

S. I. M. = Sammelbände der internationalen Musikgesellschaft, Leipzig, Breitkopf & Härtel, 1899—1914.

St. z. M. = Studien zur Musikwissenschaft, supplement of the "Denkm. der Tonk. in Österreich", Vol. I—VI. Vienna, Artaria; Leipzig, Breitkopf & Härtel, 1913—19. Vol. VII. Vienna, Universal edition 1920.

Tr. I. = "Sechs Trienter Codices", Denkm. der Tonk. in Österreich. Series VII. Vienna, Artaria, 1900.

Tr. II. = "Sechs Trienter Codices", Denkm. der Tonk. in Österreich, series XI. 1. Vienna, Artaria, 1904.

Tr. III. = "Sechs Trienter Codices", Denkm. der Tonk. in Österreich, series XIX. 1. Vienna, Artaria; Leipzig, Breitkopf & Härtel, 1912.

Tr. IV. = "Sechs Trienter Codices", Denkm. der Tonk. in Österreich, series XXVII. 1. Vienna, Universal edition 1920.

V. f. M. = Vierteljahrschrift für Musikwissenschaft, Breitkopf & Härtel, 1885—94.

Z. f. M. = Zeitschrift für Musikwissenschaft, Breitkopf & Härtel, Leipzig 1918—35.

Z. f. Ps. = Zeitschrift für Psychologie und Physiologie der Sinnesorgane, Leipzig, Barth 1890—1906.

Z. I. M. = Zeitschrift der internationalen Musikgesellschfat, Leipzig, Breitkopf & Härtel 1899—1914.

Quotations from the works of Josquin des Prés which may occur in this treatise are cited, where no other source is indicated, from Suppl. Mus. Nr. 1556 and 1578 in the National Library of Vienna. As a great part of the works of Josquin d. P. are, up to the present time, not available in modern editions, I have depended mostly upon these manuscript scores of A. W. Ambros (comprising all the printed masses and quite a number of motets of Josquin). This course, however, required a constant comparison with the older printed part-editions. In the archives of the papal chapel in Rome are found the following works, which have been scored by the author:

Andreas de Sylva: Missa (Codex 45).
Costanzo Festa: Missa de B. M. V. (Codex 26).
    „   „   Missa super "Amis des que" (Codex 26).
    „   „   Credo super "Solemnitas gloriosae" (Codex 57).
    „   „   Hymne: "Qui condolens" (Codex 18).
Ferabosco: Motette "Ascendens Christus" (Codex 54).

In giving the musical quotations, four figures are generally employed. For instance, P. I, 124, 3, 1 means: Palestrina's works, 1st volume, page 124, staff 3, bar 1. If the sign + occurs before the last figure, it signifies that the bars should be counted backwards from right to left. Thus 4, + 2 would therefore mean the 4th staff, the next to the last bar. A "d" placed after a quotation shows that it is taken from a work of whose authenticity there may be a doubt.

Preface

This book must be regarded as being merely of a preparatory nature, a preliminary treatise upon the history of dissonance treatment. Oddly enough this subject, though generally conceded as being among the most important for musical research, has not yet been taken up in any serious, scientific way. That musical scholars up to the present time have refrained from entering this field of work may be partially attributed to the lack of sources. What is needed here, first of all, is really representative selection (as complete as possible) of polyphonic musical works of all epochs in new editions.

The realization of this condition lies a long way in the future,[1] but the energetic manner in which modern "Denkmäler" work has gradually been carried on makes it already possible to begin preparatory research along this line with tolerable security. Preliminary studies are altogether, or at least for the most part, wanting. Gratitude is, however, due to the great A. W. Ambros, who in his "History of Music" touches incidentally upon this subject in such a manner as to arouse keen interest in it. Hugo Riemann in his "Geschichte der Musiktheorie" also contributes some information, but otherwise there does not exist much of importance.[2] Here and there may be found some scattered items

---

[1] Especially perceptible is the want of sufficient material to throw light upon the important harmonic-stabilizing process which occurred in English music about the year 1400, (although the "Old-Hall" manuscript has now, fortunately, been published in full). There is also great need of enlightenment concerning the transition from Netherland to Italian style, which is a matter of deep interest for the progress of musical scholarship. The works of artists such as Costanzo Festa, Willaert, Giovanni Animuccia should be seriously taken under investigation.

[2] As a valuable exception may be mentioned Glen Haydon: The evolution of the six-four chord (Berkeley, California 1933).

concerning dissonance treatment, most frequently in prefaces to new editions of older musical works, also relatively often in critical studies upon style where the characteristic signs of the different epochs are explained. It is noticeable, however, that these remarks are almost exclusively based upon a modern theoretical point of view; as a rule they concern the trespassing of the tenets of more recent text-books, (false relations, consecutive fifths, etc.) Seldom is there any attempt to regard matters in their historic continuity, to consider them in connection with temporal assumptions. This may be said of the entire didactic literature founded upon Johann Joseph Fux's famous "Gradus ad Parnassum", which in its turn is based upon Italian contrapuntal works of the 16th and 17th centuries. This literature can scarcely be blamed for being void of the genetic point of view, since its office was merely of a practical pedagogic nature. But on the other hand there are good grounds for criticizing its relation to the basis of style, which, as Fux himself makes perfectly clear, is the music of Palestrina. To this art it has but slight relation.

Altogether the contributions of the musical theorists to the history of the dissonance must only be accepted with careful reservations. The history of musical theory and the history of musical style are far from being identical. On the contrary we must take into account the constantly recurring mistakes of the theorists with regard to the description of style. These inaccuracies may be traced to certain sources of error, among the principal of which the following may be mentioned:

1. An inclination that is common to these writers to theorize on their own account (speculative methods, an exaggerated tendency to systematize).

2. The moment of inertia which causes the theorists to transfer rules from older textbooks to new without proper critical revision.

3. Inability of the theorists, when describing the practices of past times, to discriminate between these and the elements of style typical of their own contemporaries, (which was the case with Fux).

4. Pedagogic considerations, which often tend to a simplification or relaxation of the set of rules belonging to the style, but often also to a stricter rendering of these rules "for the sake of exercise".

All of this does not, however, hinder the musical theorists, provided due criticism be exercised by the reader, from contributing valuable material to musical history, or from putting us on the track of new facts and assisting in the establishment of these.

The reason that induced the author to choose Palestrina's works especially as his first field of investigation was his conviction that, in attacking a subject of such dimensions as the history of dissonance treatment, it is necessary to start from a point as central and as elevated as possible, from which the outlook is wide, and yet having close connections with the rest of the material.

In this respect Palestrina's production undoubtedly fulfils the requirements better than any other music. His works might appropriately be called a vast summary of the musical development of the preceding centuries. In them are united all the various currents,—some that spring from sources in a deeply-buried past, traceable through the more primitive phases of polyphony back to the Gregorian age. And it is finally in his music that we inherit all the forms of dissonance treatment that have been handed down from generation to generation, from France to England, from England to the Netherlands, from the Netherlands to Italy,—all fully represented, simplified, refined. He represents a turning-point in the history of dissonance treatment. Until this epoch the rules became stricter and stricter, after it they gradually relaxed.

Also with regard to later music, that after the transition of style about the year 1600, Palestrina's music affords the most advantageous starting-point. An ear, accustomed to the finest shades of dissonance treatment, is more peculiarly sensitive to a quick perception and appreciation of elements, wherein the newer music differs from that of Palestrina, than if we proceed, conversely, through the music of Mozart, Scarlatti, Carissimi and Cavalli back to the beginning of the 17th century.

On the whole it is quite evident that the characteristics of any period of art which offers a contrast or has undergone radical change, will stand out in boldest relief when compared with its immediate predecessor. Passing from an absorbing study of Gregorian music to primitive polyphonic forms, from the style of Palestrina to the commencement of dramatic music, or from Bach's polyphony to the classical art of Vienna, would be the best manner of proceeding for recognizing immediately the essential peculiarities of the new style. A chronologically ascending method would be the wise course in this case, while it would certainly be less suitable if the question were of an accurate account of the evolution of a period of style. If, for instance, we would solve the problem before us, and (contrary to the manner recommended in this treatise) begin the experiment with the first polyphonic period, advancing therefore to Palestrina, we should soon become involved in a wilderness of dissonance forms, hopelessly confusing to the mind. It would only be possible with the greatest difficulty to distinguish between essential and non-essential forms—it being most suitable in this connection to define the essential as those in which the idiomatic vitality has been preserved until the climax of the style, and which therefore are most easily recognizable there. Likewise the errors of writing and printing, that threaten the explorer into these little frequented regions at every step, will best be discovered by comparison with the typical forms belonging to the culmination of the style.

Other reasons of a more practical nature also conduced to the choice of Palestrina as a starting-point, especially the significance of this music for theoretical instruction in composition. It is an undeniable fact that the contrapuntal technique of the 16th century is to-day still regarded as the ideal, the model, of nearly every serious, scientific and practical study of this branch of art. At the same time, the rules of textbooks and those regulating the practice of 16th century composers are so little in accord with each other, that an early comparative revision is most necessary.

The history of the strict counterpoint textbook may be briefly given here.

The Italian musical theorists of the 16th century were naturally the first who attempted to compile the rules of Palestrina's style. One of the greatest of these, Gioseffo Zarlino, in his book "L'istitutioni harmoniche" (1558) treats of this style—the mode of expression already developed before Palestrina's appearance—yet scarcely of Palestrina's own production. What has been said here of "L'istitutioni harmoniche" may also be applied to Nicolo Vicentino's independently and clearly conceived work, "L'antica musica ridotta alla moderna prattica", (1555); also, even if to a less degree, to several later works, such as Oratio Tigrini's "Compendio della musica" (1588) and Gio. Maria Artusi's "L'arte del contraponto" (1598). But the first work of a similar monumental character to Zarlino's book appeared with Pietro Cerone's "El Melopeo" (1613), which especially deals with Palestrina style. Cerone, though Italian by birth, was attached to the Court at Madrid for many years as a singer, and wrote his book in the Spanish language. He was an extremely close observer with a keen eye for details. While he was not endowed with Zarlino's reflective gifts, and therefore seldom attempts to explain the reasons for his rules, he compensates for this lack by not falling into the temptation to remodel these rules in their practice, which Zarlino very often does. He had a fine sense of realities, and is able to perceive and reproduce shades of expression that escaped the other theorists of the time. When it is remembered that he treats especially of Palestrina's compositions, it will be readily understood that his work is of unusual value to investigators of style in later 16th century music.

In the following period, from about 1630, the relation to Palestrina was temporarily weakened, which fact is also evident in the theoretical works that appeared during the last half of the century, among which the most prominent are Angelo Berardi's "Documenti armonici" (1687) and "Miscellanea musicale" (1689); also Gio. Maria Bononcini's "Musico prattico" (1673) should be mentioned among this class. The publication in 1725 of the famous textbook "Gradus ad Parnassum", by the Austrian Johann Joseph Fux, marks the return to Palestrina as the standard of theoretical instruction. Fux's book is written in the form of conversations between the pupil, Joseph, and his teacher, Aloysius. The last-mentioned symbolizes "jenes vortreffliche Licht in der Musik, den Prenestinus, dem ich alles, was ich in dieser Wissenschaft weiss, zu danken habe!"[1] However, Fux is under obligations not alone to Palestrina but also to Berardi and Bononcini, from whom he borrows 17th century rules as well as the contrapuntal "species"; these he, with fine pedagogic instinct, firmly and practically systematizes so that they form a pleasant contrast to the circumstantial and planless arrange-

---

[1] Lorenz Mizler's German edition af "Gradus", Leipzig 1742.

ments of his predecessors.[1] It is therefore all the more to be regretted that he fails to distinguish clearly between the technical idioms of Palestrina's style and the peculiar characteristics of the style of his own contemporaries. Notwithstanding these drawbacks, we are indebted to Fux for his practical skill and correct judgment concerning the basis of contrapuntal instruction, while his contribution upon the subject of style is of more problematic value. The errors into which Fux falls, whether owing to the too limited amount of material at his disposal, or to his inability to free himself from the influences of the 18th century, nearly all appear still uncorrected in the new 19th century editions of his "Gradus". This remark may be extended to include Heinrich Bellermann's "Der Contrapunkt" (1862) and Michael Haller's "Kompositionslehre für polyphonen Kirchengesang" (1891) as well as to works which, even if founded upon Fux, are yet of a more independent nature than the two just named, as for instance: Joh. Georg Albrechtberger's "Gründliche Anweisung zur Komposition" (1790); Cherubini's "Cours de Contrepoint et de Fugue"; S. W. Dehn's "Lehre vom Contrapunkt, dem Canon und der Fuge" (1859); Ludwig Bussler's "Der strenge Satz" (1877); William Rockstro's "The Rules of Counterpoint" (1882); Prout's "Counterpoint" (1890) and Kitson's "The Art of Counterpoint" (1907).

The first writer who demanded a revision of contrapuntal rules regarded from a critical standpoint of style was Franz Nekes, who in an important criticism of Haller's "Kompositionslehre" appearing in the Gregoriusblatt (1891-1893), found occasion to contribute some valuable matter about Palestrina style. A promising beginning was made here, which, however, up to the present moment has not been continued. Wilhelm Hohn in his textbook, "Der Kontrapunkt Palestrinas und seiner Zeitgenossen", ("Sammlung Kirchenmusik" published by Karl Weinmann, 1918), has derived practical methods of teaching from Nekes and has personally added some observations of consequence about voice-grouping, but nothing whatever on dissonance treatment.

---

[1] Fux's "species" go back at any rate to Banchieri's "Cartella" (1614). [Refer to Zacconi's "Prattica di musica" 1622, pages 75 and 230]. Rudimentary tendencies to the "species" system may, however, be found already in Zarlino, (see Kurth's "Grundlagen des linearen Kontrapunkt" 1917, page 114).

Peter Griesbacher too treats the Palestrina style quite freshly and minutely in his comprehensive work, "Kirchenmusikalische Stilistik und Formenlehre", (I-IV, 1912-16), yet omits any mention of the genetic, historic relations of the dissonance. The same omission is noticed in the book of R. O. Morris, "Contrapuntal Technique in the Sixteenth Century", (Oxford 1922) which, notwithstanding, seems to me the best single treatise hitherto published about 16th century music.[1]

---

[1] I may, perhaps, permit myself to add that I have, some years after the first impression of this book, made an attempt to write a textbook on what I consider the true principles of Palestrina style. An English edition of this book: "Counterpoint, the polyphonic vocal Style of the Sixteenth Century" was published by Glen Haydon (Prentice-Hall, Inc., New York 1939).

Introduction

Music is, in its own way, a language. This sentence without doubt expresses one of the most important principles of modern musical science, whether the investigator recognizes it instinctively or not, and has the following natural consequence: the task of the musical historian must deal primarily with the history of this language.

The background against which such a task should be considered is of a psychological nature, viz: the projection of the human into the musical. The way to the solution of this problem leads from without inward, seeking behind the notes upon the page their deeper psychological contents.

The usage of musical language in different historical periods must first of all be made definitely clear by means of empiric-descriptive methods.[1] The next step should be, through comparison of variants of homogeneous forms of language—whether taken from contemporary or from historically separated periods—to indicate and fix common qualities, which with certainty can be supposed to possess the essential accentuations of these forms. The material thus obtained may then serve as a basis upon which to build up the laws of the language, the laws of musical evolution. These, psychologically translated, finally develop into certain regulations and directions of will—the hidden force behind these laws—which are of the utmost significance, music being perhaps the most susceptible and sensitive medium through which the human spirit ever found expression,—an invaluable material for anthropologists. Only a discipline such as that here outlined can

---

[1] In other words, the history of style, according to the standard set by Guido Adler in his books: "Der Stil in der Musik" and "Methode der Musikgeschichte", fundamental works of more recent musical history.

rightfully claim the name of Musical Psychology. The branch of science which is so called at present deals with the problem in a rather one-sided, stationary way, the objects of investigation being mostly now-living persons in their relations to musical matters, while the method of research sketched above—really historical in method and viewpoint—requires a material comprising all epochs. Its leading purpose is the pursuit of the genetic in its course, its fundamental axiom being that no deeper insight can be gained without comparing the present with the past. Therefore it is not sufficient merely to understand the manner in which modern men listen to music, but to ascertain as nearly as possible the attitude of the listener of the different historical periods in question—for the human spirit can only be acutely comprehended when considered with regard to its development in the course of time.

Entering the field of musical research work with these premises, the investigator will find an infinity of subjects awaiting solution, of which a few principal ones may be mentioned, as for instance: the two Dimensions (Homophony and Polyphony), Consonance and Dissonance, Tonality, Imitation, Variation, Cantus firmus, Ornamentation, etc.,—problems of which any single one might occupy a generation of investigators without being even approximately exhausted.

That the treatment of the dissonance was chosen as the special object of historical investigation in this work is due to the author's conviction that the attitude towards accent is the decisive point in determining the quality of expression of the different musical epochs—the fact that the dissonance forms one of the most important "accent-rousing" factors giving it a place among the most expressive and, from a historical point of view, most decisively fateful elements of style. To cite a practical example which may throw light upon the significance of the dissonance, the Cantus of the two-part Motet by Orlandus Lassus "Oculus non vidit" begins as follows:

O - cu - lus non vi - - dit

The melody is of distinguished bearing and well-balanced structure, typical of this epoch of beautiful progressions. It glides along peace-

fully at its own ease, reposeful, unconscious and unaffected by the surroundings. Its expression is characterized by simplicity and nobility,
which is in no way altered when treated in several parts, either polyphonically, as in Lassus:

or in a more harmonic arrangement:

In both cases the expressional character of the melody remains the
same as if executed in unison. The question is, substantially, one of
degree, of a fuller or richer expression of the same thing.

Quite otherwise is the result if the free dissonance is applied, a
mode of treatment, however, which would be historically as well as
musically a crime, whose commission here is only justified by the
purpose of a clearer explanation:

Immediately the whole character is changed. The former calmness
and innocence give way to a passionateness restrained only with dif-

ficulty under the quiet melodic surface. All is now tension, vibration, conscious volition, and this great alteration is due solely to the influence of the dissonance, which is without doubt one of the most potent expressional factors in music on the whole.

The truth of this assertion is also borne out historically. The most radical expressional change that ever occurred in the evolution of music, the transition to the opera, to the "passionate" music introduced in Italy towards the end of the 16th century, is really and primarily based upon a revision of the relation to the dissonance. Monteverdi, one of the leaders of the new era, baptizes the young art (which employs the free treatment of the dissonance) "la seconda practica" in contradistinction to "la prima practica",—the music of Palestrina, which maintains a strict yet delicate command of the dissonant element not equalled in any other epoch.

Musical people of that day thoroughly understood that the dissonance is the critical turning-point of style. It was therefore not accidental that Monteverdi's dissonance treatment particularly should be severely and bitterly attacked by Giovanni Artusi, a Canon of Bologna. Artusi, who was certainly neither narrow-minded nor pedantic, but on the contrary a learned and prudent man, could not understand or sympathize with the trend of the young 17th century; what he did understand, however, was that the danger that threatened the old music proceeded from the new dissonance treatment. The music of the Palestrina era is what it is because of its covenant with the dissonance; the breaking of this covenant meant the annihilation of that ancient art which Artusi loved with all his heart.

These remarks may suffice to emphasize the significance of this problem of the dissonance. Having thus briefly outlined the design of the present work, the question may arise as to where the place of the genius may be in a plan which in so high a degree contemplates the collective, the compact. The answer to this query must be, that the genius is the great language-renewer. His utterance first of all commands our attention. He speaks not alone for his contemporaries, but he also speaks more forcefully and more truthfully than any one else. We must have faith in him who masters what he wills, and to whom no convention or technical obstacle bars the way to absolute lucidity of expression, to a language of crystalline clearness.

Foundations of Style

Temporal Conditions

The musician Giovanni Pierluigi, who was born about 1525, at Palestrina in the Papal States, belongs by virtue of his artistic gifts and his noble serenity of spirit among the most profoundly influential composers of all times. His place is among those geniuses foreordained to fulfil the plan of musical historical necessity, or—more exactly expressed—he appears within the circle of those deeply inspired individuals whose mission it is to crown and bring to the highest flowering some past great epoch of art.

His life-work brought the vocal polyphonic ideals to full development,—the ecclesiastical art which had been cultivated during centuries in France, England and the Netherlands, to its final culmination. This is all that we know with certainty about him, and this may very well be regarded as his real life.

About his civil existence, at any rate, there is but little to recount.

Judging from his art he seems to have been of an earnest, quiet disposition, and to have been characterized by a certain gentle manliness combined with aristocratic reserve, and a pronounced natural aptitude for the harmonious. The few (most probably inferior) portraits that have been preserved show a finely formed head, a dignified and somewhat anchoretic expression of countenance—the whole bearing bespeaking the intellectual aristocrat. His handwriting is firm, steady, and of extraordinary beauty.

The leading characteristic of his art is his great natural genius for harmony, which is paired with an almost antique sense of the art of limitation. Ferruccio Busoni's comment upon Mozart "er hat den Instinkt des Tieres, sich seine Aufgabe—bis zur möglichsten Grenze, aber nicht darüber hinaus—seinen Kräften entsprechend zu stellen", is valid in even higher degree in the case of Palestrina,—to whom

Mozart, through congeniality of spirit, is nearly related. Proske expresses about the same in other words when he writes in the dry, yet so neat and precise manner peculiar to him: "Dass Palestrina sein lebenlanges, nach Weite und Tiefe unermessliches Kunstschaffen dem reinen Kirchenstil gewidmet, begründet die wahre Grösse seines Charakters".

As remarked before, repose and harmony are the distinctive features of his art. The little we know of his outer life offers no contradiction to this conception. He was brought up under prosperous circumstances, taken at an early age under the protection of popes and powerful clerical dignitaries, famous already as a young man, and the occupant of high offices in the principal churches of Rome. He therefore probably knew but few wordly troubles, notwithstanding contrary assertions by Baini and other early biographers.

He was a true Roman, bound by a thousand ties to the "Eternal City", from which he rarely absented himself except to visit his native home in the Sabine mountains some 20 miles away.[1] Casimiri was the first to find Palestrina's name among the choir-boys in the accountbooks of the church of S. Maria Maggiore, Rome, October 1537.[2] Evidently he served his apprenticeship in Rome. The question of the identity of his teacher cannot be settled with certainty, though in all probability it was not Claude Goudimel, as was formerly generally supposed.[3]

---

[1] An observation by Cerone according to which Palestrina, before settling upon Rome as the place of his studies, travelled about seeking the most prominent teachers, seems elsewhere not to be confirmed. El Melopeo p. 92: — saliose digo con desseo de mayores estudios y passo a Roma; mas anduvo primero perigrinando por diversas partes, buscando los Maestros mas famosos, y libros buenos que tractassen de musica.

[2] See Raffaele Casimiri: "Giovanni Pierluigi da Palestrina". Nuovi documenti biografici. Rome 1918, p. 9 and Alberto Cametti "Palestrina" p. 27 sqq.

[3] In the course of time different hypotheses have been formed concerning this question, none of which, however, have been found tenable in the long run. The first author to bring up the subject of Palestrina's master was Antimo Liberati, who mentions a certain Gaudio mell flandro as the teacher of different Roman composers— also of Palestrina—in a work dated 1685, (S. Gaetano Gaspari: Catalogo della Biblioteca del Liceo Musicale di Bologna, Bologna 1890, Vol. I. p. 85; also Fr. X. Haberl: Giovanni Maria Nanino, Km. J. 1891, 88). But as this Gaudio mell is unknown in musical history, the name is supposed to be a corruption, and this has given rise

Every effort to persuade Palestrina to accept positions abroad, (e. g. the negotiations which took place in 1567 between him and the Imperial Austrian Court,[1] and also those with Guglielmo, Duke of Mantua, in 1583[2] failed at the last moment, it seems, owing to Palestrina's secret disinclination to leave Rome. And so this peaceable, modest Italian, who was not without commercial insight and who gradually accumulated some wealth, lived on in Rome as a musician in the service of the church until his death, the 2nd of February, 1594.[3]

If we inquire what is the place of the musician Palestrina in the History of Civilization and how we are to understand his art in its relationship to period, whether it must be considered as Mediæval, Renaissance or Baroque, it is not easy to find an answer. His civil life itself leaves no room for doubt. It was lived in the Italy of the Council of Trent, under the auspices of the early Baroque era. An examination of his works gives a different result.

---

to various attempts at identification. Hawkins in his "History of Music" (1776, Vol. III., p. 170), claims that it was the Flemish composer Renatus del Melle; Baini in his Palestrina biography, published in 1828, says that it was the Frenchman Goudimel, already mentioned, while Michel Brenet thinks it was the Italian Cimello. The proofs of none of these hypotheses are well enough founded to be convincing. More recently claims have been made by Casimiri (l. c. p. 17) that Firmin le Bel, a French musician, who was conductor of the chapel at St. Maria Maggiore in 1540, (where, as noted above, Palestrina had been connected with the chorus since 1537), was the teacher of Palestrina. Unfortunately this hypothesis is likewise difficult to prove, as but few of le Bel's compositions are to be found, and a comparison of styles is therefore not possible. (See Casimiri: Firmin le Bel di Noyon, Maestro in Roma di Giov. Pierluigi da Palestrina. "Note d'archivio", Marzo 1924, p. 64 sqq.).

[1] Smijers: Die kaiserliche Hofmusikkapelle von 1543-1619, St. z. M. Heft 9. p. 47.

[2] Km. J. 1886. p. 41 sqq.

[3] His professional career, briefly sketched, was as follows: Music conductor at the church of S. Agapit in his native town 1544. Conductor of the Chapel at St. Peter's, Rome, 1551. For a few months in 1555 pontifical choir singer, then conductor of the Lateran Chapel, which position he resigned in 1561 for a similar one at S. Maria Maggiore. Here he remained till 1567, when he became Chapel Conductor to Cardinal d'Este (1567-1571), see Casimiri). He then returned to his former post at St. Peter's church, which he retained until his death. As a characteristic conservative feature of his may be mentioned that shortly before his decease he planned to go back to his first office at the cathedral in his native town (cf. Casimiri: Memorie musicali prenestine del sec. XVI, Note d'Archivio 1924, p. 15-16).

It is necessary to remember here that music has its own technical history independent of temporal conditions. No matter how truly a musician may feel himself a child of his own time, how perfectly in accord with its leading thoughts and ideas as they find expression in poetry, science or the plastic arts, nor how closely in touch with the spiritual mood of contemporary life, yet it is of no avail if, at the crucial moment when he himself must speak, he does not master the adequate means of expression. Though he may try his best, what he wishes to say he does not express, and there is a wide gulf between the actual and the desired utterance. Drastic examples of this are only too frequent. Amongst others we may cite Francesco Landino (d. 1397),[1] who to a text with all kinds of cheap madrigal appurtenances, such as "tormento", "crudeltà", etc., sets music which, so to say, has not the quality of a single responsive quiver. This remark may be extended to comprise most of the 16th century madrigal production; for in spite of ardent efforts to express the text, the relationship between the latter and the music seems very lax. Where this music attempts to express the meaning of the words, it has the effect of something inorganic, of something supplied from without.

Consequently music should be classified, not according to what it attempts to portray, but according to what it seems to express. From this point of view, European music may properly be classified under two large, general divisions: older and newer music. The dividing line may approximately be drawn at the year 1600.

An expression in words, making perfectly clear wherein the difference between these divisions lay, is probably not to be found. However Ambros' early classification as objective and subjective music gives something of the essential in this connection, notwithstanding all the recent attacks on it.

During the entire process of musical development there may be observed an uninterrupted struggle for a steadily increasing refinement of the means of expression. But it is a matter of course that, in order to express individuality, it is necessary to have a more highly differentiated and a more thoroughly mastered material than if the

---

[1] Johannes Wolf: Geschichte der Mensuralnotation, Leipzig, 1904. Vol. III., p. 124.

question concerned the expression merely of common elements. It was not till towards the end of the 16th century, however, that musicians finally were in possession of a material of this order simultaneously with an incomparable mastery of artistic means, which had been acquired in the strict Palestrinian school of style. It was then, and not till then, possible to say "I" in music.

Like Ambros and others, it is tempting to consider this musical emancipation of the individual as the Renaissance which, delayed by technical causes, finally asserts itself in music. The adoption of this interpretation, though, is hindered by the fact that the early 17th century had quite a tendency towards over-excited and uncontrolled emotions, while such tendencies were foreign to Renaissance expression, with its sense of the value of the harmonious inherited from antique art, (the immature unrest of the early Renaissance period excepted). The art of a Monteverdi plainly shows that its motto is "Movement at all costs"! And it is as grotesquely emphasized as possible. Palestrina music on the other hand is so unimpassioned, so little effervescent, that a comparison either with the Renaissance, (even though the latter, at any rate during the height of the period, shared the tactical mastery and clearness of the former), or with the Baroque, gives but meagre results. For those who desire to employ exclusively the classifications of the History of Civilization there remains but one explanation, namely, that the Renaissance and Baroque periods in music fell simultaneously, because the stage of the necessary mastery of subjective, passionate means of musical expression was not attained before the spirit of the time had already passed over into the Baroque. The inevitable deduction would be that music had passed unaffected through the Renaissance period, which negative result only seems to accentuate the impossibility of a division which at the same time recognizes both the specially musical and the historical aspects. The wisest course doubtless would be for musical historians to abandon these rather futile efforts in favour of a classification based upon the inherent claims of the art itself.[1]

---

[1] As already observed, there is really need of only one boundary line in music, between the old and the new, objective and subjective, naive and conscious. It might be well to borrow from older theoretical works the terms "Musica mondana" and

It is assuredly incontestable that, in Palestrina's cultural surroundings, phenomena and tendencies may be clearly traced which form apparent parallels to corresponding tendencies in his music. The epoch of the Post-Tridentine reforms, with its orderliness and distaste for the fantastic prolixity of the Middle Ages, is reflected in his music, just as the typical architecture of an Andrea Palladio seems to express a corresponding adequate intellectual form.

However, it may admit of some question whether such an event as the purification and ripening of vocal polyphony, which had already begun before Palestrina's time, may not have been purely a musical process which, once set in motion, had to run its course more independently of temporal relations. On the other hand, it is hardly improbable that the sympathetic contemporary surroundings, as well as the spiritual disposition of the man Palestrina himself, (which seems to have been propitiously adapted to such a task), led rapidly to an extraordinarily early climax of the style, but doubtless to its early decay also.

Probably it is with art as with fruit,—favourable atmospheric conditions may accelerate the growth, the sun may shine and rain fall in due season and quantity, as needed. Yet if the tree's own laws of life and development are not in function, the fruit will neither be large nor sweet.

It is therefore a question worthy of consideration, whether in musical art the line which leads from one musical work to another is not far more determinative and fateful than any other which may be drawn.

"Musica humana", though for use in a different sense. In reality the older music, "Musica mondana", has a quality that seems to open out upon the universe, something cosmic. It is as though this music frees itself of individualistic bonds, glides away and dissolves into space. Of the newer music, "Musica humana", it might be figuratively said that it also strikes against the limits of the individual, but is hurled back upon itself and condensed into the individually characteristic. The tension arising from this process of condensation finds its resolution in the accent, (in its strongest form, the free dissonance). The two separate at this point, for only the new music has the violent, vehement emphasis.

Rhythm

It may be confidently declared that the emotional element, which is so prominently in the foreground in musical art, is the cause of the usual disposition to lay too much stress, in explaining musical works and the conditions under which they were composed, on the matter of sentiment.

There exists, however, a certain primitive intellectual basis upon which certain requirements rest in their turn, the fulfilment of which naturally cannot fully assure the æsthetic value of a musical work, yet whose omission is followed by negative results. This fact is very distinctly illustrated in the case of rhythm.

When for instance a succession of sound impressions is produced by a delicate acoustic instrument specially constructed for this purpose,— produced at accurately equal intervals of time, and of exactly equal strength and quality of sound,—a certain systematic plan will be felt, in spite of the fact that the single impressions cannot be objectively distinguished the one from the other. After a short time it involuntarily seems to the listener that every second or third of the series is of greater strength and intensity than the rest. This phenomenon, which has long been a familiar one,[1] and which has been scientifically treated by such authors as Dietze, Bolton and Stumpf among others, is generally designated as "subjective" rhythmic accent in contradistinction to the "objective" form, which is a real accent, and not merely of psychic nature. It must, however, be noted that this systematic succession of homogeneous acoustic impressions, which follow each other at regular intervals of time, requires that these

---

[1] The mere observation of this is not by any means new. K. F. Zelter (1758 to 1832) for instance, was acquainted with it, as is evident from what he wrote to Goethe in the beginning of May, 1829: "In diesen beiden auf einander folgenden Accorden der Dominante und Tonica, oder Tonica und Dominante, finder mein individuelles Gefühl das Urelement der Metrik: arsis und thesis, oder thesis und arsis, welche mein Ohr sogar an dem Schlage der Uhr, ja des Pulses und in der stillen Bewegung des Pendels findet, wiewohl das letztere schon Takt ist, der sich zum Rhythmus wie die Enge zur Weite, wie Strenge zum Freyen verhält." Cf. also Kirnberger: "Die Kunst des reinen Satzes in der Musik". Zweiter Teil, 1. Abteilung, 1776, p. 115.

intervals should not surpass a certain length, about the duration of which opinions are still divided.[1] For if the interim between the impressions is too great, it is impossible to set them properly into mutual relationship. The sensation will only register single impressions.

Also a too rapid recurrence of these consecutive impressions makes it difficult to classify them rhythmically, and with increasing rapidity it finally becomes impossible to distinguish them from each other.[2] Dietze indicates (Untersuchungen über den Umfang des Bewusstseins bei regelmässig auf einander folg. Schalleindrücken. Ph. St. II, p. 383) that the most favourable conditions for the execution of subjective rhythmic experiments are present when the interim between the single sound impressions is 0.3-0.18 sec. (that is, from 3 to 5 impressions in a second). This indication seems to agree with the experience gained through ordinary musical observation.

The cause of subjective rhythmic perception, which, since it is not based upon exterior matters, must be of a psychological nature, is generally attributed by psychological experts to regular alternations between states of keen and diminished attention.[3] This problem being of a complicated and abstruse nature, an experimental psychological treatment of the whole matter is difficult, (though it promises better results than have been obtained otherwise up to the present); it would therefore be more prudent to employ a collective conception, such as

---

[1] Most investigators (e. g. Vierordt: "Untersuchungen über den Zeitsinn", Tübingen 1868; Ebhardt: "Zwei Beiträge zur Psychologie des Rhythmus und des Tempo", Z. f. Ps. Bd. 18; and Ettlinger: "Zur Grundlegung einer Ästhetik des Rhythmus", Z. f. Ps. Bd. 22) indicate about 0.6 to the second as the maximum interim. Meumann in his "Untersuchungen zur Psychologie und Ästhetik des Rhythmus" (Ph. St. Bd. 10). gives 0.4; while Bolton (American Journal of Psychology, Vol. VI.) names such a relatively high cipher as 1.5 to the second. Meumann objects to this, and remarks that Bolton does not discriminate sufficiently between the voluntary and the involuntary forms of rhythm.

[2] Bolton (l. c.) indicates here 0.11 sec, as the minimum interim, which approximately corresponds to Dietze's observations, (Ph. St. Bd. II.).

[3] Refer to Arps and Klemm: "Der Verlauf der Aufmerksamkeit bei rhythmischen Reizen", (Ps. St. Bd. IV., p. 505 sqq.). See also Ebhardt (l. c. p. 106), Ernst Meumann: "Beiträge zur Psychologie des Zeitsinns" (Ph. St. Bd. IX. p. 305) and Fr. Weinmann: "Zur Struktur der Melodie", Leipzig 1904, p. 4).

"activity", as Koffka does—leaving room for further possibilities—instead of the more definitively psychological term, "attention". The word activity is used here in the sense of "the feeling of activity",[1] of which attention, so far as it concerns our domain, forms a large component part.[2]

An important question arises here, whether the phenomenon of the subjective perception of rhythm—which all of our generation obey involuntarily—is something insolubly connected with human nature—something which is dependent neither upon culture nor history, but is valid in all eras.

Apparently exotic races of our day have music which does not reckon with alternating accents like ours. The material at hand up to the present is, however, too insignificant and obscure, and our knowledge of primitive psychology is still too limited to permit reliable conclusions.

With regard to the older European music, and also to the Flemish-Italian vocal polyphony, there is a strong divergence of opinions among investigators. Some maintain that the 16th century treated the accent just as the 19th century does. The leader of this party up to the time of his death was Hugo Riemann, whose conviction was that

---

[1] Kurt Koffka: "Experimental Untersuchungen zur Lehre vom Rhythmus", Z. f. Ps. 1. Abt. Bd. 52. p. 105: "Mit dem Worte "Aktivität" soll hier natürlich keine abschliessende Erklärung gegeben sein. Es soll nur gesagt sein, dass es sich um psychische Funktionen handelt, bei denen das Subject in besonderer Weise das Gefühl hat, tätig zu sein. Diese Tätigkeit und dies Tätigkeitsgefühl braucht nichts Einfaches zu sein, keine letzte, nicht mehr zurückführbare Tatsache. Weitere Analyse wird hier ansetzen müssen und sie vielleicht in eine Mehrzahl von Bestandteilen zerlegen".

[2] A popular confirmation of this view is the well known fact that in playing or singing we are predisposed to commit our rhythmical sins on the weak, or less strongly accented, beat. This fact, for the rest, is quite a familar one. Already in the 16th century a Spanish theorist, Thomas de Sancta Maria, advises beginners to pay special attention to the half bar (the second note of the measure), because mistakes most frequently occur there. (See Otto Kinkeldey: "Orgel und Klavier in der Musik des XVI. Jahrhundert", 1910, p. 30). Recently this observation has been further confirmed through experimental investigations by Arps and Klemm (Ps. St. Bd. IV. p. 518 sqq.), who, among others, proved that in objective, accentuated dactylic series (triple time), the sense of rhythmical inequalities is strongest on the first accented beat, less so on the second, and still less on the third.

the older music, taken in its entirety, had much more in common with the newer than we generally are inclined to suppose. Later on Arnold Schering has expressed similar ideas concerning the rhythm of the cinquecento in his interesting study, "Takt und Sinngliederung in der Musik des 16. Jahrhunderts."[1]

Some other investigators advance views that are diametrically opposed to the above, claiming that during the 15th and 16th centuries the so-called "freischwebend" (free-pending) accent was mainly used. This opinion has gained ground in recent years, especially through the works and essays of Adler,[2] Vogel,[3] Schünemann,[4] Kinkeldey,[5] and Orel.[6]

This hypothesis is partially based upon the following facts: firstly, the mensural vocal music of this epoch did not employ bar lines; secondly, its theorists make no mention of accentuated or unaccentuated beats; and finally, when the "measure", (considered as such), is followed, false emphasis of the text occurs very often in individual voices, which makes the bar seem an unwarranted restriction. In fact there is much to be said in favour of such a conception. For instance in the Gloria of the 4-part mass, "Sine nomine" by Palestrina (P. XI, 42, 2, + 1 sqq.) the following passage occurs:

---

[1] A. f. M. 1920, p. 469.

[2] A. St. p. 69 sqq.

[3] Emil Vogel: "Zur Geschichte des Taktschlagens", Jahrbuch Peters, 1898, p. 70.

[4] Georg Schünemann: "Zur Frage des Taktschlagens und der Textbehandlung in der Mensuralmusik", Z. I. M. 1908, p. 95.

[5] l. c. p. 110.

[6] Alfred Orel: "Zur Frage der rhythmischen Qualität in Tonsätzen des 15. Jahrhunderts", Z. f. M. 1924, p. 559 sqq.

There is no reason to suspect that Palestrina is guilty here of such a careless declamation as: "propter magnam gloriam tuam". That suspicion in this case is unjust can be proved with quite a degree of certainty.

To one only superficially familiar with 16th century vocal polyphony, the isolated crotchets on the two last syllables of "gloriam" will at once seem a breach of style. The aim and end of this music was to keep the linear character as fluent and elastic as possible, and therefore everything that would produce too harsh an emphasis or too extreme an effect was zealously avoided. But it is a fact that the sudden glimpse and disappearance of short note values possess the power to attract attention and cause emphasis or stress of great effect.[1] In order not to produce too strong an accent, they are either placed on the "weak" (less prominent) part of the measure, or the rhythm is equalized by other means. In Palestrina style, therefore, where two crotchets replace the first or third minim in duple time, the obtrusion of this phenomenon is usually neutralized in one of three ways. The first is by a preceding or a succeeding crotchet, the second, by tying the first crotchet to a preceding minim; the third is that the second crotchet must be succeeded by a syncopated minim, (probably owing to the general tendency to balance the passivity of the syncope by an energetic introduction). Care should also be taken that quavers in quarter time, when used isolated between larger note values, should not receive an accent.

Consequently when, as here, we meet this rhythmical figuration, (which is practically never in our domain of style, and especially not when employed thematically), there is no doubt that the accents do not follow the bar lines.

Admitting this, and placing these bar lines before the formerly unaccentuated beats, the whole figure immediately presents another ap-

---

[1] Kirnberger in his "Gedanken über die verschiedenen Lehrarten in der Komposition" (Berlin 1782, p. 13) expresses the same feeling in the terms of his time: "Wenn Noten von verschiedener Gattung vorkommen, so müssen nicht auf die erste Taktzeit zwey Noten gesetzt werden, und auf die andern nur eine, weil die erste Taktzeit schwer ist, und also eine Art vom Gewicht bey sich führt, die zugleich durch die leichte Note der sonst gewöhnlichen Taktzeit zu viel Gewicht giebt".

pearance. Everything falls naturally into its place, and the melody accurately follows the stress of the text:

pro - pter mag - nam glo - ri - am tu - am, tu - - am

This analysis makes it clear that the accentuated minims in Palestrina style are treated quite otherwise than the unaccentuated. This fact becomes still more obvious when we examine the treatment of the dissonance. If we count the minims from the beginning of some mensurated choral composition of the 15th or 16th century, it is apparent —more strikingly so the nearer we approach the culmination of the Palestrina period—that the dissonance as an almost invariable rule falls upon the even numbers of the minims, or on what we call the "weak" part of the measure. The only exceptions are syncope dissonances, which fall with equally as great regularity on the odd numbered minims.

It is also evident with regard to crotchets, that the dissonance was only employed on the weak beats, and that moreover the third crotchet received a less forcible accent than the first, about like this:

Melodic conditions, which we will discuss later, also plainly indicate a difference in the treatment of even and odd numbered notes. It cannot possibly be denied that in vocal polyphony those beats which modern editions designate as "accented" consistently received a different musical treatment from that of the "unaccented" beats. But why should there be this technical difference if no psychic situation lay behind it, (meaning our accent alternation, that is to say the alternate stronger and weaker moments of mental activity)?

The lack of bar lines in the older vocal part-book music constitutes no real obstacle to the acceptance of this supposition. The usage of the bar line in the musical art of the 15th and 16th centuries seems very arbitrary. They were the rule in the instrumental music tablatures of this epoch, even as far back as Paumann's "Fundamentum organisandi". Where a vocal part with mensural notation has an accompaniment of a lute for instance, bars are often used in both parts, but just as often, or even more frequently, they are omitted.[1] Also examples of lute tablatures entirely devoid of bar lines are found; moreover even in compositions of the late 17th century by Tunder and Buxtehude,[2] the bar lines are often lacking in the vocal part while appearing in the instrumental accompaniment. Yet the conclusion must not be drawn from these facts that this music, in which symmetrical group construction is often very marked, was not intended to be subject to measure and accent. The choir music of the 15th and 16th centuries, as is well known, exists only in parts, and never has bar lines. There was then no urgent necessity for these lines, for by means of the "tactus", a sign from the conductor consisting of an up and a down movement mostly covering two or three minims), the performance regulated itself. With the desire for a general outlook over the entire composition in a score, the lack of bar lines was first really felt. But even then they were not always written out. It seems to have been the ambition of every good musician of the 16th century to be able to read and play the composition directly from the voice parts as written in the choir books.[3] This playing directly from the score was made possible by the well known system of notation used in these part-books, which gave the same episode in all the voices of the composition on pages immediately opposite each other, but without bars or placing the coincidently occurring notes under each other. However, when there was the question of securing a critical estimate of a composition, even the best musicians of the 16th century now and then made use of scores. Thus Palestrina writes to the Duke of Mantua, who had sent a motet of his own composition to Palestrina, asking the

---

[1] Refer to Wolf: "Notationskunde", Bd. II. p. 77. Also to O. Körte: "Laute und Lautenmusik bis zur Mitte des 16. Jahrh." 1901, p. 102.

[2] Cf. Schünemann: "Geschichte des Dirigierens", 1913, p. 72.

[3] See Kinkeldey l. c. p. 20 Compare also the contrasting opinion of Rudolph Schwartz: "Zur Partitur im 16. Jahrh.", A. f. M. II., p. 73.

latter's opinion: "I have scored the motet myself in order to be able to judge it the better."[1]

Compositions were written out for amateurs either in tablatures or, probably more rarely, in real scores. At any rate, but few barred scores of this kind dating from the first half of the 16th century are still extant. The earliest of these seem to be comprised in Agricola's "Musica instrumentalis deutsch" (1528) and in the tract "Explicatio compendioso doctrinæ de signis musicalibus".[2] Written scores of this kind from the second half of the 16th century are found oftener; and the earliest printed scores known up to the present, date from the year 1577. These were the madrigals of Ciprian de Rore, published in Venice by Gardano, who explicitly emphasized the pedagogic purpose of the publication.[3]

Sometimes musicians with insufficient training facilitated their own playing from score by adding bar lines to the parts which, as was customary, occupied opposite pages in the old choir books. Such seems to have been the case with the Requiem of Brudieu—a composition from a not very late 16th century date.[4] A study of the famous Codex 59 in the Lateran archives is also most interesting. As is generally known, this Codex is an original autograph by Palestrina,[5] a sort of choir book, which notwithstanding its small size has seen practical use, as is shown by the singers' names written down here and there in the parts. The contents consist mainly of Lamentations and Hymns, the parts of the strictly mensurated compositions having no bar lines. But there are also a few faux-bourdon pieces in the Codex 59, such as the Improperias, Miserere and "Benedictus Dominus". In these we find that bar lines are used (at least in the Improperias and Miserere, which

---

[1] "et per meglio contemplarlo ho partito il Motetto." Bertolotti. "Musici alla corte dei Gonzaga in Mantua", p. 49. Cf. Km. J. 1886, p. 36.

[2] Refer to Bellermann: "Der Contrapunkt", 4. impression 1901, p. 67 sqq. Kinkeldey l. c. p. 189. Wolf: Notationskunde, Bd. II. p. 307.

[3] "per sonare d'ogni sorte d'instrumento perfetto et per qualunque studioso di contrapunti".

[4] See the facsimile p. 94 in: "Els Madrigals i la missa de difunts d'en Brudieu, transcripcio i notes historiques i critiques per Felip Pedrell i Higini Anglès". Barcelona. Institut d'estudis catalans, 1921.

[5] R. Casimiri: "Il codice 59 dell' archivio musicale lateranense". Roma 1919.

Casimiri gives in facsimile),—thus, bar lines in some compositions, and in others, none!

The reason for this difference can be readily explained. In strictly mensurated compositions the bar lines were not necessarily copied into the part books, as the singers only needed to follow the "tactus" and the rest came quite naturally of itself. With the faux-bourdon pieces the case was different. Here the execution was not regulated by rhythmic quantity, but more freely conformed to the textual rhythm, wherefore signs were useful to guide and keep the singers together and to insure general precision of execution. The bar lines in these Palestrina compositions did not divide them into equal time quantities, but seem, besides the function of facilitating the general survey of the works, to be intended to serve as punctuation signs similar to the "divisions" of plainsong.

We know, through the theorists of this epoch, that these lines were intended to guide with reference to the coincidental occurrence of the contents of the different parts. This, however, is the limit of our definite information from these sources; they are silent regarding the point whether the bar lines at that time, as in our own, were also accentual lines.[1]

But the musical works themselves afford unmistakable evidence

---

[1] A passage from Sancta Maria is quoted by Kinkeldey, (l. c. p. 110) as proof that the first beat was not more strongly accented than the second in the 16th century. The conclusion he draws seems doubtful to me. Sancta Maria here refers exclusively to conditions controlling the maintenance of time. He impresses, first of all, the importance of not giving more time to the down-beat than to the up-beat, secondly that the movement of the hands should not be more rapid in raising than in lowering them. Thirdly he writes, (page 8): "La tercera cosa es, que el golpe baxo o alto, y el punto que con el cayere, hiera juntamente a un mesmo tiempo, de suerte que el golpe no hiera antes ni despues del punto, ni el punto antes ni despues del golpe, sino todo juntamente a la par, para lo qual es necessario que cada golpe, assi baxo como alto, se hiera un poco rezio con impetu, y de mas desto, ambos a dos se hieran ygualdad, esto es que no se hiera mas rezio el golpe baxo que el alto, ni el alto que el baxo." It is suggested here, for the sake of precision on the part of the singers, to mark the time with a certain degree of energy, taking care that both beats should be of the same intensity. Why? Without doubt to keep the steady attention of the singers, to prevent possible rhythmical accidents, and to insure the accuracy of the time intervals between the notes of the measure. But it is certainly not the intention,

that in the 16th century, or perhaps even earlier, there was introduced a collective rhythm with regularly recurring accents, between which and the individual rhythm of the single parts there arose mutual strife and contradiction.

These very obvious contradictions seem irreconcilable. It is however scarcely worth while to try to bridge over these differences, as the phenomenon doubtless has its roots in the principal paradox of Palestrina's style, viz: the incompatibility, ideally considered, of the two Dimensions.

This conflict of the polyphonic and homophonic spheres may be symbolized in the relationship of the two kinds of listeners, of the two psychic factors with which Palestrina style deals, namely the singer of the single part[1] and the listener proper, (the receiver of the total impression). The latter, who does not take part in the singing himself, but listens at a certain distance, has a difficult—strictly speaking, impossible—task. He must assemble all the participating parts mentally and condense them into a total impression; yet he may not always be able to abandon himself freely to this total impression, but sometimes be forced, or enticed, to follow and spiritually to merge himself in single voices or parts. However, the more he is absorbed in the totality of the impression, the less distinctly will he be able to follow the course of the single lines; and the more he concentrates his attention upon the single parts, the more will his conception of the collective effect recede into the background. It is therefore possible to hear a composition of Josquin, Palestrina or Victoria, perhaps a hundred times, and each time receive a new or different impression, in proportion as this or that voice is more or less brought out or covered in the rendering. We can assuredly not reject, in advance, the assumption that the educated listener of the 16th century disposed over a greater skill in listening to polyphonic music, than is ordinarily to be found to-day; though a portion of our modern music is very horizontally conceived, and truly forms not a bad preparation for the appreciation of 16th century art. But even conceding a considerably greater degree

---

as Kinkeldey supposes, to hinder the singers' accentuating the down-beat more than the up-beat, for the question here distinctly concerns metrical matters alone.

[1] who, in this connection, also represents the principal hearer of it.

of skill to the credit of this older era, there still remains in the individual parts a number of fine melodic and rhythmic details which are fated to disappear totally in the collective impression, which only the singer of the part in question can enjoy, or perhaps some listener who has been especially attentive to this part at the expense more or less of the others—and just for whom this part preferably may have been written.

Just as melody and harmony are inclined to combat each other,—the great prominence of harmonic elements tending to absorb and efface the peculiar melodic features of the single part,—so does the "Micro" (partial) rhythm contradict and combat the "Macro" (total) rhythm. This strife has, however, scarcely had any serious consequences practically. When, for instance, in the motet of Palestrina, "Gaudent in coelis", (P. V., 96, 4, + 1), the following passage occurs:

there is no plausible reason to suppose that the executer of the tenor part here submitted entirely to the greater rhythm and sang "Christi" with a false stress. For what is there to prevent him from following the metrical accent of the text, and putting a dynamic accent on the first syllable?[1] The bar lines, at any rate, form no hindrance here, as they

---

[1] We are aware that the 16th century appreciated correct textual declamation, shown for instance in the final results of the humanistic movement on Gregorian territory: the Medicæan edition of the Graduale.

would in newer music. But it would be still more improbable to suppose, that the listener to the total effect would allow himself to be misled by the tenor's individual rhythm with regard to the macro-rhythm, which sets in at the beginning of the composition, and regularly alternates between accented and unaccented minims.[1] In this case, he would hear a free dissonance set in upon the accented minim, an effect which was considered too extreme an accentual means in this style, and therefore was prohibited as being rude and violent.[2] Probably the listener either observed the tenor enough to remark its rhythmic peculiarity, but considered it as a weaker contradiction of his own stronger vertical rhythm; or the macro-rhythm had grown so predominant in his mode of listening, that he did not catch the special rhythm of the tenor part. Whether such a manner of listening polyphonically in the 16th century may be accepted as probable, (the truth being that perhaps in certain circumstances it was realizable, in others not), or whether a freer play of forces prevailed in which every rhythm was considered good in itself, we must, at any rate, reckon with two rhythmic dimensions in Palestrina music, just as we reckon with two tonal dimensions. But if the vertical apprehension of tones corresponding to a vertical rhythm with regularly alternating accents be insisted upon, on the other hand it lies quite near to assume that these accents scarcely received so strong a stress as it pleased a later epoch to give. The reserve with regard to the melodic, the quantitative, and the harmonic accent which characterized Palestrina style, makes it seem likely that the dynamic accent was treated with similar discretion.[3] The

---

[1] The significance of the dynamic stress in proportion to the more essentially musical accent is generally exaggerated. That the dynamic is not the most important element in rhythmical apprehension is illustrated, for instance, in organplaying, which has not this emphasis, yet in which the rhythm may be irresistible and marked.

[2] Compare remarks in this treatise p. 101.

[3] A passage in Zacconi ("Prattica di Musica", I, 1596, p. 20 v.) seems applicable in support of this assumption: ".... alle volte si chiama tempo, alle volte misura, alle volte battuta et alle volte tatto .... Quelli ultimamente che lo chiamano tatto, considerano che con altro meglio il non si puo chiamare; per rispetto che il battere ricerca un atto forzato & vehemente; questa attione non essendo ne vehemente ne forzata gli pare che meglio sia di chiamarlo tatto da quel moto che in se retiene simile a un tatto gentile."

involuntary feeling of dissatisfaction with which we hear older polyphonic works rendered with too forcible dynamic accents, may be
accepted as an instinctive witness upon this point, whose attestation
can hardly be rejected.

Modes

The music of Palestrina is based upon the ecclesiastical modes, and
even upon a remarkably conservative use of these modes, considering
the time. While this modal system was tottering to its fall, while madrigal writers were employing chromatic notes in their eagerness to
lend new life and brilliancy to music, Palestrina alone stood firm and
steady in the midst of all these seething currents. He knew his own
mind, and was but little concerned about chromatic alterations. Moreover, he was not alone reserved toward the chromatic efforts of his
contemporaries, but also his attitude towards his predecessors was
critically revisional.

It is, at all events, most difficult, upon the basis of the results of
research up to the present, to form an estimate concerning the attitude
of polyphony towards chromatic alterations from the beginning of
Harmony up to the year 1600. But it does not seem improbable that
Palestrina's art may one day, when all the facts have been finally in-
vestigated and collated, be recognized as the keystone of a great process of diatonic development. At any rate it is certain, that in the
14th and 15th centuries chromatic notes were known and employed
which Palestrina avoided. Thus, for instance, in the composition for
three voices, "Bonte bialte", by Johannes Cesaris, (from the end of the
14th century),[1] both A flat and D flat occur, as also in the "Christe"
of the "Missa super Maria zart", by Jacob Obrecht:[2]

---

[1] Johannes Wolf: "Handbuch der Notationskunde" I, Leipzig 1913, p. 348. Cf. also
R. v. Ficker: "Beiträge zur Chromatik des 14. bis 16. Jahrhunderts". St. z. M. 1914.
p. 7.

[2] Obr. Zehnte Lieferung. 44, 1, 1.

The mode here is the transposed Phrygian, with A as final,—A flat and D flat thus corresponding to E flat and A flat in the original position. In v. Ficker's instructive treatise he says: "Ein ausgeschriebenes As ist jedoch in der zweiten Hälfte des 15. Jahrhunderts bis zu der Zeit Willaerts immer nur in Verbindung mit bb Vorzeichnung anzutreffen."[1] This statement, consequently, does not hold altogether, though practically considered it may be correct.

The theorists too confirm the existence of a freer employment of chromatic effects in music prior to Palestrina. We find corroboration of this in the often cited mention by Marchettus of Padua, of the halftone interval, "Permutatio", as he calls it; or in Prosdocimus de Beldemandi's "Libellus monocordi".[2]

As remarked before, it is not unlikely that there may be a slow and gradual liquidation of chromatic elements in the time prior to Palestrina, at any rate in church music,—whether this liquidation had any

---

[1] l. c. p. 11.

[2] "Lucidarium musicæ planæ". G. S. III., p. 89. Compare R. M. p. 136 and 278.

psychological features in common with the process of diatonic evolution which took place in the 11th and 12th centuries in plainsong,[1] or whether is was directly due to Gregorian influence— the latter being more distinctly evident, the nearer we approach the culmination of vocal polyphony.

However all this may be, Palestrina's music is as decidedly diatonic as any. The use he makes of chromatic alteration does not substantially exceed what was valid in plainsong. His art, on the other hand, is undeniably polyphonic. He quite understood the nature of the triad, and in a certain way how to hear the mutual relations of chords; at any rate he clearly recognized the effect of the dominant. With regard to the triad, it is noticeable that he liked the greater third (major), which was the general preference of his time. Major evidently sounded better to his ear than minor.[2] He always uses a major triad, (if at all the third is employed), as the final chord; when he begins with a full chord, which does not often happen, then this too is most frequently a major triad. Throughout his works he prefers major triads upon all more prominent passages. This desire for a major third in the final chord causes a chromatic raising of the thirds in the Dorian, the Phrygian and the Aeolian tonic triads, that is: the notes F sharp, G sharp and C sharp. To obtain major thirds (dominant effects) in the triad on the fifth interval of the Dorian, Mixolydian, and Aeolian modes, exactly the same notes are required. In the Phrygian mode, the major triad is not used upon the 5th of the scale, because the whole-tone interval between the 7th and 8th of the scale is rightly considered a principal characteristic of the mode.

All the accidentals mentioned are employed out of consideration for harmony. Otherwise, as in plainsong, only B flat is to be found, and

---

[1] Refer to Peter Wagner: "Neumenkunde" 1912. p. 292 and "Elemente des Gregorianischen Gesanges" 1917, p. 129. I allude here to the well-known fact that, after having been long occupied with a matter, and having by and by mastered the problem, one feels instinctively impelled to revise and to return to fundamental factors, discarding everything accidental or casual.

[2] The same is the case, *cum grano salis*, with races having only a primitive musical culture. Refer to B. Stumpf's experiments with a Siamese musican: "Beiträge zur Akustik und Musikwissenschaft", Heft 3, Leipzig 1901, p. 106. Likewise to Gaston Knosp: "Über annamitische Musik", S. I. M. 1907, p. 153-54.

in connection herewith E flat, though generally only in the transposed modes, (such as G-Dorian, A-Phrygian, F-ionian, etc.).

Within this limited circle of chromatic possibilities, Palestrina unfolds his sublime art. If he oversteps these bounds on rare occasions, it is only to demonstrate that he dwells "extra muros". An instance of this occurs in the motet, "Peccantem me quotidie",[1] on the words, "timor mortis conturbat me", where he can find no better means to portray the perturbation caused by agony than by employing D sharp in the cadence. It can scarcely be made more clear that to Palestrina this chromatic signified a "conturbatio" of that musical system which he thought the sole correct one.

Of similar significance is a passage in the madrigal "O che splendor de' luminosi rai", (P. XXVIII, 115, 3, + 1). Here he employs a G sharp, (the mode being G-Dorian, this in reality is D sharp), since he had to express something as extraordinary as "una dolcezza smisurata e nuova"; without doubt the G sharp is especially meant for "nuova", but "smisurata"—immeasurable—has surely also had its influence here.

To my knowledge, A flat does not occur in Palestrina's compositions. In a single instance it is written,[2] (to the text "pien di miseria e male"); but in reality this is not an A flat, but a disguised E flat— the mode being the transposed Dorian with its fixed B flat.

Besides their vertical function, which was to procure major triads and, in addition, to eliminate discordant elements from accords, (for instance, the diminished triad in its root position,) accidentals were used for melodic reasons, (as in plainsong), either to avoid the direct tritone or tritone-like phrases, to follow the rule "una nota super la" —, or to render leaps possible that ordinarily were prohibited—for instance, lowering the ascending major sixth a semitone, which alteration made the movement legitimate.[3] Consequently when we take into consideration the strict attitude of the style towards dissonant features, *a priori* it would seem improbable that accidentals in Palestrina's com-

---

[1] P. II, 75, 1, + 1.

[2] In the madrigal "Amor, senza il tuo dono". P. XXIX, 61, 3, + 1.

[3] Cf. this treatise p. 52.

positions were employed for the express purpose of rendering dissonant leaps possible.

Nevertheless the chromatic semitone step may be found here and there in the works of Palestrina and other 16th century composers. A citation from the motet "O lux et decus Hispaniae" Pars II (P. III, 48, 3, + 3) follows:

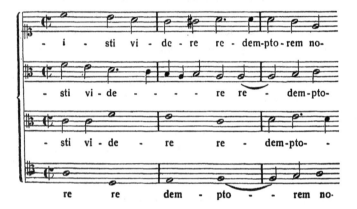

Similar passages may be found in the following motets: Beatae Mariae (P. I, 55- + 2- + 1); Lapidabunt Stephanum (P. I, 85, 2, 2 and + 3, and likewise 85, 3, 2); "Canite tuba" (P. II, 44, 2, 4); furthermore in the third volume of the complete edition (containing the third book of motets from 1575) in which such instances occur comparatively often: 5, 3 + 3; 8, 2, 2; 8, 3, 3; 10, 2, 3; 26, 1, 7-8; 53, 2, 3; 67, 3, 3; 70, 2, 4; 76, 3, + 4; 81, 2, 2; 101, 2, 2; 132, 1, 2; 134, 3, 1; 139, 1, 4; 140, 1, + 4. Examples may likewise be found in the 8-part masses from 1601: P. XXII, 111, 2, 2-3-4- + 2- + 1; 118, 2, + 1; 126, 3, + 2. Refer also to the madrigal: Vergine tale (P. XXIX, 37, 3, 4-. + 3).

All these instances have the quality in common that the change of chord does not take place simultaneously with the chromatic alteration, and are therefore not to be classed with modes of expression like the next example:[1]

---

[1] P. XXXII, 120, I. This composition, and others similar, are by Marc Antonio Ingegneri, and are consequently incorrectly included in the Palestrina collection, as Haberl himself proved, (Km. J. 1898, p. 78).

Plan - ge, plan - ge qua - si vir - go

Plan - ge, plan - ge qua - si vir - go

Plan - ge, plan - ge qua - si vir - go

Plan - ge, plan - ge qua - si vir - go

Here the change of chord coincides in time with the chromatic semitone alterations. The feeling of conscious chromatic alteration is also much stronger in this example. The aim here is to enhance the richness and metallic lustre of the chords—in reality only triads with "third-related" roots, which anticipates, in the cinquecento, an effect of which Romantic composers of the 19th century were very fond. This phenomenon assuredly signified the same in both eras—over-ripe homophony!

As previously stated, the examples quoted from Palestrina are all of another kind. Only one of them, (an antiphon, "Lumen ad revelationem", P. XXXII, 145, 3, 2) resembles the passage cited from Ingegneri, this resemblance being strong enough to characterize the already dubious composition as not being a genuine Palestrina work.

The query arises, however, whether all these instances of chromatic progression cited from Palestrina's works, should really be taken seriously. Alfred Einstein in his study. "Claudio Merulo's Ausgabe der Madrigale des Verdelot"[1] calls attention to the fact that in Verdelot's second book of madrigals, (1538) several passages with chromatic semitones occur which are reprinted without these in later editions of the same collection, (e. g. Gardano's edition 1556, and Merulo's edition 1566). Likewise v. Ficker, in his study of chromatic alterations already mentioned, goes critically to work regarding similar modes of expres-

---

[1] S. I. M. 1907. p. 232.

sion in the literature of the early part of the 16th century. Probably
the phenomenon may arise out of a misapprehension of the manner of
notation in the old printed editions; at any rate this supposition holds
good as far as Palestrina is concerned. It is common knowledge among
musicians, that the composers of that time were not very exact about
the application of accidentals. In cases where the latter were considered self-evident, they were not written out at all, and in other instances they were very imperfectly noted. For instance, when it was
desired to signify that several notes of the same pitch should all be
either raised or lowered, it was seldom thought necessary to give each
note an accidental, but only a single note was so marked. Usually this
accidental was placed before the first note, sometimes, however, it was
placed between the first and second notes. That both notations signified the same, is shown by the following facts.

The instances of chromatic semitones cited from the first volume
of the complete edition of Palestrina's works, (which was based upon
the first book of multipart motets from 1569), are all removed from
the second edition of the same motets (Venice 1579). Where the 1569
edition has a sharp placed between the first and second notes, in the
1579 edition it is only placed before the first note.

As further evidence may be cited the theme of the 8-part mass,
"Confitebor tibi Domine", P. XXII, 111, 2, 2:

which later on, in the same part, has:

There is not a doubt, therefore, that the sharp in the first example
is intended for the first F. We get a similar result if we compare, in the
same mass, the tenor part of the first chorus (118, 1, + 2) with the

tenor part in the second chorus (118, 2, + 1); or if we compare the passage, "Domine Fili unigenite", (Cantus, 118, 2, + 1 sqq.) with the corresponding passage, (P. II, 135, 2, 2,) in the motet upon which the mass is based.

Though it seems beyond question that all the examples so far chosen from the complete edition are due to mistakes of the editors, still it cannot be denied that a few instances occur in which the semitones cannot be eliminated. But in these cases the semitone is a "dead" interval, that is, its notes do not belong to the same musical phrase.[1]

In the motet already mentioned, "Peccantem me quotidie" (P. II, 74, 3, + 2), we find an interesting mode of expression:

It is plain that the breve in the third bar of the upper voice must be G and not G sharp, because the following note is F. Raising the G would give an augmented second, which is otherwise never employed. It is, at all events, conceivable that the F might be changed

---

[1] In cases like this, there were not so many scruples about the kind of interval. For instance, the otherwise forbidden major sixth may sometimes be encountered "dead": P. II, 25, 1, + 4; P. III, 164, 3, 2; P. IV, 52, 3, + 1; 62, 2, 3; 147, 1, 3; 147, 3, + 4; P. V, 104, 2, 2; 127, 4, 2; P. IX, 107, 2, 2; P. X, 171, 1, + 3; P. XI, 4, 2, 2; 144, 2, 5, etc. The seventh may also occur as a "dead" interval. Compare, for example, the alto in P. XI, 149, 2, 6-7.

into F sharp; but this would necessitate an F sharp in the bass instead of F, which would be a melodic impossibility, owing to the B flat expressly indicated in the last bar. The passage cited is also of interest as a proof that, even as early as the 16th century, composers clearly felt the difference between major and minor, just as modern composers do, (the small triad on "timor" being without doubt a tone-picture).[1] Passages where the chromatic semitone is used as a "dead" interval, may be found, furthermore, in P. XXVI, 23, 1, 4 and XXVIII, 6, 2, + 1.

Palestrina's attitude towards chromatic alteration on the whole is of a noticeably negative character. What he omits is in reality of more interest than what he allows. It is, however, of importance to observe his procedure in this domain, for he reveals himself a master in selecting and rejecting,—as one to whose art there adheres no particle of anything casual.

Treatment of Words

The relation to words is perhaps that in which the tendencies of modern art come out most strongly, and in which its expressional will, intensified to extremity, is most pronounced.

To our ears the sixteenth century's primitive efforts at word-painting seem rather childish and superficial. However, it should be remembered that they originated in the intense desire for the expressive.

---

[1] Similar practical examples by Palestrina may be found for instance in P. V, 137, 3, + 4 ("Heu") and P. V, 181, 2, + 3 ("morte"). The theorists too certify to the correctness of this opinion: Zarlino, "Istitutioni" p. 223 (221): "— — percioche (come ho detto altroue) quando si pone la Terza maggiore nella parte graue, l'Harmonia si fà allegra; & quando si pone nell'acuto si fà mesta." Refer also to p. 191, p. 293 and p. 306 l. c. Pietro Pontio "Dialogo", Parma 1595 p. 58: "— — Quando adunque vorrà, che la sua cantilena sia mesta, si servirà di tai moti tardi, & anco della Terza minore, la qual rende assai mestitia. Se poi vorrà la sua compositione allegra, si servirà delli moti veloci, come si puo vedere nelle compositioni volgari; & in luogo della Terza minore si servirà della Decima maggiore; et di altri movimenti, che fanno la Musica allegra!" Furthermore, see Vicentino: "L'antica musica, ridotta alla moderna prattica" p. 33 v., and Artusi: "L'arte del contraponto", Venice 1598, p. 38.

Generally the result was that the composers merely succeeded in securing a snip of the garment, though their intentions were of the best.

Even the great, far-seeing Zarlino (1517-1590), who was one of the most distinguished musical thinkers of any era, looks upon this phenomenon with loyal tolerance. In his work, "L'istitutioni harmoniche" (1558), he advises composers to avoid extremes, and also against dwelling too long either in the high or low registers in their works, except for the accomplishment of special aims[1]—"which is the intention of modern composers, (whom only the overwise would allow themselves to blame), when they descend in the scale in melodies to texts depicting anything deep or gloomy, such as descent, fear, lamentation, tears, etc., while they ascend in tones expressing elevation, vehemence, ascent, joy, laughter." Altogether the theorists thoroughly understood that in this period the end and aim was expression above all, and that the strictest rules could be relaxed when such vital features were at stake. E. g. in his "L'antica musica ridotta alla moderna prattica", Rome 1557, (a title which shows how far back the Hellenizing tendencies of the 17th century reach), Vicentino says that in setting music to madrigals and the like, one need not be too scrupulous about keeping to the mode: "ma sarà solamente obligato à dar l'anima, à quelle parole, & con l'armonia dimostrare le sue passioni, quando aspre, & quando dolci, & quando allegre, & quando meste—" (l. c. p. 48). The tritone also may sometimes be employed in syncopes when it is desired to express harshness: "alcune uolte nelle compositioni s'usa

---

[1] See "De tutte l'opere del R. M. Gioseffo Zarlino", Venetia 1589, Vol. I, p. 253: "Hò detto; senza proposito; percioche i compositori moderni hanno per costume (il che non è da biasimar, se non da quelli che sono troppo sauii) che quando le parole dinotano cose graui, basse, profunde, discesa, timore, pianti, lagrime & altre cose simili, fanno continuare alquanto le lor modulationi nel graue; & quando significano altezza, acutezza, ascesa, allegrezza, riso & simili cose, le fanno modular nell' acuto." Refer also to "Sopplimenti musicali" l. c., p. 319. On the part of authors in "La seconda practica", we find a much less tolerant attitude than Zarlino's to this form of artistic expression. Both Vincenzo Gallilei and G. B. Doni are its decided opponents, while Pietro Cerone, (though in point of time belonging to the new era), agrees with Zarlino here, as in numerous other instances. Reference is advised also to Alfred Einstein: "Augenmusik im Madrigal", Z. f. M. XIV, p. 8 sqq.

comporre il Tritono sincopato, in luogo di quarta; & si fa à due, & à tre uoci, & perche è di natura aspra, le parole moueranno il Compositore à far quello" (p. 31 v).

Palestrina's attitude towards this was steadily marked by self-control, though he wrote madrigals, (for which he later thought fit to apologize), and also church music which showed that he had not been able to keep himself entirely free from the influence of contemporary secular music. That he understood, "il dare spirito vivo alle parole", appears not only from a letter to the Duke of Mantua,[1] but also, and even still more clearly, from his compositions.

It is for instance self-evident, that to the musicians of that time the meaning of the words "up" and "down" corresponded to ascending and descending movements of tones. Palestrina also found it difficult to say "descendit" without going down, and "ascendit" without rising.

It is, however, word-painting of the most flagrant order when Palestrina places a general rest on words like "sospiro",[2] or when in the motet, "O patruo" (P. IV, 94, 2, 2), he musically interprets the adjective "longa" by means of the "Longa" note-value. Besides this, he lets the full six-part chorus sing the second part of the motet "Vidi turbam magnam", (P. I., 134), because the text begins "Et omnes angeli stabant", and on the other hand he only uses a four-part chorus when the text later says "et quatuor animalium".

The declamation of the text is artistically more significant and finely characteristic of Palestrina than this rather superficial word-painting.

It is clear though, with regard to declamatory technique, that it mainly shows to advantage in homophonous compositions. In contrapuntal web-work, where the single voice or part is very apt to be covered by the others, Palestrina is not so scrupulous about textual emphasis, though he is still a great deal more careful in this respect

---

[1] See Bertolotti l. c. p. 49.

[2] Numerous cases of this kind, and others similar, are cited in Peter Wagners "Palestrina als weltlicher Komponist", Strassburg 1890, p. 34. Refer to V. f. M. 1892, p. 446, Theodor Kroyer: "Die Anfänge der Chromatik im italienischen Madrigal des XVI. Jahrhunderts", Leipzig 1902, p. 34 sqq., also to Alfred Einstein l. c., a fine collection of examples!

than either the Josquin or the French school, or than his great contemporary, Orlandus Lassus.

From the very earliest period of musical history, note-against-note
has always been considered as especially characteristic of Palestrina
style.

From old records it appears that the triumph of the Marcellus mass
must be attributed particularly to the distinctness of the text, which,
in its turn, was due to the strong influence of note-against-note. Speaking of this matter, Prätorius says that the earlier composers, in contradistinction to Palestrina, thought "allein auf die Fugen und Noten und
nicht auf die Affectus und Gleichförmigkeit der Wörter".[1] Burney, who
really was the first to analyze more closely the individuality of style
in the Marcellus mass, forms his observations as follows:[2] "I can
venture to assert, that it is the most simple of Palestrina's works: no
canon,[3] inverted fugue or complicated measures have been attempted
throughout the composition, the harmony is pure, and by its facility
the performer and hearer are equally exempted from trouble."

The Marcellus mass the most simple of Palestrina's works! Correctly as Burney has judged here in one way, he can still thank
a lucky chance that he remained right. In reality he did not,
and could not possibly know all this master's compositions; for
at that time the greater part of them were still undiscovered treas-
ures. Nevertheless, as remarked before, his assertion is true to a
certain degree.

The requirements of the church at that time, with regard to polyphonic liturgical music, primarily concerned the intelligibility of the
text.

It is quite obvious that, in the case of the mass, these exactions
especially related to the long, wordy texts of the Gloria and Credo.
In the Kyrie, Sanctus and Agnus Dei, it was of less consequence that
the texts were sometimes veiled by the music, the words here being

---

[1] "Syntagma musicum" III, 1619, p. 150.

[2] Burney: History of Music, III p. 190.

[3] It is evident that Burney had the mass in the form transmitted by Santarelli,
without the 7-part Agnus Dei II, (which is also lacking in the 1567 edition), and in
which two canons occur simultaneously.

few, and therefore easily caught and found coherent. Besides, the shortness of these texts necessitated repetition in most cases; hence there was no need to avoid imitations, which otherwise might cause inconvenience in extended texts of an epic nature, and make it difficult for the listener to follow them.

A minute examination of the Gloria and Credo of the Marcellus mass reveals, at first sight, the fact that note-against-note is employed to an extraordinary degree in these pieces, while imitation is limited to a minimum. This is especially true of the Gloria, this mode of treatment not being carried out quite so strictly in the Credo.

This Gloria, indeed, ranks high above all the other pieces of Palestrina's masses, both with regard to distinctness of text and intelligibility of declamation. The following schematic plan may serve to throw some light upon these relations:

Name of mass.	Where found	A	B	C	Total number of cases
1. Ad fugam	P. XI p. 57	8	75	203	286
2. Brevis	P. XII p. 52	61	93	124	278
3. Ut re mi fa sol	P. XII p. 168	168	83	52	303
4. Beatus Laurentius ..	P. XXIII p. 52	147	72	38	257
5. Assumpta est Maria .	P. XXIII p. 101	169	109	47	325
6. Papæ Marcelli	P. XI p. 131	204	114	31	349

The Glorias of the six masses indicated were used as basic material for this analysis.

An investigation of Palestrina's total Gloria production led to the selection of the numbers from 2 to 6 in the above plan, these being especially chosen because they make extremely little use of imitation. On the other hand, the Gloria of the "Ad fugam" is included for exactly the opposite reason.

An attempt has here been made to procure, if possible, numerical evidence that the supposition, formed mostly from general considerations, of the greater or less distinctness of the text, is correct.

Here as elsewhere, figures *per se* will prove nothing about psychological phenomena of a higher degree of development; yet they may serve to support the correctness of purely practical estimates.

Should the pieces chosen be analyzed with regard to textual intelligibility, then it must be done by examining the intelligibility of the single syllables, since that alone will insure the intelligibility of the whole text, at any rate in Palestrina music, which always uses syllables which belong together in conspicuous proximity to each other, and, (contrary to the custom of earlier Netherland composers), avoids separating syllables of the same words by too prolonged ornamentations, and still less allows the dismemberment of words through pauses.[1]

It may be affirmed without hesitation that syllables which occur either in one part, or coincidentally in all the parts, assert themselves most distinctly. In the foregoing plan, the places where entries of this kind occur in the masses cited have been counted, and the respective numbers have been placed under section A. Conversely, syllables which are introduced in one or several voices coincidentally with the maintenance of quite different syllables formerly introduced, have a less intelligible effect, (Group B, in the plan), while different syllables entering at the same time will be still less distinctly understood, (Group C). In order to facilitate the comparison of the groups, the numerical relations are given in percentages in the following:

	A	B	C
Ad fugam	2.8 %	26.22 %	70.98 %
Brevis	21.94 %	33.45 %	44.6 %
Ut re mi fa sol	55.45 %	27.39 %	17.16 %
Beatus Laurentius	57.2 %	28.0 %	14.79 %
Assumpta est Maria ...	52.0 %	33.54 %	14.46 %
Papæ Marcelli	58.45 %	32.67 %	8.88 %

The text of the "Ad fugam" is least intelligible, which was to be foreseen, because this Gloria (of all this kind of Palestrina's compositions), is the one in which the imitation of the voices is most consistently carried out, (the piece being constructed as a strict double canon).

In the "Missa brevis", which has one of Palestrina's simplest and

---

[1] See, in this connection, Theodor Kroyer: "Zur A-cappella-Frage", A. f. M. 1920, p. 53.

polyphonically least elaborate Glorias, the corresponding percentage amounts to 21.94. The figures of the other 4 masses lie very close to each other. "Papæ Marcelli" ranks highest with its 58.45 %, which only surpasses the Missa "Beatus Laurentius" by an insignificant fraction.

However, it is neither the A nor the B group, (each so nearly of equal importance as to render closer distinctions practically superfluous), which contributes the most weighty evidence towards an estimate concerning texual intelligibility. Upon this point, preponderance lies with group C, under which all vague and confused passages, arising out of the simultaneous entry of different syllables, are collected.

If now we examine the numerical relations of group C, we clearly see the distinctive position of the Marcellus mass; for it is apparent that the latter has only 8.88 % of the kind of cases mentioned, while the mass nearest approaching it, "Assumpta est Maria", has as much as 14.46 %, "Missa brevis" has 44.6 %, and "Ad fugam" 70.98 %.

That the Marcellus mass occupies a quite distinctive position in its creator's production, may thus be considered proved, since the figures in this case confirm a supposition reached in a purely practical, intuitive way.

Baini, (who, notwithstanding his high merits, has in the course of time been placed in a semi-comical light because of the ten different kinds of style which he, in his orderly way, thought he could point out in Palestrina's production), is not altogether wrong in believing it necessary to reserve a particular kind of style solely for the Marcellus mass, (unfortunately, however, without any further explanation of his motives).

Considering the fact that this work in certain ways stands isolated, and that it seems as if even Palestrina himself did not think it necessary to carry out the principles of style asserting themselves here in his subsequent production—later publishing a number of masses in which relatively little attention was paid to the intelligibility of the text—the hypothesis of a change of style, with this composition as its starting-point, is highly improbable. It seems more like a demonstration. Undoubtedly in the Marcellus mass more than in any other of his masses, Palestrina endeavoured to make the text as distinct as possible; the style of the Marcellus mass is not contingent

merely upon purely artistic and musical demands, but also upon exterior, practical exigencies. It is evident that Palestrina himself was
conscious of the peculiar character of this style from the expression
"novo modorum genere", (see the dedication in P. XI. p. III), and moreover from a letter to the Duke of Mantua, in which he inquires whether
the latter wishes the mass, (which he had engaged Palestrina to write),
to be "long or short, or composed so that the words may be understood."[1] The latter case, therefore, is not considered a matter of course,
but dependent upon a distinctive mode of writing which could be employed at will. That Palestrina maintained this mode of writing in the
Marcellus mass with such consistency, (whatever the external, purely
practical circumstances may have been), must doubtless be considered
in connection with the views on liturgical music, expressed at the
Council of Trent, ("ut verba ab omnibus percipi possint", as remarked
in a proposal regarding the reform of church music),[2] and perhaps also
in connection with an event which happened in the short reign of
Marcellus II.[3]

Such a supposition is confirmed by the fact that fragments of masses by other composers, which form the nearest approach hitherto
known to the style of the Gloria in the Marcellus mass, are found in

---

[1] Bertolotti l. c. p. 48: "se li piacerà comandarmi, come la voglia, o breve o
longa, o che si sentan le parole".

[2] S. Weinmann: "Das Konzil von Trient und die Kirchemusik". 1919 p. 4.

[3] Ludwig von Pastor, the Austrian ecclesiastical historian, in his "Geschichte der
Päpste", Bd. VI, 1913, p. 345, calls attention to a passage in Massarelli's "Diarium
VII". Angelo Massarelli, who was on intimate terms with Pope Marcellus, and who
described his life in almost microscopic detail, relates here that on Good Friday,
April 12th, 1555, on the third day of his pontificate, Marcellus had the singers called,
and enjoined them to pay heed in future that the music on Good Friday be selected
in conformity with the serious character of the day; moreover he demanded that the
texts of the songs to be performed should be intelligible. (Consilium Tridentinum,
Friburgi Brisgoviae MCMXI. Pars secunda. p. 256:—pontifex ipse, vocatis ad se can-
toribus ipsis, eis iniunxit, ut quae his diebus sanctis in misteriis passionis et mortis
Christi recitanda erant, ea rei condecentibus, vocibus referrent, atque etiam ita referrent, ut quae proferrebantur, audiri atque percipi possent). It seems not improbable
that this event, at which Palestrina probably was present in his capacity of pontifical
singer, gave the impulse, as Weinmann supposes, to the composition of the Marcellus
mass.

a collection of masses published in 1580 by Vincenzo Ruffo, musical conductor at the Cathedral in Milan, and expressly characterized by him as "novamente composte seconda la forma del Consilio Tridentino".[1]

Still we must take into consideration that in the Marcellus mass we are not dealing with a little, bloodless experiment, but with a work of art of magnificent proportions,—a marvel whose like is scarcely met with once in a century.

The problem here was not only how to bring out the text to the polyphonic music most clearly—in that case, any half-grown chorister could have quickly solved it—but how to secure textual intelligibility at the same time as the artistic value remained unimpaired. In other words, how was note-against-note to be treated in order to hold the æsthetic interest, even when this mode of writing was continued throughout long periods?

Palestrina solved this question with the utmost elegance especially by the exhaustion of the rich, sonorous possibilities which composition for 6 parts offers. He lets groups of voices, differently combined, succeed each other in reciting the text, and refreshes the ear with ever new sound-combinations, and shades of new and delicate colours. At the same time, he employs note-against-note in a peculiar manner, giving striking preference to the upper voice, and endeavouring to indue it with special beauty.

In contrast to the usual rather recitative-like, stationary note-against-note of the Netherland school, the form he employs is distinguished by its high quality of plastic art in melodic construction, by the beauty of its outlines. But it is not our intention to claim that this form was Palestrina's own invention, or that it was used here for the first time. It is true of this, as of the technique of sonorous alternations on the whole, that both were known and used by older masters, yet scarcely before with such intensity as in the Marcellus mass.

The stress which these artistic means received through their fre-

---

quent use in this widely renowned work—which cardinals and musicians alike hailed with joy as the model of true ecclesiastical music—may reasonably be considered influencing the development of the note-against-note motets, which, (in a delicate, sonorous treatment, and with a more modernly developed upper voice), came into notice about 1570.[1]

Thus far it might be said that exterior circumstances exerted an influence on the evolution of this style. But the style of Palestrina certainly did not arise out of any decree of the Tridentine Council. Even if the legend that the Marcellus mass was written especially for the Council should be true,[2] it cannot be denied that other works by Palestrina and his contemporaries, which show relations to imitation and declamation altogether different from those of the Marcellus mass, belong nevertheless to the purest Palestrina style. Perhaps the sympathy for distinct textual rendering to which those high prelates gave utterance at the Council of Trent, may possibly have forwarded the distinctive position of the mass in this regard. But that which gives real significance to the Marcellus mass and other masterpieces of this epoch, their eminent artistic culture, cannot be explained by any single event in general history. The problem resolves itself finally into an inner musical matter, the adequate explanation of which can be found only in the works themselves.

---

[1] Prominent examples of this kind are, among others, the well known motet, "O bone Jesu", which is attributed to Palestrina, but which without doubt owes its origin to a later master; "O crux benedicta" by Pietro Vinci (in a collection of 5-part motets from 1572) incorrectly cited under Goudimel's name in Bellermann's "Der Contrapunkt"; and Simon Molinari's "Adoramus te Christe". In comparison with older vocative motets, (the preference from the 14th to the 16th century being for homophonous modes of writing to vocative texts), these may be recognized, besides from the above-mentioned qualities, by their brief, gracefully rounded, almost song-like form. Cf. my essay: Das isometrische Moment in der Vokalpolyphonie (Peter Wagner-Festschrift. Leipzig 1926, p. 87 sqq.).

[2] Cf. my essay: Wann entstand die Marcellus Messe? (Guido Adler Festschrift. Wien 1930, p. 126 etc.).

The Style of Palestrina

In Palestrina style the starting point is the melodic line, and the technique of this art consists mainly in inventing and combining such independently conducted and conceived lines. The art of Palestrina is therefore of a pronouncedly polyphonic nature, and consequently it is characterized by the tension between melodic and harmonic elements. However, it is especially in the variable strength of this tension that one polyphonic style differs from other historical styles of similar structure, and the dissonance is without doubt the most sensitively indicative manometer upon this point. This criterion of style, besides the above-mentioned general value for musical historical research, consequently has a special function of the greatest importance. However, before undertaking an examination of the degrees of tension starting from the dissonance, it will first be necessary to consider separately the causes of this tension, viz: the harmonic and the melodic ideals of the 16th century—the two conflicting powers, the outcome of whose mutual struggle constitutes the style.

Melody

If we judge the different historical styles by the course of the melodic curve, it is really surprising to remark the very characteristic and deeply-rooted differences that appear. The curves of elevation or undulation in the melody, which characterize all musical art, show a striking variety in different epochs and reveal much of the psychologically fundamental contents of the style,—indeed they seem to lead into the inmost recesses of the latter.

There are two types of movement, mutually contrary to each other, which especially strike the eye here.

The first might be graphically illustrated thus,

 and the second thus,

Schweitzer and Ernst Kurth recognized the first type as characteristic of Bach, who liked to give his melodic curve developments a broad, slowly ascending and gradually intensified movement, and then—having finally reached the culmination point, breaks off, and suddenly rushes downward in a precipitate, cataract-like fall:[1]

J. S. Bach, Orgelpartita: Sei gegrüsset Jesu gütig.

The second type has a short, scarcely noticeable ascent followed by a very gradual and calm floating downward—much like a bird which is suddenly seen in the sunlight, a shining stationary mark high up in the air, and which then glides downwards on outstretched wings, softly and almost without moving:

Kyrie: Te Christe Rex supplices. (Graduale romanum. 1908, p. 69*.)

Ky - ri - e   e - le - i- son.

This curvilinear form, which is found particularly often in Gregorian melodies, on its part doubtless signifies just as genuine and characteris-

---

[1] Albert Schweitzer: J. S. Bach (p. 760): "Wichtig ist es zu beobachten, dass in den gewaltigen Tonperioden, in denen Bach seine Themen konzipiert, der Hauptakzent durch eine oder mehrere vorhergehende Betonungen vorbereitet und ebenso ausgeleitet wird, nur dass die Vorbereitung gewöhnlich viel länger ist als die Ausleitung."—Kurth: Grundlagen des linearen Kontrapunkts. 1917, p. 251: "Ist einmal bei Bachs einstimmigen Linienausspinnungen der Höhepunkt solcher breit angelegten Steigerungen erreicht, so hat die lang verhaltene Auslösung der zur Kulmination entwickelten linearen Spannkraft dann meist etwas Explosives an sich, und die Bewegung stürzt von der Gipfelung des Linienzuges sehr rasch und jäh in die Tiefe zu einem Ruhepunkt hinab."

tic an expression of the style-creative powers and ideals of plainsong, as the other form, on its part, roots deeply in the psychological background of the dramatic-expansive Bach style. In these striking curvilinear contrasts one is rather inclined to see typical criteria of a certain mystic contrast of style—which contrast is as easy to comprehend intuitively as it is difficult to define in conception and words, whether it be termed ascendent-descendent, ecstatic-contemplative, or in conformity with Nietzsche "dionysisch-apollinisch".

On the one side: the Will to accentuate vehemently, to give vent in tempestuous and explosive manner,—on the other: the Endeavour to adjust the forces in a clear and harmonious way.

In the former the interest is strongest in the genesis of things, the rapture of experiencing the evolutionary course is dominant—in the latter the stress falls upon the concentrated appreciation of the stationary, harmonically limited forms.

Palestrina style, properly speaking, belongs to neither of these two groups. It does not incline either to the very intense expansion of energy gradually surging up against heavy pressure, or to the practice of the extended, long-sustained downward sweep.

Palestrina's typical curvilinear form would approximately be:

Motet: Sicut cervus. P. V, p. 148.

As seen here, the ascending and descending movements counterbalance each other with almost mathematical accuracy. This is very often the case with Palestrina, though seldom of course so completely as in this example. Especially the preference of the ascending curve is unusual, the trend of Palestrina being otherwise rather towards the broader, downward tendency of plainsong. The curvilinear course of energy in Palestrina music might appropriately be likened to serenely flowing waters which, checked in their progress at a certain point, quietly and unobtrusively glide out over hindrances and (to retain the influence of the ethos of the style in the simile) spread themselves as over fertile fields.

Proportion and serenity are the principal tendencies of Palestrina's music, and there is perhaps no other musical style in which the passionate momentum, (in the sense of violent and extreme excitement) seems to be so restrained—even so consciously excluded—as in this field of art.

However, the principal means of expressing passionate emotions, in spoken language as well as in music, is the violent and sudden accent —the inordinately strong, high or rhythmically striking tone or harmony. One might certainly also say: the great consumer of attentive energy, for there exists, beyond a doubt, an intimate connection between the passionate emotions and the violent activity of the attention. That which attracts our attention suddenly and intensely, affects us as an expression of extraordinary activity, and involuntarily creates a wave of passion within us.[1]

The attitude of Palestrina towards the accent is characterized by the strictest self-control and the most exquisite refinement. Musically and technically this is shown by the subtile discrimination with which everything is avoided that might make too strong a claim upon the attention, and consequently create the impression of too great activity. In order to throw a clearer light upon this relation it will, however, be necessary first to draw up the following leading principles, which are partly directly self-evident, and partly of a more hypothetical nature—for which reason they should be interpreted merely

---

[1] The possibility of a negative accent is based upon the connection between the attention and the accent. Just as the disproportionately high tone forces itself upon the attention and can therefore produce the effect of an accent, so the disproportionately deep tone may take on the character of an accent when it occurs in circumstances where it is striking in effect. We find this negative melodic accent especially often in the figurative style of Bach. Refer also to Riemanns Musiklexikon 1929, p. 21: "Eine Art negativen Akzents ist nach vorausgehendem crescendo die Ersetzung des Höhepunkts der Tonstärke durch ein plötzliches piano, ein Mittel, dessen bereits von Joh. Stamitz gefundene faszinierende Wirkungen besonders Beethoven zur Geltung gebracht hat." Here too it is the unexpected occurrence of the effect in question which excites the attention by its suddenness, thus creating the accent.

as apparently the only possible explanation of certain technical facts in music, which will be touched upon later.

1. Larger melodic leaps arouse more attention and are consequently felt to be expressive of stronger psychical activity than smaller intervals.

2. The same is the case with higher compared to deeper notes, and, consequently, likewise with ascending in relation to descending movements.

The melodic material of Palestrina is, according to section I, relatively limited. Only the following intervals are regularly used: the major and minor second and third, the perfect fourth, the perfect fifth, the minor sixth (ascending only), and the octave. The reason why the minor sixth is only used in ascending movements is not easily explained; we will therefore let this question rest until various presuppositions, not yet touched upon, have been discussed. Taken altogether, the intervals employed in Palestrina are identical with those of plainsong, only the minor sixth ascending and the octave have been added in polyphonic music.[1] But it would be a mistake to suppose that the Gregorian intervals remained intact during the whole polyphonic period up to Palestrina's time, and that only the minor sixth and the octave had established themselves by the end of this period. In reality the melodic art of Palestrina signifies rather a return to the stricter melodic fashion of plainsong with regard to intervals. In the music of the first and second Netherland schools,[2] for instance, the following intervals are found

Missa: O rosa bella (Tr. II, 15, 5, + 2.)

De - us pa - ter om - ni -

---

[1] The noted descending sixth in the "jubilus" of the Hallelujah verses, "Multifarie", seems a "hapax legomenon" in plainsong.

[2] When not otherwise expressly noted, "dead" intervals are not taken into consideration in this treatise, as they cannot be reckoned as real leaps.

Also in Tr. II, 90, 2, 2; 93, 1, + 2; 97, 5, 3. Tr. III, 38, 4, 3; 141, 4, + 2; 142, 3, + 3; 150, 3, 1.

Josquin des Prés, Missa: Una musque de Biscaya. Gloria, bar 4.

Refer also to Josquin: Una musque de Biscaya. Crucifixus, bar 121. Andreas de Sylva: Missa. Credo, bars 34 and 43. Is. III, 45, 6, + 3. Obr. II, 88, 3, 2. Obr. VII, 32, 1, + 2. Claude Goudimel: Credo of the mass "Le bien que j'ai". (See P. Wagner: Geschichte der Messe, I, p. 268), Goudimel: the end of the motet "Domine quid multiplicati"; (Burney: History of Music, Vol. III, p. 270) and Credo of the mass "Audi filia" (according to Goudimel's: Missae tres. Paris, Adrien le Roy et Robert Ballard, 1558) at the "Qui cum Patre".

Though the two latter examples from Goudimel approach in their effect "dead" intervals, yet the tones of the 7th are rhythmically so placed that they must undoubtedly be understood as melodically related to each other.

The ninth also occurs, though only in isolated instances:

Jouquin des Prés, Missa: Malheur me bat. "Qui tollis", bar 55.

Compare Josquin, Missa: Una musque de Biscaya Kyrie II, bar 28, and also Ambr. III, p. 127. Is. II, 65, 1, + 3.

The occurrence of the tenth 'is comparatively less rare. An instance is

Heinrich Isaac: Dixit Dominus. Is. 1, 118, 3, + 2.

Compare also Obr. II, 125, 2, 1; 161, 3, 2. Obr. IV, 3, 3, 3; 62, 3, 3; 162, 3, + 2. Obr. VI, 103, 1, + 3. Josquin des Prés, Missa: Didadi, Gloria (Domine Deus), bar 12; in the same work, the Sanctus, bar 21; Missa: Lomme armée sexti toni. Credo, bar 62. Missa: Sine nomine. Osanna, bar 22.

At all events it is a question whether these large leaps in Pre-Palestrina compositions are due to instrumental practice or to the influence of instrumental music itself, as is asserted most emphatically by Arnold Schering.[1]

This supposition may seem probable in itself, all the more since it may be considered as proved that instrumentalists also assisted in the performance of ecclesiastical compositions in the 15th and 16th centuries.

Yet it is questionable whether this instrumental practice exercised a really serious influence on style. At any rate it should be kept in mind that these large leaps, which were not used in Palestrina style, were also only used in exceptional instances by the early Netherlanders, (in their masses and motets, as well as in instrumental tablatures). If these melodic progressions had been based upon the greater extent and mobility of musical instruments, it might be justifiable to suppose that they would be found much oftener in the in-

---

[1] "Die niederländische Orgelmesse im Zeitalter des Josquin" (1912) p. 4 sqq. Refer also to the controversy between Hugo Leichtentritt and Schering. Z. I. M., September and October 1913. Cf. also Theodor Kroyer: Das A-cappella-Ideal. Acta. 1934, p. 152 sqq.

strumental music of the period than is the case. But they remain the
exception here as elsewhere, and assuredly may be assigned a place
among the licences about which composers in the 15th and early 16th
centuries were not so strict,—just as there was less appreciation then
of the fine reserve of the style than during the florescence of the
Roman school.

We find neither sevenths, ninths nor tenths used as real intervals
in Palestrina's works.[1] Of irregular intervals he only uses (extremely
seldom) major sixths, thus a major ascending sixth[2] in the

Motet: Parce mihi. Pars II. (P. IV, 116, 1, 4. Compare likewise P. XXIX, 157, 1, 1.)

O   cu-stos   ho-mi-num

Such sixths (and also descending minor sixths) are also not often
used by the Netherlanders, though more frequently than by Palestrina.

Josquin des Prés, Missa: Sine nomine. Osanna, bar 17.

See also Josquin, Missa: Gaudeamus, "Et in spiritum", bar 29; Agnus III, bar 19; Missa: Sine nomine, Agnus I, the third from the last
bar; Obr. II, 46, 3, 2. Obr. IV, 47, 3, 2; 70, 2, 2; 153, 1, 3. Obr. V, 27, 5, 1.
Obr. VI, 29, 2, + 2.

Palestrina often employs both major sixths and descending minor
sixths as "dead" intervals.[3] This is also frequently done by the Nether-

---

[1] The tenth in the mass, Ave Maria (P. XV. 141, 3, 3, Altus I.) should be eliminated
as, according to the original edition of the sixth book of masses (Gardano 1596), it
is a misprint. The first two notes of the bar should be D and B flat, instead of B
flat and G.

[2] The major descending sixth, P. XIX, 127, 3, 3, is surely a misprint; doubtless the
first note of tenor I (E) should be D.

[3] See for instance P. X, 141, 3, 4; 171, 1, + 3. P. XXVIII, 40, 2, 3. P. V, 104, 2, 2.
P. XI, 4, 2, 2; 144, 2, + 3. P. I, 11, 2, + 1. P. XII, 126, 2, + 2. P. II, 25, 1, + 4.
P. III, 164, 3, 2. P. V, 127, 4, 2. P. XIII, 18 3, + 4; 31, 2, 3. P. IV, 62, 2, 3; 147, 1, 3;
147, 3, + 4. P. XXVIII, 87, 2, 1; 92, 1, + 2; 95, 1, + 4; 104, 3, 2. P. XIV, 4, 3, 4.

56

landers. The example from Clemens non Papa which Griesbacher cites
in his "Kirchenmusikalische Stilistik und Formenlehre" (Vol. II, p. 44),

Pr. II, 65, 1, + 1. Motet: Vox in Rama.

- - - tus plo - ra - tus

shows a "dead" interval of the sixth of this kind, which, consequently,
is not very exceptional.

The legitimate leaps larger than a fifth are not excessively employed by Palestrina, but when it does happen they are always ef-
fectively used. An example among others of the minor sixth is found in

P. IX, 16, 1, 1. Offertorium: Tui sunt coeli.

Tu - i sunt coe - li

Concerning octaves we find that they are used both in the ascending
and the descending direction. Bellermann is not altogether willing to
admit the descending octaves, but finally concedes that they too were
used in contrapuntal parts: "Dass man die Oktave aber, auch abwärtssteigend, als wesentlichen und charakteristischen Bestandteil eines
Themas benützt hätte, ist mir nicht bekannt".[1]

Nevertheless they occur, used in this way:

P. III, 90, 3, 1. Motet: Domine Deus. Secunda pars.

-o, ut ca - dat ro - bur

P. XXVII, 43, 1, 2. P. IX, 107, 2, 2. P. XXVI, 43, 3, 3. P. XV, 6, 3, + 1; 67, 4, 3.
P. XVI, 45, 4, 5; 59, 1, + 2. P. XVII, 20, 4, + 4. P. XIX, 125, 1, + 3. P. XXI, 81, 1,
+ 2; 102, 1, 1.

[1] "Der Contrapunkt", 4. Aufl. (1901), p. 110.

P. IX, 150, 3, 1. Offertorium: Si ambulavero.

ex - ten - des ma - - - num

That Palestrina also uses the descending leap of the octave thematically where, in contradistinction to the two foregoing examples, there is no question of a tonal picture, is evident, *inter alia*, in the following example:

P. XXIV, 95, 3, 1. Missa: Benedicta.

ple - ni sunt coe - li et ter - ra   et

In Palestrina style, however, other elements than extent can also have a limiting effect upon the use of intervals. Thus, as is well known, augmented and diminished intervals are not employed, or at any rate only as "dead" intervals.[1] This circumstance may be owing to these intervals being considered too striking modifications of the simpler, diatonic intervals current since the time of plainsong.

Palestrina's melody is extraordinarily interesting seen from the viewpoint of our second axiom: Higher notes arouse more attention, and therefore are felt to express stronger psychologic activity than deeper notes.

This thought leads us into a domain where we approach the common origin of spoken language and music. It is thus a philological fact, that stress and relatively high notes most frequently, though not always, are related.[2] This rule has also a certain validity with

---

[1] With composers prior to Palestrina this also was different; both augmented fourths and diminished fifths are used, though only as exceptions. Compare Tr. III, 63, 3, 4. Is. I, 27, 4, 2. Obr. IV, 28, 2, + 2. Josquin: Una musque de Biscaya, Credo, bar 132. Compare also the end of the same mass, (Ambr. III, p. 125). Missa: Fortuna desperata, Osanna, bar 14. The younger contemporaries of Palestrina in this respect as in many others also act more freely than Palestrina himself. Thus Victoria quite frequently uses diminished fourths descending.

[2] Otto Jespersen: Lehrbuch der Phonetik, 2, edition, Leipzig 1913, p. 226: "Je stärker wir eine Silbe oder einen Laut aussprechen, desto höher sind wir auch geneigt, ihn zu machen."

regard to music, and has exerted great influence upon the development of this art. As Robert Lach expresses it, "Das Hauptmittel aber der Lautverteilung und -anordnung, das Grundprinzip aller Gliederung überhaupt, ist das Akzentuierungsprinzip: indem der Akzent einerseits betonte von unbetonten Silben scheidet, andererseits der betonten Silbe eine höhere Tonstufe zuerkennt als der unbetonten, wird er so zur Grundwurzel und zum Ausgangspunkt jener rhytmischen und tonalen Differenzierung, die in der Musik einerseits als musikalische Architektonik, andererseits als Aneinanderreihung verschiedener Töne zu einem neuen, einheitlichen Ganzen, d. i. zur Melodie, zutage tritt".[1] The phonetic rule that "the more weight the thought places upon the word, the higher the note it will be given"—which rule may be disputed, since stress (i. e. strength of tone) for instance may have the same function as pitch—is at all events musically valid in its inversion "the higher the pitch of a melodic point, the stronger the impression of mental energy".[2] The well known rhythm-creative effect of high or relatively high notes is founded upon this principle.[3] But in music as in language, other factors besides pitch and strength of tone may also produce accentual effects, especially duration of tone.[4] In addition we

---

[1] Studien zur Entwickelungsgeschichte der ornamentalen Melopöie (1913) p. 569.

[2] Compare with this the experimental results in Ohmanns "Melodie und Akzent". Kongress für Ästhetik und allgemeine Kunstwissenschaft. 1914, p. 479.

[3] Meumann Ph. St. Bd. 9, p. 307: "— — es scheint nämlich, dass hohe Töne uns intensiver erscheinen als tiefe von gleicher objektiver Schallstärke. Dies fällt besonders ins Gewicht bei schroffen Übergängen von tiefen Tönen zu hohen und umgekehrt .... ein einzelner Ton, der beträchtlich höher oder tiefer liegt als die unmittelbar vorausgehenden und nachfolgenden Töne, erscheint in seiner Bedeutung für die Markierung des Zeitfortschrittes gesteigert" etc. Perhaps there is a connection between this greater effect of the higher notes and their shorter periods of reaction. Compare Gustav Kafka: "Über das Ansteigen der Tonerregung". Ps. St. II, p. 292: "Die akustische Erregung bedarf einer messbaren Zeit, um ihre volle subjektive Intensität zu erreichen, und zwar beträgt diese bei geringen, objektiven Intensitäten ungefähr 1.5 Sekunden, mit wachsender Intensität (und anscheinend auch wachsender Tonhöhe) nimmt die zur Erreichung des Maximums erforderliche Zeit immer mehr ab. Der Anstieg erfolgt zuerst rasch, dann immer langsamer." Götz Martius: "Über die Reaktionszeit und Perzeptionsdauer der Klänge." Ph. St. VI, p. 415: "Die Reaktionszeiten auf Klänge nehmen mit wachsender Höhe derselben, soweit sich die bisherige Untersuchung erstreckt hat, ab."

[4] Just as we often mark very important words by speaking in a slow, solemn

have the typically musical factors: harmony, dissonance, ornamentation, and probably several other elements constructive of rhythm.[1]

These different factors show a certain tendency to co-operate, to appear simultaneously. For instance, it is a generally recognized and experimentally proved fact that in playing we are involuntarily disposed to broaden out the dynamically accentuated notes somewhat more than is strictly correct.[2] Thus we have the co-operation here of the dynamic and time accents.

Likewise there is no doubt that there is a tendency to an exaggerated dwelling upon the relatively higher notes, which means a combination of the melodic and the time accents.[3]

The relations of the dynamic and melodic accents are especially important in musical form construction. As already stated, their combination in language, though often a fact, is not altogether necessary.[4]

---

tempo with what Jespersen calls "Wertdruck" (stress of value), seeking thus to draw the attention of the listener to that which seems to us of importance, so also we are inclined to interpret as the bearer of the accent in music such notes as stand out conspicuously on account of their duration. The contrary, however, is also possible, e. g. when a series of equally long notes is followed by a few rapid short ones, the attention is aroused by the latter and we experience the mystic, active state which we call "accent".

[1] O. Abraham and E. v. Hornbostel: "Phonographierte indische Melodien." Sammelbände für vergleichende Musikwissenschaft I, p. 285: "Neben den bereits erwähnten Kriterien der *dynamischen Akzentuierung* (Intensitätsunterschiede) und der *relativen Tondauer* (temporale Unterschiede) wird unsre rhythmische Auffassung (Gruppierung durch Verteilung subjektiver Akzente) noch durch eine Reihe *qualitativer* Faktoren geleitet. Ein Ton mag sich ceteris paribus durch Tonhöhe und Klangfarbe oder was immer von einer Reihe andrer Töne unterschieden, immer wird die Aufmerksamkeit durch die Abweichung in Anspruch genommen, und der betreffende Ton erhält so ein psychisches Übergewicht (*psychologischer Akzent*)."

[2] Compare Meumann l. c. p. 309. Consult also Kurt Ebhardt: "Zwei Beiträge zur Psychologie des Rhythmus und des Tempo" (Z. f. Ps. vol. 18, p. 139 etc.).

[3] We have only to observe a large assembly united in singing to see how they hold on to high notes of the melody, or, when such a high note is near, rush on over intervening less prominent notes, taking no heed of rhythmic requirements, hypnotically fascinated by this luminous attraction—one of many other proofs of the power of high notes to arouse attention.

[4] Otto Jespersen l. c. p. 226: "Jedoch darf man nicht Ton und Druck als zwei Dinge auffassen, die einander notwendig begleiten, oder gar als ein und dasselbe— eine Auffassung, die zu vielen unglücklichen und verwirrenden Benennungen wie

Something similar holds good in music. There is an obvious disposition at any rate to place high notes on dynamically (or rhythmic-psychologically) accented points; and it is probable that if we were to go through our entire musical literature, counting the cases where the ascending movement goes from the unaccented to the accented beat, and comparing these with the number in which the opposite takes place, we should substantiate a majority—though, may be, not a great one—for the first group.[1] A closer examination would show that very different kinds of technique in this respect are found in the different epochs. It is especially interesting to observe this technique in Palestrina music—characteristic and eloquent of the psychologic atmosphere of the style.

It is a well known fact that minims were employed mainly as time units in the middle of the 16th century. Usually there were four of these minims in the bar, of which the first and third were stressed, while the second and fourth were unaccented. It often happens that the melodic culmination points fall upon the stressed parts of the measure, thus causing a descending movement from the heavy to the light minims. But it also happens very often that there is a gradual movement upward from the accented beat; likewise it is quite usual, (though not so frequent as the opposite case), that an upward leap from the dynamically accentuated beat occurs. For instance:

P. XIX, 17, 1, + 3. Missa: In illo tempore.

Sa - - - - - - ba - oth

"Hochton" u. dgl. und besonders "Betonung, betont" geführt haben, wo nur von Druck die Rede sein sollte. Ebenso wie in der Musik ein tiefer Ton forte oder fortissimo und ein hoher Ton piano oder pianissimo sein kann, ebenso kann in der Sprache eine starke Silbe tiefen Ton und eine schwache Silbe hohen Ton haben — — — "

[1] Todoroff confirmed this supposition through statistics, the material used embracing among other things Schubert's "Müllerlieder". (Kosta Todoroff: "Beiträge zur Lehre von der Beziehung zwischen Text und Komposition". Z. f. Ps., 1. Abt., Vol. 63, p. 401). Also Ohmann (l. c. p. 478) came to similar results. Refer likewise to Kurt Huber: "Der Ausdruck musikalischer Elementarmotive." Leipzig 1923, p. 164 sqq.

The general statement may doubtless be made that there is no very intimate correlation of the dynamic and melodic accents in Palestrina, at any rate where the movement progresses in the time units. But on considering the style with regard to crotchets (half time-units) we meet with the astonishing fact, not previously observed, that a rule (almost without an exception) forbids the leap upward from an accentuated crotchet. Downward it is, however, legitimate, as the following ornamentations show:[1]

[1] The melismata cited may be found in the following places: 1 = P. XII, 146, 3, + 3. 2 = P. IV, 142, 3, 3. P. XXX, 176, 2, + 3 (d.); 176, 3, 1 (d.). 3 = P. V, 3, 2 + 1; 122, 1, + 1 etc. P. XIX, 43, 3, + 1 etc. 4 = P. XXXII, 39, 3, 1. 5 = P. II, 148, 2, 4. P. IV, 35, 2, 1; 35, 3, + 3; 111, 3, + 1. P. VIII, 15, 5, + 3; 160, 2, 3. P. IX, 101, 2, + 3. P. X, 156, 3, 3. P. XI, 49, 1, + 2 and + 1. P. XIV, 47, 4, 1; 109, 3, 1. P. XVI, 84, 2, 3. P. XVII, 63, 1, + 2. P. XVIII, 125, 2, + 1. P. XIX, 41, 2, 4. P. XX, 51, 1, + 3. P. XXII, 36, 3, 4; 36, 4, + 3; 37, 1, 4; 37, 2, 2, + 3; 56, 2, 1; 98, 2, 1; 107, 3, + 3. P. XXIII, 46, 2, + 3; 97, 2, + 2; 97, 3, 2. P. XXXII, 10, 1, + 1 sqq.; 42, 3, 3; 81, 3, 1 (d.); 82, 4, + 3 sqq. (d.); 90, 3, + 2 sqq. (d.). 6a = P. III, 52, 2, 3. P. VIII, 20, 5, 2; 90, 3, + 1. P. IX, 194, 2, 2. P. XIII, 27, 2, + 3. P. XIV, 47, 4, 2. P. XXI, 62, 2, 4. P. XXXI, 57, 1, 2 (d.); 57, 3, + 4 (d.); 153, 1, + 2 (d.); 153, 2, 1 (d.). 6b = P. XXIII, 138, 3, 5. P. XXXII, 147, 4, 1 (d.). 6c = P. XVIII, 98, 3, + 2. 7 = P. III, 117, 1, 1. P. XXIII, 68, 2, + 1. 8 = P. I, 25, 3, 1; 29, 3, 1. P. IX, 51, 1, + 3. P. XXVII, 253, 1, 1 (d.). 9 = P. XXI, 89, 1, + 1. P. XXX, 170, 4, + 1 (d.). 10 = P. XXXII, 83, 1, 2 (d.). 11 = P. IX, 94, 2, 3. P. XXIV, 98, 1, + 1. 12 = P. XXI, 14, 4 + 3. 13 = P. I, 126, 3, + 4. P. II, 55, 2, + 1. P. IV, 22, 3, 1; 79, 3, 3. P. XII, 31, 4, 1 etc. P. XVI, 95, 2, 4. P. XVII, 16, 4, + 3. P. XXII,

134, 3 + 2. P. XXIII, 79, 1, + 2. P. XXIV, 137, 1, 1. P. XXVII, 69, 4, 2. **14** = P. I, 84, 1,
+ 3. P. II, 133, 2, + 2. P. IV, 17, 2, 3; 24, 2, 2; 41, 1, 3; 42, 1, 2; 82, 2, + 2 and + 3; 82,
3, 3 and 4; 104, 2, 1; 107, 3, + 3; 108, 2, 1. P. V, 30, 2, 1; 151, 1, + 2. P. VIII, 11, 2, 4; 28,
2, + 4 and + 2; 92, 2, + 2; 116, 2, + 3; 131, 3, 4; 175, 4, + 3. P. IX, 3, 3, + 4; 48, 2, 1;
59, 2, + 4 and + 2; 59, 3, 2 sqq.; 60, 1, 2; 118, 2, + 4 sqq.; 125, 1, + 2; 135, 1, 1; 138, 2,
+ 1; 148, 2, 4; 149, 3, + 2. P. X, 9, 3, + 4; 14, 6, 4 and + 3; 15, 1, 1 and 4; 15, 2, 1; 18,
1, 3 sqq.; 32, 2, + 2; 37, 1, 2 sqq.; 48, 4, 2 sqq.; 71, 5, 1 sqq.; 101, 3, 4; 139, 3, 3. P. XI,
31, 3, 3; 50, 4, + 1; P. XIII, 46, 3, + 2; 74, 2, + 2; 76, 3, 4. P. XIV, 33, 3, 3; 35, 4, 3; 39,
3, 1; 46, 4, + 4; 124, 2, 1. P. XV, 37, 4, + 1; 38, 1, + 3; 55, 4, + 3 and + 1; 69, 1,
+ 3 sqq.; 98, 2, + 2. P. XVI, 18, 3, + 2. 79, 2, 3 sqq. (14 times). P. XVII, 7, 3, 4 sqq.; 10,
2, 2 and + 3; 12, 2, 4 and + 2; 12, 3, 4 and + 2; 13, 3, 1; 17, 4, 1; 19, 2, 2 sqq.; 20, 1, 4
and + 1. 20, 2, 2 and + 1, and + 3; 60, 3, 4; 75, 3, 2; 81, 4, 3. P. XVIII, 12, 4, + 1; 18,
3, + 1; 57, 3, + 3; 59, 2, + 4; 60, 2, + 3; 86, 3, + 2; 91, 2, 3; 114, 3, 4 sqq. P. XIX, 76,
1, 1. P. XX, 13, 1, 1; 7, 4, + 3; 75, 1, 1. P. XXI, 11, 2, + 3; 17, 3, + 4; 71, 3, 1; 103,
1, 2; 103, 1, + 3; 103, 2, 1. P. XXII, 65, 2, 2. P. XXIII, 37, 4, 3 and 4 and + 2. P. XXIV,
134, 2, 3; 140, 3, + 2. P. XXVII, 20, 1, + 2; 25, 1, 2; 33, 4, 1 and 2; 52, 1, 3 and + 2; 62,
3, 3. **15** = very common, e.g. P. XXIV, 47, 3, + 1; **16** = P. II, 45, 3, + 1. P. V, 24, 2,
+ 2; 89, 2, 1; P. VII, 35, 1, + 1 (d.); 57, 1, 2 (d.) (imitations). P. IX, 80, 2, 2; 154, 2, +
2. P. X, 35, 4, + 1. P. XIV, 2, 2, 1. P. XV, 120, 1, 2. P. XVI, 16, 4, + 2. P. XVII, 7, 2, 3.
P. XVIII, 73, 3, 3; 132, 4, + 2; 133, 1, + 4; P. XX, 44, 2, + 4. P. XXI, 85, 1, + 1. P.
XXIII, 37, 2, + 3 and + 2. P. XXVII, 171, 1, 1 (d.). P. XXVIII, 47, 4, + 2. **17** = P. XVII,
96, 1, 1. P. XXII, 77, 3, 3. P. XXX, 188, 1, + 4. **18** = P. II, 60, 3, 1. P. VII, 170, 2, + 2
(d.); 171, 1, 1 (d.). P. XVI, 91, 3, + 2. P. XXI, 27, 1, 4. **19** = very common. e.g. P. IV,
9, 2, + 2. **20** = P. II, 27, 3, 1. P. IV, 33, 1, + 2; 53, 1, + 2. P. XI, 126, 1, + 4. P. XII,
158, 3, + 2; 159, 2, + 3. P. XVI, 56, 2, + 2. P. XVIII, 56, 3, 2 sqq. P. XIX, 104, 2, 4. P.
XX, 27, 3, 3; 33, 3, + 2. P. XXI, 106, 3, + 3; 129, 1, 3. P. XXIV, 73, 3, 2 sqq. **21** = P. I,
66, 3, 4; 86, 1, + 3; 107, 3, + 3; 126, 3, + 4; 128, 1, + 3; 146, 2, 3. P. II, 23, 1, 3; 23, 3,
+ 1; 27, 3, + 4. P. IV, 7, 1, + 3; 13, 1, 2; 102, 2, + 3 and 3, + 3. P. XVII, 70, 3, 3; 71,
2, + 2. P. XXIV, 3, 1, + 1. **22** = P. I, 82, 3, 5. P. II, 32, 3, + 1; 168, 2, 3. P. III, 8, 1, +
4; 47, 3, 2. P. IV, 15, 2, 4. P. XVII, 70, 2, + 1. **23** = P. XI, 127, 3, 2. P. XII, 18, 4, + 3;
61, 5, 2. P. XVI, 36, 3, + 3. P. XVIII, 1, 4, 4. P. XXVIII, 16, 2, + 1; 16, 4, 1. **24** = P. I,
94, 3, 1. P. II, 68, 1, 2 and 3, + 2. P. IV, 39, 2, + 3; 53, 1, 4. P. V, 49, 1, 1; 58, 2, + 2;
86, 4, 3; 105, 1, 2. P. VIII, 115, 2, 4. P. XI, 7, 1, 4; 12, 2, + 2; 20, 2, + 3; 71, 3, + 1; 81,
3, + 4. P. XII, 49, 3, + 4. P. XXIV, 3, 3, 4. **25** = P. XIV, 27, 4, 3 and 4; 28, 1, 1 etc. **26**
= P. I, 42, 3, 5; 124, 2, + 1. P. II, 60, 3, + 4. P. V, 38, 4, + 3; 65, 1, + 4. P. VIII, 102, 4,
+ 2; 111, 4, + 2. P. XII, 68, 2, + 4; 77, 3, + 2; 78, 1, + 1; 166, 3, + 2. P. XIV, 14, 2,
+ 2; 135, 1, 2. P. XVIII, 35, 1, 1; 88, 3, 4 and + 3; 91, 2, + 1; 127, 1, + 3. P. XXI, 7, 1,

These modes of expression are as commonplace as their inversions
are rare. An ornament like

is obviously quite a harmless inversion of the perfectly legitimate
motive in No. 3; yet I have never encountered it in Palestrina (at any
rate where the time units are minims), nor do I know, up to the present,
of more than one single instance in works dating from the florescence of
Italian vocal polyphony:

M. D. II, 407, 1, 1. Costanzo Porta, Motet: Vidi turbam magnam.

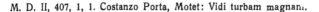

3 and 4. P. XXII, 15, 1, + 3; 27, 4, 1; 147, 3, + 3. P. XXIII, 50, 1, 4; 124, 3, 2; 125, 2,
+ 3; 128, 2, 3; 150, 2, 2. P. XXIV, 24, 2, 3; 79, 1, 2. P. XXIX, 189, 1, + 2. P. XXXI, 163,
1, 4. **27ª** = P. II, 152, 2, 3. **27ᵇ** = P. VIII, 170, 4, 2; P. XXI, 96, 1, 2. **28** = P. IV, 102, 2,
3. P. XVI, 63, 1, 4. P. XX, 107, 1, 4. **29** = P. IV, 7, 1, + 3. P. IX, 94, 2, 4; 131, 1, 4; 141,
3, + 1; 159, 1, + 4. P. XI, 76, 1, 4. P. XV, 65, 4, + 3. P. XVIII, 13, 2, + 3. P. XXII, 100,
4, + 2. P. XXIX, 131, 1, 3; 157, 3, + 3. **30** = P. II, 51, 2, 4. P. XII, 183, 1, + 2. P. XIII,
107, 1, + 2. P. XXV, 182, 2, 4. P. XXIX, 82, 2, 4; 83, 1, + 3. **31** = P. III, 36, 3, 4. P. XIV,
129, 2, 5. **32** = P. I, 17, 3, + 4; 27, 1, + 2; 125, 3, + 2; 151, 1, + 3. P. II, 143, 1, + 2. P.
III, 83, 3, 4. P. IV, 11, 2, + 2. P. V, 59, 3, + 4; 163, 3, 4. P. VI, 78, 2, 1. P. VIII, 15, 3, 3
and 5; 44, 3, + 3; 158, 3, 1 and 2. P. XII, 84, 3, + 2; 117, 3, 2. P. XVII, 67, 1, + 2. P.
XVIII, 28, 3, 3; 35, 4, 1; 78, 1, 1. P. XIX, 2, 1, + 1. P. XX, 111, 2, + 3. P. XXI, 128, 1, + 3.
P. XXIV, 3, 3, 3; 42, 1, + 2; 75, 3, + 3. P. XXVII, 61, 4, + 1; 62, 3, 1; 63, 1, + 3. **33** =
P. XXVIII, 48, 4, + 1. **34** = P. IV, 20, 3, + 3. **35** = P. XXVI, 86, 2, + 3. P. XXIX, 164, 3,
+ 2.

It is clear, however, that there was a dilemma about this phrase, the G of the bass being mainly intended as a means of avoiding consecutive fifths, which would otherwise arise between the bass and the alto.

A very significant fact also is that, although the ornamentation in No. 15

is one of the most commonly used in this style and occurs innumerable times in Palestrina's own compositions, its inversion in the 16th century is so rare that I can only refer to six such examples from Palestrina's authentic works.[1] In two of these instances the leaps of the third ascend from the third crotchet in order to avoid faults in composition, such as fifths and octaves:

P. IX, 92, 2, 1. Offertorium: Confirma hoc Deus.

For instance, the continuation here of the F as a minim in the second measure of the tenor would cause consecutive fifths between the tenor and alto. A similar case is the example P. XXII, 47, 4, + 2. Also figures like

---

[1] P. I, 159, 1, 3. P. IX, 92, 2, 1. P. XV, 55, 2, 3. P. XVIII, 119, 3, 4. P. XXII, 47, 4, + 2. P. XXIII, 19, 5, 4. See likewise P. XXX, 170, 1, 4 and + 1 (d.). P. XXXI, 2, 3, 2 (d.).

when found, (which is extremely seldom), are used for the most part to evade unwelcome parallels of this kind or difficulties in the textual distribution.[1] When such difficulties arise, it may happen moreover that a leap larger than a third, and ascending from an accentuated crotchet, is risked.[2] An irregularity of this kind may also be occasioned by the exigency of moving the melody to a higher and vocally more grateful position;[3] it may depend also upon other factors, as for instance the contraction of two themes, whereby a rhythmically constrained situation is brought about, (P. VIII, 145, 2, 2), and finally also upon "Austerzung" (equipment of thirds, P. IX, 5, 1, + 3).[4]

It must, however, be emphasized that all these cases just cited, if the great quantity of material which has been examined is taken into consideration, only amount to the isolated exceptions that prove the rule which I will call the "high-note law" of Palestrina style: *An avoidance as far as possible of ascending leaps from accentuated to unaccentuated crotchets.*

Yet it is incontestable that still further exceptions to this rule than the above-mentioned may be found in the works of Palestrina and his contemporaries; but these licences, (which will now be explained), are of such a clear and comprehensible character, that they do not at all influence the general validity of the rule.

It has previously been stated that time units (minims) are treated more freely by Palestrina than crotchets, for it not infrequently happens that he leaps upward from an accentuated minim. But in Palestrina style the syllables usually can only be placed upon time units,

---

[1] See a) P. II, 131, 3, 3. P. III, 14, 1, + 4; 46, 1, 4. P. XX, 26, 2, 1. P. XXXIII, 67, 3, + 4. b) P. XVIII, 60, 1, 2. P. XXIV, 66, 1, + 1.

[2] See P. XIV, 130, 1, 1. P. XXIII, 11, 2, + 3. P. XXVIII, 92, 3, 3; 182, 1, 3 (d.). P. XXIX, 135, 1, 1; 187, 1, + 2.

[3] Compare P. X, 8, 3, 4. P. XXI, 65, 2, 3.

[4] The queer, uncalled-for leap of the ascending fourth (P. XX, 120, 2, + 3) should be eliminated, for according to the original edition of the 11th book of masses (Venice 1600) it is a misprint, the first note in the alto not being dotted, and the second a minim.

evidently because the change of syllables on such short values as crotchets was considered impractical. Nevertheless it sometimes happens that the movement of the syllables takes place on crotchets simultaneously in all the parts. Whole compositions (usually madrigals) may be thus contrived; but this technique may also be found employed momentarily in works, (though extremely seldom in Palestrina's), where the time units are mainly minims: P. V, 172, 3, + 1, Motet: Pueri Hebraeorum. (Compare likewise Victoria I, 144, 3, + 2, in this treatise p. 243).

ob - vi - a - ve - runt Do - mi - no

ob - vi - a - ve - runt Do - mi - no

ob - vi - a - ve - runt Do - mi - no

It is probable that the passages were performed with a ritardando, for which reason it is understandable that the crotchets were employed in the same manner as minims. Perhaps it was also a significant fact that these crotchets do not belong to the same syllable, which weakens their mutual connection.

Another exception to the given rule is less directly explicable. In the works of Palestrina and his fellows we relatively often encounter passages like the following

P. XX. 71,3,3. Missa: Quando lieta sperai.

- - - - ctus

in which an upward leap from an accented (tied) crotchet also occurs.[1]

---

[1] Refer to P. I, 137, 3, + 1. P. III, 77, 3, + 3. P. IV, 107, 3, + 3. P. V, 179, 1, 1. P. XII, 173, 2, 4. P. XIII, 69, 1, + 4; 120, 2, 1. P. XIV, 26, 4, + 3; 74, 2, + 2; 81, 4, 3; 89, 1, + 2.

On closer examination, however, all these cases are found to have as the feature in common that it is a dotted minim in an ascending leap of a third (generally a minor third), which then takes a step of the second downward, followed most often by still another step of the second in the same direction. Thus there is here a conventional mode of expression of an obviously ornamental character. However, this must be looked upon as archaism in Palestrina, a rudiment inherited from the Netherland school; for in the works of masters like Obrecht, Josquin and Isaac it is found much oftener than in the second half of the cinquecento.

On the whole, ascending leaps starting from accentuated crotchets are not very uncommon with transalpine musicians and become perceptibly more frequent when we go back into the polyphonic period.[1]

P. XV, 76, 4, 4. P. XVI, 30, 2, + 3. P. XVIII, 22, 3, + 2; 41, 3, 3. P. XIX, 40, 2, 4; 40, 3, 4; 46, 2, + 1 and 3, 4; 74, 2, 2. P. XX, 22, 3, 1; 32, 2, 3; 59, 2, 3; 64, 1, 4; 69, 3, + 4; 73, 1, + 4. P. XXI, 77, 2, 3; 87, 1, + 1. P. XXII, 5, 1, + 2; 20, 4, 3. P. XXIII, 19, 3, 4; 19, 3, + 2; 41, 3, + 4. P. XXVII, 84, 4, 2; 101, 3, 1; 130, 3, + 1. P. XXVIII, 151, 3, 1; 180, 1, + 2. P. XXXIII, 13, 3, 3; 28, 2, 3; 81, 2, 2 (d.). Noticeable here is the almost invariable tendency towards forming a conclusion—the only exceptions I know being P. XXI, 32, 4, + 3 and P. XXXII, 53, 1, + 2 (d.).

[1]) Compare Obr. I, 46, 1, + 2; 119, 3, + 1; 119, 4, 1; 129, 4, + 3; 141, 3, 1; 175, 1, + 1 sqq.; 188, 2, 3; 199, 3, 2; 226, 2, + 1; 226, 4, 1; 241, 2, + 1. Obr. II, 85, 4, + 1; 123, 3, 2; 134, 3, 2; 135, 3, 1; 136, 1, 2; 136, 4, 1; 145, 4, 3 (with the semibreve as time unit) 158, 5. 1. Obr. III, 40, 4, 1; 44, 4, 1 sqq.; 148, 1, 2; 148, 3, 1; 172, 4, + 1; 173, 4, + 1; 178, 2, + 2; 203, 4, 2. Obr. IV, 46, 2, 2; 60, 2, 2; 137, 4, 2; 138, 3, 2; 191, 4, 1; 200, 1, 1; 214, 3, 2; 218, 4, + 1. Obr. V, 35, 1, + 2; 45, 3, 2. Obr. VI, 14, 2, 2; 20, 3, + 1; 21, 2, 2; 29, 2, + 2; 30, 1, 1; 30, 2, 1; 52, 3, 2; 55, 2, 2; 78, 1, 1; 78, 2, 1; 136, 2, 3. Obr. VII, 58, 3, + 2. Is. I, 100, 2, 4; 111, 4, + 2; 137, 2, + 1; 142, 2, 4; 187, 4, 2; 218, 1, 3; 221, 4, + 2. Is. II, 2, 4, + 2; 18, 5, + 2; 54, 5, + 2; 58, 4, + 3; 79, 1, + 4 sqq.; 127, 2, + 4; 128, 4, 4; 132, 3, + 3. Is. III, 6, 5, 2 and 4; 13, 2, 4; 55, 3, + 2; 77, 5, + 3; 90, 4, + 3; 117, 5, 3; 118, 3, 3; 133, 3, + 1; 144, 1, + 4; 148, 6, 4; 157, 2, + 3; 157, 5, 1; 190, 5, 1; 191, 1, + 3. Jos. I, 30, 3, + 2. Jos. II, 5, 4, + 2. In view of this practice the following passage should also be considered, a phrase that so far as I know occurs nowhere else in Palestrina's works:

P. X. 20, 3, + 4 sqq. Missa: Ecce sacerdos magnus.

That this figure should be found in probably the oldest work of Palestrina that has

The following observation may serve to give an insight into the psychology of these ornamental exceptions. Palestrina's 5-part mass "Nigra sum" (P. XIV, 81, 4, 3) has the melodic passage:

i - te - rum ven - tu - - - - rus est

But this theme had already in the same mass (68, 3, 4) been given the following rhythmic form:

Ky - ri - e e - lei - -

We notice that the minim is dotted in the first, but not in the second case. Concerning Palestrina's mass, "Nigra sum", I may call attention to the fact that the basis of this mass (hitherto unknown), is a motet of the same name by l'Heritier.[1] In this motet the original form of the phrase is

in de - o di - lex - it me

been preserved, and the one that shows the influence of Netherland art most markedly, is surely not a mere accident. We find exactly the same effect in Josquin des Prés' mass, "La sol fa re mi", Et in terra, bar 32 sqq.:

do - mi - ne————— . De - us

and in the Gloria of the mass "Amis des que" by Costanzo Festa.

[1] Printed in the collection: Secundus liber cum quinque vocibus. Impressum Lugduni per Jacobum Modernum de Pinguento, Anno MDXXXII, a work from which it is known that Palestrina extracted the bases of several of his masses, (see Killing: Kirchenmusikalische Schätze der Bibliothek des Abbate Fortunato Santini, and P. Wagner: Geschichte der Messe, p. 447). At the same time I should like to call attention to the fact that the mass which Haberl published in the 32nd volume of the Palestrina collection as "Missa sine titulo", in fact has a title. A comparison with the 4-part mass (Vol. XII, p. 26 sqq.) shows that the two masses were composed upon the same basis viz: Ferabosco's 4-part madrigal, "Io mi son giovinetta".

Hence it would seem that the essential feature of this ornamental phrase lies in the melodic form, while the rhythm seems a more casual circumstance which could not change any inherent element in the situation.

But even if the exceptions to the "high-note law" prove less significant and relatively easy to explain, the true origin of the law itself is rather obscure. We should, however, scarcely be far wrong in supposing it to be connected with the accent. Even in the mere comprehension of two time units the flowing back of the attention upon the socalled "weak" beats claims consideration. The relation of the individual historic style towards these natural claims for the most part exercises a decisive influence upon its entire expressional character. In general terms it might be said that the greater delicacy with regard to these psychic tendencies gives the style a certain character of naturalness and dispassionate calm, (not identical, however, with apathy), while the opposite makes a more active—even defiant—impression. This "contra-time" accent has on this account been termed the "pathetic" accent, since it "häufig dem Ausdrucke leidenschaftlichen Widerstandes, erregten Kämpfens dient".[1] The leap upward from an accented crotchet would, however, represent such a melodic "contra-time" accent, (the "weak" crotchets being accentuated through pitch), and it is easy to understand that the extremely sensitive Palestrina style excludes even the slightest degree of this effect. The reason that the "high-note" rule is for the most part only applicable to crotchets (half time units) and properly speaking not to the minims, is to be found in the fact that crotchets (M. M. 144) in the normal Palestrina tempo (Minim = c. 72)[2] lie quite near the limit of tempi in which the most favourable conditions for subjective rhythm are present, (M. M. 200—300);[3] the minims on the contrary are rather

---

[1] Heinrich Rietsch: Die Grundlagen der Tonkunst, 2. edition. 1918, p. 22. Eugen Tetzel: Das Motivleben und sein Einfluss auf den musikalischen Vortrag, Z. f. M. 1924, p. 646: "Bei der "Gegentaktbetonung" dagegen haben wir die Empfindung eines ruckartigen, gewissermassen eines abwehrenden Gegenstosses, mit dem man eine bedrängende Gewichtsmasse abschleudert."

[2] Refer to Schünemann: S. I. M. 1908, p. 88.

[3] See this treatise, page 19.

distant from this zone, and consequently their rhythmical connection is not so perceptible.

Just as the leap may be made downward from an accented crotchet, it is likewise possible to leap downward from an unaccented; however, the ascending leap is also possible here:

¹ **36** = This phrase (cambiata) is so common that it is hardly worth while to recapitulate the places where it may be found. **37** = P. XVII, 57, 4, 4. P. XVII, 99, 2, + 3. P. XXII, 130, 4, 4. P. XXIV, 6, 1, + 2. **38** = P. VIII, 64, 2, 2. P. XIV, 16, 4, + 2; 34, 3, 4. P. XVI, 50, 1, + 2. P. XVII, 59, 3, + 2. P. XX, 24, 1, 4. P. XXI, 64, 1, 3. P. XXIII, 59, 4, 2. P. XXIX, 154, 1, 2. P. XXXII, 81, 3, 4 (d.). **39** = P. XXII, 42, 1, + 2. P. XXIII, 9, 3, 4. **40** = P. XXI, 12, 1, 1. P. XXIV, 143, 2, + 1; 143, 3, 3. P. XXXII, 81, 5, 4 and + 2 (d.). **41** = P. XXII, 42, 2, 2. **42** = P. II, 29, 1, + 2. P. III, 12, 3, + 3; 28, 3, 2. P. IV, 52, 3, + 3; 65, 3, 4; 129, 3, 4. P. V, 49, 3, 2; 94, 1, 1; 177, 2, + 1; 180, 1, + 4 etc. P. VIII, 17, 4, 1; 99, 4, 2; 160, 4, + 3. P. IX, 80, 3, 1; 136, 1, + 4; 160, 2, 2; 161, 2, + 3; 161, 3, + 3; 177, 3, 2; 188, 3, + 4; 189, 3, 4; 197, 2, 2; 206, 2, 4. P. X, 46, 2, 2; 49, 2, + 1; 67, 1, + 3; 93, 1, + 3; 97, 2, 2; 103, 1, 4; 103, 3, 4; 125, 3, 2 and 4; 137, 1, 4. P. XI, 5, 2, + 1; 28, 1, + 1; 36, 3, 2; 41, 4, + 3; 76, 3, 3; 103, 2, + 1. P. XII, 8, 2, + 1; 13, 5, + 3; 31, 5, 1; 33, 3, 3; 58, 3, 4; 60, 2, + 4; 66, 3, + 4 etc.; 69, 4, + 4; 105, 2, 2; 118, 1, 3; 129, 2, + 1; 146, 2, 4. P. XIII, 2, 2, + 3; 8, 1, 2; 10, 1, + 3; 12, 1, + 3; 19, 4, + 1; 37, 1, + 4; 37, 2, + 1; 48, 4, 3; 51, 3, + 4; 62, 2, + 2; 71, 1, 3; 72, 3, + 2; 80, 3, + 3; 96, 2, 4; 111, 3, + 2; 125, 1, 2; 125, 4, + 1; 128, 3, 3; 129, 2, 1; 131, 4, + 2; 137, 1, 2; 139, 2, 3. P. XIV, 8, 4, 4; 12, 1, + 1; 26, 2, + 3; 31, 3, 3; 38, 4, 2; 69, 3, 4; 72, 1, 1 and 3; 78, 3, + 4; 80, 2, 3; 91, 2, 3; 94, 3, 5; 110, 2, 3; 139, 1, 3. P. XV, 2, 4, 3; 2, 4, + 2; 9, 2, + 3; 18, 3, 1; 24, 3, + 1; 29, 1, 3; 39, 2, + 3; 51, 3, 1; 52, 1, 1 and 2; 53, 2, + 2; 55, 3, 1; 71, 1, 3 etc.; 77, 3, 4 and + 2; 77, 4, 1 etc.; 78, 3, 1; 78, 4, 2; 80, 4, + 2; 94, 2, 2; 104, 3, + 2; 106, 2, 1; 112, 2, 3; 129, 3, + 1. P. XVI, 9, 2, + 1; 15, 2, 4; 19, 1, 4; 19, 2, 2; 25, 3, + 1; 25, 4, + 3; 27, 3, 2; 30, 1, + 3; 31, 3, 1; 32, 1, + 4; 45, 2, + 3; 69, 2, + 1; 78, 1, 2 and + 3; 78, 2, 1 and 3; 80, 2, 3; 80, 2, + 1; 80, 3, 2; 86, 3, + 1; 105, 1, 3 etc. P. XVII, 1, 1, + 1; 2, 1, 3; 9, 1, 4; 9, 4, + 1; 13, 1, 4; 17, 1, + 2; 65, 1, 2; 99, 4, + 3. P. XVIII, 2, 3, + 3; 18, 3, 2; 94, 1, 1; 97, 1, + 1; 107, 3, 4; 108, 1, + 3; 116, 2, + 2; 125, 3, + 4. P. XIX, 1, 2, + 1; 7, 1, + 4; 8, 4, 2; 14, 4, + 2; 15, 1, 3; 37, 3, 2; 41, 3, 3; 44, 1, + 2; 60, 1, + 3; 86, 3, + 1; 91, 1, + 3; 97, 4, 3; 109, 3, + 3 and + 4; 110, 1,

Morris gives the following rule for the melodic treatment of crotchets in his "Contrapuntal Technique in the Sixteenth Century" (p. 36): "The student should remember that the minim is normally the smallest harmonic unit in $^4/_2$ measure, and that consequently a crotchet

1 and 2; 132, 3, + 1; 133, 1, 2; 133, 3, 4; 137, 1, + 3. P. XX, 21, 2, 2; 22, 2, 4; 28, 3, + 2; 32, 2, 2; 60, 3, 2; 77, 1, + 2; 111, 2, + 4; 125, 3, 1. P. XXI, 28, 4, 1; 30, 1, + 2; 31, 2, 4; 68, 2, + 2; 83, 1, + 3. P. XXII, 12, 3, 2; 16, 2, + 2; 35, 1, 2; 59, 3, + 1; 59, 4, 3; 65, 4, 4; 130, 4, + 1; 141, 2, + 3; 148, 1, + 2. P. XXIII, 6, 2, 4; 10, 1, 1; 12, 1, + 3; 47, 1, + 4 and + 1; 48, 2, 1; 49, 2, + 2; 62, 3, + 3; 67, 2, 1. P. XXIV, 63, 1, 2; 65, 2, 1; 72, 3, + 3; 73, 1, 1 sqq.; 81, 2, 4 sqq.; 104, 3, + 2; 147, 3, 1. P. XXV, 8, 4, 3; 42, 3, 2; 43, 2, 2; 44, 3, 2; 105, 3, 1; 110, 1, 4; 113, 3, + 3; 117, 1, + 1; 177, 2, 1; 206, 2, 3. P. XXVII, 13, 4, + 3; 22, 1, + 3; 35, 1, 3 and + 2; 44, 1, + 3; 47, 3, + 2; 71, 1, 3 and + 4; 73, 4, + 3. P. XXVIII, 54, 3, 3. P. XXIX, 132, 2, 2. P. XXXI, 140, 2, + 3. **43** = P. II, 54, 2, 2. P. IV, 92, 2, + 1; 103, 1, + 3; 153, 3, 1. P. V, 31, 4, 2; 45, 1, + 2; 54, 1, 3; 55, 4, + 2; 67, 1, 3; 74, 4, + 4; 93, 1, + 3; 97, 2, 3; 124, 1, + 3; 125, 4, + 3; 173, 2, + 4; 173, 4, + 1; 175, 2, + 3; 175, 4, 2; 180, 3, 3. P. VI, 21, 2, 3. P. VIII, 14, 3, 1; 14, 4, + 2; 25, 2, + 2; 27, 2, + 1; 31, 4, 2; 39, 1, 4; 47, 2, 4; 51, 3, + 2; 54, 4, 2; 75, 1, + 2; 89, 3, 2 and + 1; 96, 2, 1; 106, 3, + 3; 116, 2, + 2; 120, 4, 3 and + 3; 161, 4, 1; 171, 4, 2; 175, 2, + 1; 176, 3, + 2. P. IX, 6, 3, + 2; 32, 2, + 3; 32, 3, + 3; 78, 3, +1;99, 2, 1 and + 4; 99 3, 3; 107, 3, + 1; 109, 2, 2 and + 3; 133, 2, + 4; 135, 2, + 4 and + 1; 135, 2, + 1 etc.; 136, 1, + 3; 158, 2, + 3; 186, 2, + 2; 205, 3, + 2. P. X, 4, 1, + 3; 4, 2, 3; 12, 4, 3; 39, 3, + 1; 47, 4, 3; 63, 3, 2; 72, 1, + 3; 98, 4, 3; 120, 3, 1; 122, 2, 1; 127, 2, + 1. P. XI, 3, 4, + 3; 8, 1, 1; 26, 1, 1; 49, 3, + 1; 51, 3, 1; 83, 2, +4; 122, 4, 2; 150, 1, 1. P. XII, 16, 3, 3; 19, 3, 1; 31, 3, + 3; 79, 2, 2; 90, 1, 3 and + 3; 107, 3, 2 and + 3; 148, 2, 4; 163, 1, + 2; 180, 1, 3. P. XIII, 10, 2, + 4; 36, 4, + 3; 51, 4, 1 and 2; 70, 3, 2 sqq.; 75, 3, + 3; 83, 1, 2 sqq.; 112, 1, 4; 118, 2, 1; 134, 1, 1; 134, 2, 1; 138, 2, 2 and 3. P. XIV, 9, 3, + 3; 12, 4, 1; 13, 2, + 2; 23, 5, + 3; 27, 4, + 3; 31, 4, 2; 37, 4, 3; 40, 2, + 2; 40, 3, 2; 41, 2, + 4; 46, 1, 3; 50, 3, 3; 50, 5, 4; 77, 1, 2; 106, 2, 1; 117, 3, + 3; 125, 2, + 4; 133, 1, 3. P. XV, 17, 1, 3 and + 1; 17, 2, + 1; 35, 4, + 1; 36, 4, 1; 39, 2, 1; 40, 1, + 1; 83, 2, + 3; 96, 1, 1; 129, 2, 1. P. XVI, 7, 3, 3; 41, 2, + 2; 46, 2, + 3; 55, 3, + 3; 56, 2, + 4; 85, 2, 4; 103, 1, 2; 104, 2, + 3. P. XVII, 2, 3, + 4; 4, 3, 1; 7, 3, 2; 11, 3, 4; 12, 4, + 1; 12, 5, + 3; 50, 2, 4; 79, 1, 2; 99, 2, 3; 105, 2, + 1; 105, 4, + 1; 106, 1, 3; 125, 1, 3; 131, 1, 1; 135, 2, + 2. P. XVIII, 22, 3, 2 and + 2; 22, 4, 3; 27, 2, 3; 36, 1, + 3; 36, 3, 3; 38, 1, + 3; 51, 3, 4; 84, 2, + 1. P. XIX, 2, 3, 2; 3, 1, + 2; 4, 4, + 3; 8, 1, + 1; 22, 1, + 3; 33, 4, + 2; 48, 1, 3; 62, 2, 2; 63, 2, + 2; 83, 1, + 4; 96, 1, 1; 109, 3, 4; 124, 4, + 2; 138, 2, + 2. P. XX, 7, 2, 2 and + 1; 7, 3, 4; 16, 2, 4; 18, 3, + 3; 18, 4, 4; 23, 3, + 3; 24, 2, + 1; 24, 3, + 4; 34, 1, + 2; 35, 3, + 4; 36, 1, + 2; 36, 2, 2; 45, 1, + 2; 47, 3, 2; 119, 3, + 3. P. XXI, 2, 2, 2; 3, 2, + 3; 3, 3, 2; 5, 3, + 1; **8, 4, 1 and 4;** 11, 3, 1; 14, 4, 2; 17, 4, 3; 19, 2, 4; 35, 2, + 4; 74, 4, 3; 105, 3, 2; 107, 2, 1. P. XXII, 1, 1, 4; 6, 3, 4; 11, 4, 1; 20, 4, 2; 29, 3, 4; 34, 1, + 3; 59, 1, 4 and + 3; 103, 4, + 2; 105, 4, + 3; 145 3, 4. P. XXIII, 3, 1, 4; 3, 2, 1; 7, 2, 3; 18, 1, + 1; 34, 3, 2 and + 3; 59, 3, + 4; 77, 1, 4; 105, 1, + 3; 118, 2, 1; 139, 1, + 4. P. XXIV, 12, 4, + 1; 13, 3,

72

that looks like a new harmony note may have to be treated technically
as a discord, i. e. quitted in conjunct movement only. .... Exceptions
to this rule can be found, but they are very rare." According to this
opinion whenever, in the vocal style of the 16th century, an unaccented crotchet is introduced by a conjunct movement from an accented crotchet (in a $^4/_2$ measure), it is necessary to continue this progression by steps (also in cases where it does not cause a discord, for
then at all events there must be a change of harmony). The ornaments

---

+ 1; 14, 3, + 2; 14, 4, 1; 23, 2, 3 and + 1; 23, 3, 2; 95, 4, 4; 122, 2, + 2; 124, 3, 1;
125, 3, + 4; 134, 3, 3; 143, 1, 1; 147, 2, + 2; 151, 3, + 2. P. XXV, 12, 3, 4; 30, 2, + 3;
107, 2, + 3; 141, 3, 2; 201, 1, 4. P. XXVII, 9, 1, 4; 9, 2, 1; 9, 4, + 4; 13, 3, + 2;
23, 1, 3; 28, 3, + 2; 37, 2, + 4; 42, 3, 2; 48, 3, + 1; 49, 1, 4; 52, 3, 4; 53, 4, + 3; 65, 1,
+ 3; 66, 4, 4; 73, 3, 3. P. XXXI, 142, 3, 3. **44** = P. II, 104, 2, + 4. P. III, 3, 1, + 4.
P. V, 122, 4, + 3; 124, 4, + 2; 158, 4, + 3. P. VIII, 36, 3, 4. P. IX, 17, 2, + 1; 23, 1, 3;
97, 3, 3. P. XI, 111, 1, 1. P. XIII, 77, 3, + 2. P. XIV, 31, 3, + 3; 84, 2, + 2;
111, 3, + 3. P. XVI, 37, 3, + 4; 106, 2, 1. P. XVII, 6, 4, 3 and + 4; 17, 3,
+ 3; 17, 4, 1 and + 3; 19, 2, 2 sqq.; 50, 1, + 2. P. XIX, 65, 2, 3; 66, 3, 4; 115, 2, + 1.
P. XX, 12, 3, 4; 120, 4,3. P. XXII, 57, 2, 2. P. XXIV, 33, 2, 3; 71, 3, + 3. P. XXV, 193,
2, 3. P. XXVII, 5, 2, 2. **45** = P. XXXII, 135, 1, 1 (d.). **46** = P. III, 83, 3, 2. P. IV,
50, 3, + 4. P. V, 52, 2, + 3. P. VIII, 43, 2, 3. P. XI, 19, 3, + 4. P. XIV, 34, 2, 1. P. XVII,
1, 2, 3; 1, 4, + 3; 16, 4, + 3; 108, 1, + 1. P. XIX, 64, 2, + 3. P. XXIII, 135, 2, + 2.
P. XXVI, 73, 2, + 4. **47** = P. I, 112, 1, + 3. P. III, 121, 1, + 3; 121, 2, 1. P. IV, 20, 3, + 4
and + 2; 48, 3, + 3; 73, 3, + 4; 105, 2, 4; 126, 1, 2; 134, 3, + 4; 147, 3, + 2. P. V,
19, 4, + 2; 20, 1, 1 and 3 and + 2; 29, 2, + 2; 81, 2, 4; 138, 1, 3; 147, 3, 4; 151, 2, + 3.
P. VIII, 21, 1, 1; 30,1, 4; 73, 4, + 1; 95, 4, 3; 102, 2, + 3; 127, 2, 1. P. IX, 81, 2, + 1;
96, 3, + 3; 159, 1, + 4. P. X, 71, 5, + 3. P. XI, 140, 3, 3. P. XII, 38, 4, + 2; 54, 2, 2; 58,
3, + 4. P. XIII, 7, 3, 3; 70, 3, + 1; 76, 3, + 3; 85, 3, 1; 94, 1, + 3; 97, 4, 3; 130, 2, 2. P.
XIV, 60, 2, 1; 121, 3, 1; 130, 2, + 2; 130, 3, 4. P. XV, 20, 1, + 1; 57, 3, 2; 68, 4, 4; 73, 4, 3;
98, 3, + 3; 130, 4, + 3. P. XVI, 9, 3, 1; 26, 2, 3; 33, 3, 3; 36, 2, + 3; 38, 5, + 2; 45,
1, + 2; 93, 1, 2; 105, 3, + 2. P. XVII, 3, 2, 4; 44, 1, + 2; 44, 2, + 4; 49, 2, + 1;
87, 2, + 4; 90, 2, + 1; 121, 2, + 1. P. XVIII, 12, 1, + 2; 12, 2, 3; 26, 3, + 3; 45, 3, 4;
69, 2, 2; 79, 3, 1; 125, 1, + 3; 125, 3, + 3; 126, 1, 4. P. XIX, 24, 1, 3; 39, 2, 3.
P. XX, 9, 4, 3; 12, 3, + 4; 13, 1, + 3; 20, 3, 1; 37, 1, + 1; 37, 2, 2; 37, 3, + 1; 50, 3,
+ 2. P. XXI, 16, 2, 4; 17, 1, + 3; 26, 1, + 4; 33, 2, 3 and + 4; 50, 1, 4; 53, 3, 3. P. XXII,
51, 1, 3; 51, 2, + 4. P. XXIII, 5, 2, + 4; 121, 1, 3; 129, 2, 1. P. XXIV, 3, 2, + 2; 57, 1,
+ 3; 95, 6, 2; 104, 1 + 3; 130, 3, 3 sqq.; 149, 1, 3. P. XXV, 81, 2, + 3; 127, 2, + 1; 206,
4, + 2. P. XXVI, 46, 4, 3; 85, 1, + 3. 88, 4, 4; 89, 1, 4 (d.); 93, 2, + 2; 93, 3, 2. P. XXVII,
47, 2, 1; 73, 2, + 3 and + 1; 73, 3, 3. **48** = P. XVI, 75, 2, + 1. **49** = P. IV, 48, 3, + 3.
P. XXIX, 188, 3, 2. **50** = P. XXVI, 13, 2, + 2. Compare also the Ornam. 4, 5, 6, 7, 10, 12,
20, 21, 22, 23, 24, 25, 26, 27, 29, 30, 31, 32, 34, 35 p. 61 sqq.

cited above, (36—50), in which the leap always takes place from the second (unaccented) crotchet, which is introduced by steps, contradict the above rule of Morris by reason of their great number.

The exceptions here can surely not be counted as "rare" even in Palestrina style. Yet it must be conceded that a still more common practice in this style is the continuation of step-progression in crotchets when once begun. The reason, however, seems really to be a purely melodic one, and doubtless has nothing to do with a change of chords or the like.[1]

An investigation of the melodies of Palestrina's time will speedily demonstrate that, where the melody moves constantly in the same direction, conjunct movement is preferred. Notwithstanding, it often happens in such a situation that step-progressions and leaps, or larger and smaller leaps in the same direction, occur by series; in this case the following facts will be noticed:

1. In ascending, the larger movements are ordinarily placed at the beginning of the curve, while the smaller ones come later. For instance:

P. V, 79, 1, 4. Motet: Dum aurora.

2. In descending, the smaller movements, on the contrary, are generally placed first; as an example,

P. XI, 95, 1, + 1. Missa: Aspice Domine.[2])

---

[1] Such an apprehension besides being but imperfectly in accord with the preeminently linear character of Palestrina style, is also contradicted by numerous examples, for instance: P. XII, 5, 2, + 3; 21, 1, + 1; 34, 1, + 1; 45, 4, + 2; 116, 1, 5; 154, 2, + 4; 160, 2, 4. Assuming that the unaccented crotchet which does not belong to the preceding chord should be treated as a dissonance, these instances—where the unaccented crotchet is introduced disjunctly, notwithstanding the change of the chord—would be wrong.

[2] See P. VIII, 134, 2, + 1. P. IX, 30, 1, 2; 44, 2, + 2; 91, 2, 1; 136, 2, 2; 144, 1, 4 P. XII, 49, 3, 2; 155, 1, 3. P. XIV, 26, 4, 2. P. XX, 83, 1, 1. P. XXI, 111, 1, + 1 etc.

In conformity with our leading principles 1 and 2, these two observations with respect to style can be explained thus: in ascending movements a larger leap cannot very well be made after steps or smaller leaps, because the ascending movement increases the projection of attention, and consequently larger leaps (which are in themselves of striking effect) are perceived as the outcome of an exaggerated and undisciplined activity when used in this manner. Likewise larger descending leaps followed by smaller intervals create disproportionate effects, for here there is a decrease in the projection of attention, therefore the larger leaps that are placed thus appear too glaring in relation to the smaller. In Palestrina, however, all melodic laws are generally strict with regard to the movement of crotchets; for as already observed, the most favourable time-conditions for a musical comprehension are present here. Consequently it can easily be explained why phrases like the following will be sought in vain in Palestrina music:

and still less figures of this kind:

As shown by the citations of the ornamentations 5, 10, 12, 13 (p. 61 sqq.) and 39 (p. 70), even phrases which have the correct succession of intervals with respect to size are rarely found. The only figure of this kind generally used is the ornament No. 36 (the so-called "cambiata"). The preceding discussion should make the reason for its preference to the following figuration perfectly clear:

---

[1] The only exceptions that I know of are the ornamentations No. 41, (p. 70) and the very unusual figuration P. VIII, 24, 1, + 2. Compare also ornamentation No. 50.

[2] Compare J. G. Albrechtsbergers sämtliche Schriften. 2nd edition, Wien 1837, Vol. 2, p. 51. Also Ebenezer Prout: Counterpoint (10th impression, p. 22), and C. H. Kitson: The Art of Counterpoint, Oxford 1907, p. 32.

Indeed these leaps, after the step-progression has first been introduced and one has become accustomed to the lower level of activity,
have for the greater part something striking about them, aside from
their direction etc. It is therefore comprehensible that the continuation
of the step-progression (as far as a note whose value exceeds a
crotchet), which produces a more even and a calmer effect, was preferred, and this is probably the explanation of the observation made
by Morris.[2] In this way it is also explicable that one had to exercise
more care with leaps which succeeded several crotchets in step-progression, than when they were used after only one or two of these
notes of lesser value. While phrases like the following are very commonplace with the early Netherlanders,

they are a great rarity with Palestrina.[7] On the other hand the leap

---

[1] Most likely the recurrence of the identical tone on the 2nd and 4th note, giving
a certain melodious monotony, may have been a concurrent cause here.

[2] Refer to Andres Lorente: "El Porque de la Musica". Alçala 1672, p. 310: "Y la
razon porque ha de parar en figura sossegada, y de mas valor que las que son
puestas en la carrera, es, porque una carrera para ser buena, ha de ir via recta, y
para firmes, y sossegadamente."

[3] Is. I, 45, 3, + 2.

[4] Is. I, 12, 3, 4.

[5] Is. I, 57, 2, + 4.

[6] Josquin des Prés. Missa: Dung aultre amer. Sanctus, bar 13.

[7] Fig. a): Of similar phrases by Palestrina only the following can be cited: P. III,
28, 3, 2. P. IX, 193, 3, 4; 195, 2, + 3. Fig. b): P. XVI, 9, 3, 1. P. XVII, 20, 2, + 3; 121,
2, + 1. P. XVIII, 69, 2, 2. P. XX, 9, 4, 3. P. XXIV, 3, 2, + 2. Fig. c): P. XIV, 23, 5, + 3.

to the unaccented minim was not regarded by Palestrina as a breach even if preceded by several crotchets. For the more marked the concluding tone of the leap, the more striking was the effect, (e. g. P. XII, 107, 3, + 3, p. 203 of this treatise). For this reason also it was not at all rare that leaps were made from accented to unaccented minims after a longer progression of crotchets; for example:

P. V. 57, 3, 2. Motet: Quae est ista.

P. V. 46, 3, 4. Motet: Magnus sanctus Paulus.

In the last example, to be sure, there is a leap of the fourth from an unaccented crotchet to an accented minim; but the level of the movement in both these instances has been extended by the preceding leap of the third in the opposite direction, which mitigates and neutralizes the larger leaps—a technique which on the whole is employed rather often with larger crotchet leaps. Therefore if leaps succeeded by other leaps in the opposite direction belong to the altogether legitimate methods of Palestrina, on the other hand, a superficial glance will show that the alternation of leaps and step-progressions is still more common, and better in keeping with his melodic ideals. As an example,

P. V, 107, 3. Motet: Exaudi Domine.

The passage P. XII, 106, 1, + 3 (according to the 3rd Book of Masses, Venice 1598) is misprinted, the third and fourth crotchets being B and A instead of A and G. Doubtless the passage P. XVII, 1, 4, + 3, notwithstanding it conforms with the original edition of the 8th Book of Masses, (Venice 1609), should be changed so as to correspond with the passage P. XVII, 16, 4, + 3. Phrases like d) are not to be found in Palestrina, unless I have overlooked them.

P. I, 56 3, + 3. Motet: Beatae Mariae.

vi - vum ab in - fe - ris

The last cited example is particularly interesting. The leap from G down to its octave is not succeeded by an ascending step-progression, but by an ascending leap of the sixth from G to E flat. After this leap of the sixth the part is conducted downward by steps, and then taking a leap up to the fourth, it again descends to the second below. Thus it would seem that leaps upward are succeeded more regularly by conjunct movement in the contrary direction than leaps downward. And in fact it is so; though the upward leaps are not invariably answered by seconds below, yet it is quite clear that exceptions to this procedure are much rarer than in instances where the leaps descend.

While phrases such as

in - gre-di me - ru - i [1]

in minims represent an ordinary phrase in Palestrina style, (but an extremely rare one with crotchets, as already noted), passages like:

-a be - a - ta Vir - go [2]

are not found quite so often—the leap of the third here being generally filled out. A typical mode of expression is:

. a . . . . . dae [3]

With leaps still larger, such as sixths and octaves, the difference in the treatment of ascending and descending intervals is distinctly

---

[1] P. I, 63, 2, + 3.

[2] P. I, 64, 2, + 2.

[3] P. I, 92, 3, + 2.

greater. Here we find the explanation of the fact, to which allusion has already been made (p. 52), that in Palestrina a leap of the minor sixth may go up but not down. Inasmuch as the larger ascending leaps are succeeded in most cases by the second below, this custom makes it possible to perceive the minor sixth in relation to its second below (the perfect fifth), not so much as an independent interval, but rather as an energetic expansion—a kind of logical function of the perfect fifth. Such a perceptive method of hearing was not natural in cases of descending leaps, since the relation here to the second above is much more vague, and it is for this reason explicable that the descending leap of the minor sixth was not risked.

However, the reason why leaps downward could better be succeeded by leaps in the opposite direction than when the leap first went upward, lies in the fact that in the first case the note to which the leap is made is "deep-note", while in the second case it is "high-note". Therefore ascending leaps were more conspicuous than descending, and consequently accompanied by less actively operative phrases, since the situation otherwise would assume a too unquiet and not sufficiently disciplined character. But when the leaps descend, these intervals being less distinctly remarked, (as already noted), do not require so much toning down through the succeeding musical incidents; a continuation of the disjunct movement in the contrary direction may therefore be more readily permitted.

Griesbacher, (the first, I believe, to make this observation), calls attention to the interesting fact that while the figuration

is often encountered in Palestrina style, the inversion of this phrase does not belong here:

---

[1] "Kirchenmusikalische Stilistik und Formenlehre" II p. 305: "Umkehrungen der eben behandelten Formen, Melismen von der Art, wie sie Witt in so vielen seiner

Yet Palestrina himself occasionally uses this melisma,

P. XXIII, 97, 3, + 1. Missa: Assumpta est Maria.[1])

which at the same time is rare enough to rank absolutely among the exceptions. Neither did the masters of the second and third Netherland schools make much use of it, at all events not in ecclesiastical music; it is more likely to be found in lute and organ tablatures from this period. On the other hand, it is of very frequent occurrence in the works of the Italian "ars nova", with which style it immediately became a pet phrase; for instance,

M. Rosso de Chollegrana: Tremando più che foglia.[2])

The cause of its suppression in the course of the 15th and 16th centuries may be attributed to a tendency to depart gradually from the perihelitic melodic principles (paraphrase of single tones) which according to Lach were noticeably prevalent in this period.[3] As melodic

---

Werke kirchlichen wie weltlichen Genres so häufig beliebt, dass Verfasser noch als Student bei einem Referat über Aufführung des Op. 36b für die bei ihm typische Sequenzfigur:

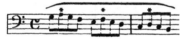

den gewagten Terminus 'Neuma Witticum' mit Rufzeichen in sein Tagebuch malte, wird man, obwohl gar kein vernünftiger Einwand denkbar ist, in alten Partituren vergeblich suchen. Wenigstens in dieser Form. Vor einer Synkope ist allerdings die Obersekunde als Wechselnote nicht unbekannt."

[1] See also P. VIII, 119, 3, + 3. P. IX, 39, 2, 4. P. XXI, 123, 2, + 3. P. XXII, 48, 1, 3. P. XXIII, 102, 3, + 2. P. XXVI, 110, 2, + 3. P. XXIX, 30, 1, + 3. P. XXX, 114, 2, 1 and 2. P. XXXII, 85, 2, + 2 etc.

[2] Wolf: Geschichte der Mensuralnotation. III p. 143.

[3] "Entwickelungsgeschichte der ornam. Melopöie" p. 427.

culture by degrees was brought to a higher state of refinement, the character of this phrase with its identical second and fourth notes was found empty and dull. Berardi[1] expresses this in terms more adjusted to the harmonic conception of the 17th century, as follows: "Si proibisce ancora quella modulatione, che vien chiamata girandoletta, overo gioco, particolarmente quando il canto fermo stà sopra d'una medema corda":

Thus Berardi thought that all such turns should be prohibited in curt and clear terms, especially where the second voice lies stationary, which causes a repetition of the vertical intervals also. But a comparison of 16th century practice with Berardi's rules makes it clear that Berardi generalizes too much—for instance in not differentiating between phrases in which the turn is made with the second above, and figurations where the second below is used:

Yet in this apparently immaterial difference lies the reason why a

---

[1] Angelo Berardi: "Miscellanea musicale". Bologna 1689, p. 136. Also Berardi: "Il perche musicale". Bologna 1693, p. 32: "La ragione, per la qual si proibisce la Girandoletta, ouer Gioco, particolarmente, quando il Canto fermo non si muoue, è questa, perche si sentono due ottaue, ouero due quinte replicate sopra di una medesima corda; oltre di questo nelle tirate di semiminime, si deue procedere con la modulatione, la quale uien chiamata Conducimento, che è quando si procede di grado uerso l'acuto, e dall' acuto, al grave — — —."

number of melodic phenomena were altogether acceptable to Palestrina, while others were rarely used here or avoided entirely. A comparison for instance of the numeric relations of the figurations 37, 38, 39, 42, 43, 44, 45, 46 and 40, 41, 47, 48, 49, 50 (p. 70) will show that the latter group, in which the leap is made from the high-note which is introduced from below in step-progression, is decidedly in the minority. Doubtless the explanation of this fact is that the high-note, especially in unaccented places (where in reality it does not belong) is particularly prominent, (see our leading principle no. 2); therefore the attention is especially directed to its continuation, and as a consequence it must be treated with great care. For this reason it is more difficult not to hear the somewhat thin effect of note repetitions in phrases where the turn is made with the second above than where the subtonal form is employed.[1] This observation explains why the following phrase is very common in Palestrina style,

P. XVII, 98, 2, + 4. Missa: Dum complerentur.

Et ho . . mo

while its inversion is so rare that I only know of a single example of its kind:

---

[1] When melodic is furthermore combined with rhythmic monotony, the triteness of the phrase is doubly felt. It is consequently comprehensible, as has been previously remarked by Griesbacher, that the turn with the second above can better be made where the note to which this second returns is a minim, than if it is a crotchet, like the two foregoing notes.

[2] Also P. I, 94, 2, + 1; 96, 3, + 4; 106, 1, 4. P. II, 72, 2, + 3; 129, 3, + 2. P. XVI, 26, 4, + 1; 103,2, 1 and + 2 etc. P. XVII, 92, 3, + 3. P. XVIII, 40, 3, 4; 86, 1, 2 etc. 93, 3, + 3; 141, 3, 3. P. XIX, 97, 4, 3; 107, 1, 2 etc. 126, 1, 4. P. XX, 8, 2, + 2 etc. 100, 2, 4; 119, 2, + 4. P. XXI, 56, 4, + 3; 116, 2, 2 etc. 126, 1, 1. P. XXIII, 116, 2, 1 etc. 119, 2, 4. P. XXIV, 145, 2, + 4; 152, 1, 2. P. XXVII, 8, 3, + 1; 15, 2, 2. P. XXIX, 62, 2, 2 etc.

P. XII, 66, 3, +1. Missa: De Feria.

Likewise we meet with the following figuration in Palestrina, though seldom:

P. XV, 99, 3, +2. Missa: Dilexi quoniam.[1])

while its inversion:

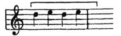

is very sparsely used by the earlier Netherlanders and, to my knowledge, is nowhere to be found in Palestrina's works.

Some phrases, akin to the above-mentioned, are occasionally encountered in ultramontane compositions, such as:

---

[1] Cf. also P. I, 159, 2, 4. P. IV, 153, 1, + 2. P. VIII, 29, 2, 1. P. XV, 99, 3, + 2. P. XXI, 72, 1, 2. P. XXIII, 17, 1, 4; 101, 3, + 3. P. XXIV, 134, 2, 3. P. XXVII, 91, 4, 1. P. XXX, 136, 1, + 3. P. XXXII, 80, 4, 2.

but are not employed by Palestrina.[3] This is not remarkable, since three notes are repeated here, which greatly impoverishes the melodic contents. Also the following very harsh outline by Orlandus Lassus, who is rather robust at times,

M. D. II. 149, 2, + 2. Motet: Christus resurgens.

would never come from the delicate pen of Palestrina, even in a tone-picture.

A noble repose and simplicity are the foremost and fundamental criteria of Palestrina's melody. Here is indeed an art of fine transitions which keeps every vulgar element at a distance,—but without weakness or degeneracy, a style which pursues its expressional aims with the marvellous energy and consistency peculiar to all great art. Above all it is, however, characterized by its directness of aim, always seeking the shortest way and employing the simplest and least conspicuous means, never failing in its wonderful obedience to the claims of nature. Out of these springs a serene gentleness—unmistakable token

---

[1] Is II, 66, 6, + 3; 70, 6, + 4; 78, 4, + 3; 110, 4, + 5.

[2] Obr. IV, 255, 1, + 2.

[3] The only exception (previously noted) is the altogether rather peculiar passage P. VIII, 24, 1, + 2.

of supreme culture.[1] Palestrina's style is an art of placid movement—
without harsh effects or violent contrast. In an elementary psychologic
mode of expression, it might be designated as a certain equalized ab-
sorption of the attention—translated into musical terms: a free and
unobstructed flow of melody without sudden effervescent outbreaks
or forced climaxes, with no unprepared cessation or exhausted fall,—a
calm alternation, as devoutly accepted and borne as the alternation of
the hours of the day—a culture which completes the orbit of its course
by becoming nature again: *cortesia!*

Harmony

In any style whatsoever, the presence of tension between the
horizontal and vertical musical conceptions may be substantiated; but
in the one style, the primary interest lies in the line—in the other, it
lies in the chord; in the first, one has to do with melodic impulses,
which recoil from the impact with the sonorous requirements—in the
second, with the sense of sonority, which finds an æsthetic corrective
in the linear demands.

The line is undoubtedly the starting-point of Palestrina's style. The
exactions arising out of harmonic aspects are really only intended to
ensure the sonority of the individual harmonic moments. "Harmonic"
does not signify here any independent sphere of interest; chords had
not yet reached a stage where they had their own vigorous life, as in
Bach's works.

All that was required of the vertical in Palestrina's time was clearness and sonority; the real æsthetic incidents were sought in other
directions. With Bach it was quite otherwise. It is as if the fundamental

---

[1] Jespersen (l. c. p. 229) most pertinently notes an analogous phenomenon in
language: "— — — die Sprache der Wilden charakterisiert sich durch grosse un-
beherrschte Tonübergänge, während die Zivilisation den Leidenschaften und ihren
Äusserungen in Gesten und Rede einen Dämpfer aufsetzt. Die Höflichkeit verlangt,
dass man keine groben Mittel gebraucht, um sich bemerkbar zu machen; der fein
ausgebildete Geschmack gibt sich auch in einer Vorliebe für kleine, feine, ausdrucks-
volle Nuancen zu erkennen, in welchen der Aussenstehende nichts als grobe Ein-
förmigkeit zu sehen vermag — —."

compository forces here may be traced back to certain chord-like, modulative and emotional impulses, which break like light through a prism into a myriad of shimmering colours—a multitude which is seen, on closer inspection, to be illusory. With Bach the vertical requirements are expressed in the exaction of a precise, logical succession of the keys, an exact arrangement of the modulations. With Palestrina, who writes in the ecclesiastical modes and knows nothing of modern modulatoric contrasts, the vertical ideal was, in plain words, Consonance—that is to say, (if the passage is in more than two parts): the full triad.

Already Zarlino teaches that one should always endeavour, as far as possible, to employ in harmony the third, the fifth (or sixth) besides the tonic:[1] "Osseruarà adunque il Compositore questo, c'hò detto nelle sue compositioni; cioè, di far più ch' ello potrà, che si ritroui la Terza, & la Quinta, & qualche fiate la Sesta in luogo di questa, ò le Replicate; accioche la sua cantilena uenghi ad esser sonora & piena; & accioche contenga in sè ogni perfettione d' harmonia". And Artusi says also in plain terms that the full triad should be used when there are more than two parts:[2] "Dirò di più, che per regola infallibile, deue il studioso, nel componere le sue Cantilene, auertire, che mentre, che à più di due voci, le parti cantano insieme, sempre habbino li suoi accordi, che sono la Ottaua, Quinta & Terza, che quando sono priue, ò della Quinta, o della Terza: s'addimandano quelle Cantilene pouere, d'Harmonia, debbe perciò cercare ogn' uno, la richezza dell' Harmonia, & non la pouertà."

Unquestionably this sense of "la richezza dell' Harmonia" has deeply influenced musical development. If we went through the literature from the Netherlanders up to Palestrina, counting instances, we should observe that the percentage of incomplete, empty-sounding chords steadily decreases. That this tendency exerted a deep influence upon the historical development of the linear course, admits of no question.

It is indeed remarkable to observe how an eminent technicist like Palestrina is able, (upon the basis, it is true, of a skill that it had taken generations to perfect), to devise themes which fully meet the require-

---

[1] "Institutioni harmoniche" l. c. p. 301.
[2] Arte del contraponto p. 36.

ments of both Dimensions—so admirably adapted, for instance, to Imitation, that in their development the best sonorous effects that could be imagined are spontaneously accomplished. Thus the beginning of the 4-part motet, Ave Maria (P. V., 164):

The theme here, very exactly carried out in imitative manner, is based upon a Gregorian motive,[1] but rhythmically it is Palestrina's own; his hand is also evident in certain remodellings of the melody, which is much more freely treated here with regard to the plainsong than, for instance, the same theme in the 4-part mass, "Ave Maria".[2]

The imitation is conducted, with all conceivable regularity, in unison and in such wise that the voices succeed each other with interims of two breves' length. The result of this horizontal accuracy, considered from the opposite standpoint, is that the voices unite whenever the opportunity offers, (i. e., when the third voice sets in), in the full triad. Even if the composer had been entirely unrestricted, he could scarcely have found a more beautiful solution.

It is on the whole interesting to note the importance which Palestrina attaches to contriving that the imitation in the third voice should form a full triad with both the preceding, either in supplementing a previously placed third,[3] (a favourite effect):

[1] Liber antiphonarius pro diurnis horis. Roma 1912, p. 220.
[2] P. XVI, 1.
[3] P. V, 137.

or in a movement of all 3 voices to the triad:[1]

Both the last 2 examples have interims of unequal length between the incidence of the voices; in the first, 1¹/₄ breves between the 1st and 2nd incidence, (though in reality only 1 breve, as the theme actually begins with a minim which is extended the first time to the duration of a semi-breve, since the custom of that time forbids a pause as a beginning). On the other hand, there is an interim of 2 breves between the 2nd and 3rd incidence, and similarly between the 1st and 2nd in the second example, while there is here an interim of only 1¹/₂ breves between the 2nd and 3rd incidence.

The 3rd voice thus awaits a favourable opportunity for its entrance; that it actually comes too soon in the last example is due most probably to the major third, which, (automatically produced in the imitation on the last semi-breve of the 4th measure) through its relation to the first tone of the third appearance of the theme acts like a magnet. How much stress Palestrina laid upon having the B flat triad just where it is, is shown by his altering the imitation in

---

[1] P. V, 148.

the 5th measure in the next to the upper voice; for, introducing the theme so early in the upper voice, the fourth in the voice next to the upper (between the last syllable of "cervus" and the first of "desiderat") could not be retained, and this alteration also gave rise to other small changes.

It is unquestionable that harmonic considerations have exerted a decisive influence here. In spite of this, it is admirable how well Palestrina succeeded in retaining the essential in the outlines of the altered voice. The notes which fall upon the declamatory centre of gravity, "Sicut cervus desiderat ad fontes", and which at the same time form the top notes of the musical line, remain intact in their characteristic relation, (second and fourth), to the first note of the theme. We may here refer to a place where the regard to harmony is demonstratively distinct, viz. in the 4-part mass, Ave Maria (P. XVI, 20)

We have here a break in the imitation for the sake of a full triad at the entrance of the 3rd voice. The first note in the 4th measure of the lower voice ought, in conformity with the theme, (based upon a plainsong motive, cf. p. 86) to be F, but is replaced by a D, which (supplementing the third in the upper voice with the tonic), gives the full triad. That the melodic progression is still excellent, notwithstanding the change, is another matter. Like most great men, Palestrina was an opportunist of genius who understood how to make the most of the circumstances, whatsoever they might be. To the above examples is added still another, (P. V. 54):

The note F in the 5th measure of the Alto (next to the upper voice) is used here solely because it is the third of the D minor triad, and it is desired to fill out the empty fifth which would otherwise arise. There is but little reason to suppose that it is dictated out of regard to the line; on the contrary, it does not seem particularly well motived if the voice is considered in relation to the melodic antecedents.

The notes F and E in the 5th measure are an exact repetition of notes in the preceding measure. This is a breach of the rule concerning "fresh-notes", which rule forbids the use of previously employed notes on all important melodic points, since the interest in the melody is weakened by a repetition of these notes.

The special reason why the repetition in the 5th measure produces such a weak effect is that the motive in the 4th measure is so prominent in interest, (probably owing to the "memory-accent" of the similar motive in the 2nd measure upon this 4th measure), that its notes have become quite exhausted, and are therefore too weak for an effective repetition.

The attractive force of harmonic principles is not, however, the sole reason for the deviation of the line from its course, determined by individual, inner laws. Rhythmic as well as harmonic impulses influence the style-complex of Palestrinian music also.

The existence of a vertical macro-rhythm as opposed to the horizontal individual rhythm has already been mentioned. A conception concerning the totality as an independent rhythmic organization must naturally affect the individual rhythms, and thereby the independence of the individual voices.

The rhythmic requirements on the part of the totality are mainly evident in the exaction of steady, fluid movement in which the rhythm of one voice fits into the others in such a manner as to avoid stoppage, and that the greater note-values in one voice are offset by shorter notes in the others,—the whole to result in a uniform, steadily flowing stream.

When the movement has once begun, it is requisite, as a rule, that at least one voice, (either by means of a new note or syllable), should mark every single beat, (i. e., in the usual Alla-breve time, every minim). It is not considered good musical form for two or more voices to remain stationary at the same time, as for instance, in syncopation. Vicentino[1] remarks with regard to this:

"Et s'auertirà che nel procedere di più d'una ò due note insieme sincopando, non si facci con tutte le parti; perche non parerà Sincopa, imperò che la Sincopa si può discernere almeno per cagione d'una parte che canti nella battuta."

A passage like the following, from Josquin des Prés' "Pange lingua" mass, was not therefore considered good form in Palestrina's time[2]:

---

[1] l. c. p. 33.
[2] Ambr. V, p. 81.

In Palestrina one of the voices would for the most part be required to move, while the others at the same time lie stationary to form the syncopation, so that it would always be perfectly clear where the accented or unaccented beats lie. The rhythm of one voice is thus contingent upon the other, and the one voice influences the other's course, so that we can, strictly speaking, no longer talk of independence. This is very distinctly seen in the following example, the beginning of the motet: Dum aurora finem daret (P. V, p. 77)

It will be noticed that in the last measure of the upper voice the theme has a minim-rest after the word "daret", after which the melody is continued in purely thematic tones. In the Alto (the middle voice) the minim-rest is omitted, most likely because the syncopated F in the Soprano would otherwise hang suspended in the air, and the accentual requirements could not be satisfactorily met. Probably also the greatly extended F in the Soprano acted as a splendid invitation— like a canvas too tempting to the painter.

A comparison with the beginning of the 4-part mass: Spem in alium (P. XII p. 3), shows that such an assumption is justified:

It will be noticed that the second half of the 4th and the first half of the 5th measures of the motet correspond exactly to the second half of the 2nd and the first half of the 3rd measures of the mass. The fact that in both cases the counterpoint is set to the same cantus firmus (given to the upper voice in both instances) shows beyond doubt that the counterpoint here is formed with a view to the theme rather than for its own sake, and that it also must be characterized as a function of the rhythmic character of the theme. In all probability the exceptionally favourable opportunity for conjunct development of the melody, and of an excellent contrary motion in the parts, exerted a decisive influence upon the progression of the lower voice.

In every art which employs the two dimensions, divergences from the strict polyphonic principle of independence may be found. They also occur in Palestrina's works, as presumably demonstrated.

In conclusion one more example is presented, Jos. III, p. 4: Ave Maria,

It cannot be denied that this vocal line, in each and every part, is as beautiful as can be conceived. Just the single trait that the Tenor, (the next to the lowest voice), takes the A and not the C as the first note in the 3rd measure, shows plainly enough that the linear requirements were paramount. From a vertical view-point there should be a C to fill out the otherwise incomplete triad, but this would spoil the vocal progression of the tenor part; it is the A which gives character to the part, and coincidentally produces a fine contrary motion with the upper voice. In contrast to the foregoing examples from Palestrina, the linear considerations here outrank the vertical.

No similar examples from Palestrina have been given, simply because there are so many that it seems superfluous to draw attention especially to them.

We thus see the tension between the two dimensions already distinctly expressed here; but it becomes still more striking when we consider the style from the point where the two spheres of ideas collide with the greatest force: the dissonance.

Dissonance

Phases of Dissonance Treatment

In the history of dissonance treatment we recognize three phases of decisive importance:

1. Dissonance as a secondary phenomenon, (melodically induced accidental dissonance).

2. Dissonance as a primary phenomenon ("musical" dissonance in conscious, deliberately stressed contrast to consonance).

3. Dissonance employed as a means of poetical expression.

Though the order of succession in the disposition made here is contingent upon time, it must not be understood that the one of these phases definitively supersedes the other. What has once been attained is retained and employed co-ordinately with the new. Nor may we venture to mark the divisions of the periods too exactly. Although the beginning of the first phase may be put as simultaneous with the earliest regulated polyphony, the second phase at about the year 1400, and the third at c. 1600, still the germs of the later phases may be traced back quite naturally to the earlier. At the periods mentioned, the characteristic instances increase so inordinately, both in number and distinctness, that the basis of a historic division seems to be present.

In the first phase, the dissonance has merely the character of an accompanying phenomenon,—what might be called a melodic function. It is tolerated out of consideration for melodic development, but no stress of significance is attached to it. Consonance is preferred upon all accented points; dissonances are, as far as possible, packed together upon unaccented beats. In its most highly developed form, this order of dissonance becomes the passing note (or passing discord). This rather negative sort of dissonance conception leads, in the highest phases of dissonance treatment, to the strict execution of the principle of the passing, or conjunctly moving, dissonance.

In the second phase the dissonance is desired for its own sake, and it is consciously employed as a co-equal contrast to consonance. The practical consequence of this highly developed conception is the dissonance of the syncope—suspension.

Finally, in the third phase, dissonance is employed as an expressional factor, most often to symbolize painful or pathetic emotions.

These three phases are all represented in Palestrina's compositions, though instances of the third phase are very rare. In an account of the relation of the Palestrina style to the dissonance, it would therefore be quite natural to classify the material according to these phases,—which classification indeed has been made the basis of the following treatise.

Dissonance as a Secondary Phenomenon

a). The Passing Dissonance

One of the oldest notations of West European polyphonic music that come to light up to the present seems to be found in the tract "Musica enchiriadis",[1] commonly ascribed to a monk from a Flemish cloister, St. Amand, by the name of Hucbald (d. c. 930). However, this tract dates from such a late part of the 10th century that it is more likely that a younger theorist, and not Hucbald, was its author.[2] The musical examples contained in "Musica enchiriadis" demonstrate the so-called "Organum"—2-part compositions that, according to Hucbald, may be extended to 6 parts by doubling the octaves—which is produced by setting a lower voice to a Gregorian melody, the counterpoint accompanying this melody mainly in similar motion with fifths and fourths. In the earliest Organum, however, there is a preference for fourths above all other intervals, while later fifths predominate. It is thought by some that this music is not to be taken seriously at all. Raphael Kiesewetter's remark as to its "moral impossibility" is a classic expression of this view.

---

[1] G. S. p. 152.

[2] Consult Karl Müller: "Hucbalds echte und unechte Schriften über Musik", 1884.

But more recent scholars also express the supposition that "Organum" merely represents rather awkward theoretical efforts according to antique theoretical recipes,[1] which aimed at the correction of the current musical practice, that is supposed to have taken quite another and freer form in popular use, far removed from all the anxious clinging to parallel motion, and moreover with a probable preference for thirds and sixths. Since then, however, the rather new branch of Comparative Musical Science has really rendered these interpretive efforts superfluous by proving that fourths and fifths are commonly used by races in a primitive stage of musical development, for example by certain negro tribes of East Africa,[2] the Burmese[3] and the Chinese.[4] The Icelandic "Tvisang" too bears significant testimony in favour of the theory of the living force of "Organum".[5]

Should there, consequently, be little reason to doubt that singing in fourths and fifths existed also as a musical reality in Western Europe, the problem of the origin and antecedents of this form of song is one of high interest. Assuredly it must have been preceded by an extended period of freely improvised polyphony, which has been designated, by a term borrowed from Plato, as Heterophony.[6] In this, a kind of pseudo-polyphony arises through all the voices singing what is really the same melody, only with variants in the different voices. Naturally these voices often move in unison or the octave, and continue in these intervals at great extent, likewise generally beginning and ending with them. But it often happens also that one or another of these parts leaves the beaten path, and proceeds in notes diverging from the leading melody. As a rule, however, they do not venture very

---

[1] R. M. p. 30. Riemann later expressed the opinion that the preference for fourths came via pentatonic considerations. Consult: Handbuch der Musikgeschichte I, 2 p. 145.

[2] H. Z. p. 299 (Hornbostel).

[3] Refer to Carl Hagemann: Spiele der Völker, 1920, p. 121.

[4] Lavignac: Encyclopedie de la musique I, p. 121. See also S. I. M. 1911, p. 191 (Fischer: "Beitr. z. Erforschung d. chines. Musik").

[5] Consult Angul Hammerich: "Studier over islandsk Musik". 1900, p. 37 sqq.

[6] See Guido Adler: "Über Heterophonie", Jahrbuch der Musikbibliothek Peters, 1908. Also Erich v. Hornbostel: "Über Mehrstimmigkeit in der aussereuropäischen Musik", H. Z. p. 298 sqq.

far from the terra firma of this tune, but commonly keep within a prudent proximity to its borders.

Polyphony of this sort may be found among many exotic nations, for example among the Chinese, Siamese, and Javanese; according to the testimony of Plato and Aristoxenos of Taranto, it was known also in ancient Greece.[1] Indeed, it is said that music of this kind is still to be heard in Greece, and heterophony plays an important role at all events in Russian folk music.[2]

Concerning the transition from heterophony to parallel singing it is difficult to form an opinion. It may be that the sense of hearing notes together was developed through heterophony. After singing heterophonically during centuries—probably mostly occupied with the individual singer in his ornamental extravagances, (though perhaps also with appreciation of the rhythmic variety), it probably occurred one day to some ingenious soul that the combination of this and that musical note in itself had a striking effect. This item was then taken under special observation—special treatment—and in this way the vertical process of selection was finally worked out. It may also be that it came about more accidentally—as Hornbostel, with several others, assumes—for instance where a single voice and a chorus alternate in singing, and one of them sets in by mistake on the concluding note of the other: or where players upon instruments happened to touch adjacent strings simultaneously with those they were to play upon. As already noted, such casual circumstances may have led to the first ray of light in this domain. In such an involved question, however, we can but surmise; the only absolute fact that we know at present is, that in the 10th century there was a clear comprehension in Western Europe of the conception "consonance". The relation to dissonance was beyond doubt very uncertain, however, and naturally there existed nothing whatever of dissonance treatment proper. It is true that "Musica enchiriadis" gives a rule which limits

---

[1] Stumpf: Gesch. des Konsonanzbegriffes, I, p. 18 and 47.

[2] See Eugenie Lineff: "Über neue Methoden des Folklores in Rusland", H. Z. p. 233 sqq.; also Guido Adler: "Die Wiederholung und Nachahmung in der Mehrstimmigkeit", V. f. M. II, p. 343, and Robert Lach: "Vorläufiger Bericht über die .... Gesänge russischer Kriegsgefangener", Sitzungsberichte der philos.-hist. Klasse der kais. Akad. der Wiss. in Wien, 183. Bd., Wien 1917.

the extent of the free lower voice in order to avoid dissonant fourths, (tritones).[1] However, this rule, in the first place, was not strictly kept (not even by Hucbald himself, as is exemplified, for instance, by the augmented fourth in G. S. I, p. 171, last example); in the second place, it leads to intervals of the second in many cases—a dissonance which is much harsher to our ears than the one it was to replace. The possibility that these intervals sounded different to the people of that time from what they do to-day, however, cannot be refuted. Moreover it seems quite probable that they may have had an especially strong perception of these dissonances because of their divergence from the usually preferred fourths.[2]

At any rate, there is no question here of any dissonance treatment in the real signification of the term, but at most of a predilection for certain consonances, and a not entirely consistent rejection of an individual dissonant relationship. It was not until the appearance in the 12th and 13th centuries of Mensural music, "Ars antiqua", that regular rules for the employment of dissonance were introduced. With the *Franconian law,* propounded about the middle of the 13th century by a certain Franco, (probably from Paris?), in a tract called "Ars cantus mensurabilis", there came, in a monumental form, the first, and altogether one of the most important, of the fundamental laws governing dissonance treatment. It is to this effect: "In omnibus modis utendum est semper concordantiis in principio perfectionis, licet sit longa, brevis vel semibrevis".[3] That is to say, that in the beginning of a measure, (Franco using "perfectio" here in the sense of "measure", as all the musical works of his time seem to prove),[4] there should be consonance in all the "modi", (certain metrical series), whether the first note be a longa, brevis or semibrevis. This is a rule which, with one single modification, (the tied dissonance, suspension), stood firm and un-

---

[1] R. M. p. 40.

[2] There may perhaps also be a connection between this phenomenon and the melodic "horror tritoni" of Gregorian chant.

[3] G. S. III, p. 13. It is found already, but in less decisive form, in Johannes de Garlandias "De musica mensurabili positio" (C. S. I, p. 107) which is generally supposed to be a little older than "Ars cantus mensurabilis".

[4] Consult R. M. p. 181. Also Gustav Jacobsthal: "Die Anfänge des mehrstimmigen Gesanges im Mittelalter". Allgemeine musikalische Zeitung 1873, p. 644.

changed throughout the entire florescence of vocal polyphony up to the hour of destiny, the year 1600. It was, however, comparatively late that sufficient mastery of the material was attained to make a strict execution of the rule possible.

In Franco's own time it obviously took serious efforts to reduce this material to a state of subjection. If, for instance, we go through the c. fifty motets from Ms. H. 196 (Fac. de méd. Montpellier), which Coussemaker published in his work "L'art harmonique aux XIIe et XIIIe siècles" (Paris, 1865), we receive the impression of a constant struggle towards the goal of keeping the accentuated beat free from dissonance; but, for the most part, the technical difficulties proved insuperable.[1] These difficulties were by no means inconsiderable, especially in motets. This musical form, the most diligently cultivated of that time, was constructed by composing 2 or 3 melodies of a consciously musical independence, to a cantus firmus in the lower voice, (either a Gregorian fragment or a secular melody), which independence was further emphasized by giving to each individual voice its own special text.[2]

Thus it happens quite often that there is a dissonance upon the principal accented beat of the measure, though there are several motets in the Montpellier Ms. which are entirely free from dissonant accents, (in Coussemaker's collection, Nos. 34, 35, 39, 41, 42), or in which there only occurs a minimum of instances, (as in Nos. 12, 21, 22, 27, 28 and 38, also from Coussemaker). When, in this connection, we refer to a piece as being free from dissonance, it means that only the following tonal combinations occur upon its first beats: the octave, fifth, fourth and third with their respective inversions, in the forms usually reckoned as consonant. It may seem arbitrary to include the fourth and third, in spite of the uneasy and uncertain feelings with

---

[1] An interesting case is that of the motet "Chançonnete va t'en tost", which appears in the Bamberg Ms., (Aubry: "Cent motets du XIIIe siècle." No. XI) as a 3-part composition without any accentuated dissonances at all, while a fourth part (Quadruplum) is added in the same motet in the Montpellier Motets (Coussemaker l. c. No. 49). The new voice here forms harsh, dissonant relations with the other parts in several places, proving that three parts—but not more—could be managed.

[2] Consult Friedrich Ludwig: "Studien über die Geschichte der mehrstimmigen Musik im Mittelalter". S. I. M. Jahrg. IV, V und VII.

which the early polyphonic theorists regarded the latter interval, and the unsettled character of the fourth on the whole, which, however, only became more apparent about the beginning of the 15th century.

My classification, however, is based more upon practice than upon the dogmas of the theorists. It is a matter of fact that the beginning and conclusion, (and especially the conclusion),[1] of compositions dating from the early polyphonic period, made specially rigid demands with regard to consonance. These are also the points which held their own the longest against the recent ever increasing invasion of the dissonance. That which has the conclusive faculty, or is appropriate as a beginning, is the thoroughly reliable consonance. But in the 12th and 13th centuries, (and, for that matter, up to the 16th century), the usual opening and concluding chord was—to use modern terms—the bare triad (without the third).[2] Of the 51 motets published by Coussemaker, 46 begin in unison, with fifths or octaves, or a combination of these intervals, while 48 of them conclude in like manner. One single motet, (No. 35), begins with a major third, (the same composition with the same opening intervals is given in Aubry's edition of the Bamberg motets as No. XXII.), while Nos. 41 and 51 begin respectively with the full major and minor triads. There are also in Aubry's collection several pieces that begin with the full minor triad, (for example, Nos. XXI, XXXII, LXXVII). Nos. 2 and 29 in Coussemaker's collection close upon an interval of the fourth with the bass,[3] while Aubry's No. LXXVIII begins in a similar manner—so it is not unreasonable to assume that major and minor thirds, as well as perfect fourths, were considered consonant in the practice of the "Ars antiqua" period, and consequently their employment upon accented beats was not a breach of the Franconian law.

---

[1] Consult Franchinus Gafurius, Practica musicae (1496), Liber III, cap. III: "Principia uniuscujusque cantilenae sumantur per concordantias perfectas — — — Verum hoc primum mandatum non necessarium est sed arbitrarium: namque perfectionem in cunctis rebus non pricipiis sed terminationibus attribuunt."

[2] One of latest instances in classic music of the occurrence of this effect is in the closing chord of the introductory chorus of Mozart's Requiem, where it certainly signifies Atavism rather than Archaism.

[3] Temporary conclusions of a similar character may be found in Coussemaker, i. a. 41, 2, 10; 67, 2, 7 and 75, 2, 1.

It is difficult to ascertain the relation of the sixth in this regard; it does not occur, to my knowledge, either in opening or closing chords, and theorists of that date considered it much inferior to the third. "Ars cantus mensurabilis" ranges the major and minor thirds among the imperfect consonants, while on the contrary the major sixth is reckoned among the imperfect dissonants, the minor sixth even as a perfect dissonant. Though it may seem rather illogical, especially to modern ears, still I thought it safest, in my inquiry into the observance of the Franconian law, not to count the sixth as a consonant interval.

It would exceed the scope of this treatise to follow the fate of the Franconian rule throughout the changing periods up to the time of Palestrina. For the present it will only be noted that this law was never lost sight of, even if it cannot be said that there was any increasingly strict observance of its tenets. In the beginning of every new period there are generally a lot of new problems which, as the particular constructive factors of that period, are of such absorbing interest that other, secondary matters are allowed to glide along as best they can. Yet as soon as the modern factors have been fairly assimilated, the requirement for consonance upon the accentuated beats arises anew. For every period through which this demand fought its way, it became steadily stronger, ever more imperious in character. In Palestrina it reached the climax of its power.

In all the works of Palestrina there does not exist a single example of any infringement of this law. Apparently a few cases may be found; however, these are all due to faults of transcription or misprints. As these faults are generally overlooked, and as it is also of practical importance to have them corrected, I seize this opportunity of drawing attention to them.

In Haberl's edition of the mass "Ecce sacerdos magnus" (P. X, 30), the "Agnus Dei" begins:

The time units are minims here. The accents are therefore upon the 1st and 3rd minim in each measure, the 2nd and 4th being unaccented. Now it will be noted that there is a fourth in the third measure upon the 3rd minim, thus an accented dissonance introduced in the tenor voice. At first sight one might believe this to be an archaism, as the "Ecce sacerdos" mass is perhaps the earliest of Palestrina's works. A comparison with the original 1554 print, however, shows at once that we have to do here with an error in transcription.

In the original, the tenor sings:

As the mensuration is perfect here, each breve has the value of 3 semibreves. The signature having a line through it, (and consequently, in transcription, the note values being halved), this means that the first note should in reality only have the value of 1½ semibreves instead of the 2 semibreves given by Haberl. The 2nd and 3rd notes, both semibreves, are placed between 2 breves; being thus isolated, the second of these notes must, according to the rule, be altered, (doubled).

The passage appears then:

The fourth falls upon the second minim, and the whole moves quite regularly.

In the motet, "Valde honorandus est", in the first book of the 4-part motets, (1563), Espagne's edition, (P. V, 9, 1, 2), the following occurs:

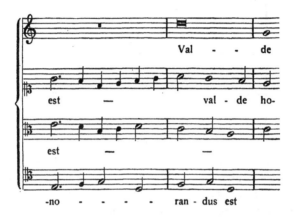

Here the next to the lowest voice has C on the first minim of the second measure, which produces a dissonant relation with D of the upper voice. There is no sense in this extremely harsh effect, which is without doubt a misprint. Unfortunately it seems that the first edition of these motets is no longer extant, and of those still to be found I have only been able to examine the following editions: 1613 (Phalesius, Antwerp); 1622 (Lucas Antonius Soldus, Rome), together with a copy of the edition 1595 (Scotus, Venice; Staatsbibliothek Berlin: L. 195). In the 1622 edition, (which agrees with L. 195, while the 1613 edition corresponds to Espagne's, and the latter also to Proske's edition in "Musica divina", which in its turn is based upon the edition of 1574 [Gardano, Venice]), the tenor is written thus:

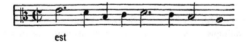

with this result:

As we may clearly see, all falls naturally into place. The dissonance is pushed aside—away from accented beats—and receives only a light, transient character. The tenor's progression also wins in beauty and flexibility in this form, in which the sudden stiffness, (due to the series of 3 minims succeeding the crotchet progression), is finely neutralized. There can be no doubt that this is what Palestrina intended, and that the mode of interpretation adopted by Proske and in "Ges.-W", (no matter how accurately they may follow older editions), is based upon misprints.

Finally, we find in P. XVI, 53, 4, 1, that according to the edition from 1594 (Franciscus Coattinus, Rome), of the 7th volume of masses, the second note of the tenor should not be B flat, but A, whereby a harsh dissonance on the third minim disappears.[1]

The very few other instances of the freely treated dissonances that occur in Palestrina's authentic works cannot be reckoned as breaches of the Franconian law, but must be classed partly under the heading of pedal dissonances, and partly as expressional dissonances, in connection with which forms they will later be examined.

---

[1] The place, P. XXI, 89, 2, 3, which exactly agrees with "Praenestini: Missarum cum quattuor, quinque et sex vocibus. Liber duodecimus. Scotus Venet. 1601" is unquestionably due to a misprint in the original edition. The free fourth, which falls upon the first beat of the measure, is not only most irregular, but it brings about a harmonic combination which in its helplessness sounds highly improbable. Perhaps the first note in the upper voice of 89, 2, 2 should be changed to a minim and the second note in the following measure to a semibreve?

Even if the full and undoubted validity of the Franconian law in Palestrinian music is proved, this says but little of the essential features of dissonance treatment in this art—just as we can scarcely characterize the state of justice in a highly civilized community by proving that certain primitive notions of right, (be they ever so fundamental), are respected there.

One of the foremost exactions of "Ars antiqua" was that all accented beats should be consonant. The unaccented beats had to get along with either consonance or dissonance, as it might chance. In contradistinction to this, Palestrina style subjects everything— even to the minutest item—to the rules. Here it was no longer sufficient merely to consign the dissonance to an obscure point; the laws of accentuation in themselves not yielding a sufficient guarantee of the intelligibility and clearness of the musical impression, much more was exacted with respect to the melody, rhythm, and harmony.

The melodic requirement was, in brief, the passing dissonance. In other words, the unaccented dissonance was to set in by degrees, and continue in conjunct movement in the same direction as the entrance, (occasionally, though more rarely, it might return to the tone upon which it began.[1]

It seems to be the rule that the new means of musical expression generally exist, and have been in practical use for some time, before the arrival of what might be termed the decisive process of "*psychological precipitation*". These expressional means appear mostly in the guise of secondary effects, (by-products), which are apt to be overlooked (or at least scarcely noticed), until suddenly the above-mentioned crucial moment of precipitation brings them into the full light of day.[2]

Music after all is a process of the inner man. The physical possibilities have probably been the same in all eras. Aboriginal people have perhaps perceived the same tonal combinations in natural sounds —the howling of the wind, the tinkle of falling drops of water—with which our own generation have recently been familiarized through the works of the composers of to-day. It is only the psychological

---

[1] The term. "returning-note" will here be used for these forms of melodic movement.

[2] A typical example of this is the history of the chord of the 7th.

possibilities that vary, the capacity to hear intensively and connec-
tively, and the increasing skill in mastering ever more complicated
phenomena, the description of which constitutes the real history of
music. The same tonal combinations may symbolize quite different
things in different periods of time; not what is actually written on
the paper, but what lies behind it, is the question. The manner of
perception characterizing the people of any period is determining with
respect to a correct historic estimation of its musical works.

We meet with the passing dissonance, at any rate pro forma, in a
very early stage of polyphonic music. As soon as note-against-note,
Organum's rhythmic constructive principle, is abandoned for an occasional replacement by two notes against one, the passing dissonance
arises quite automatically; for conjunct melodic progression, (unquestionably the most natural and the most usually employed) is extremely
apt to produce dissonances of this order. It is therefore problematic
whether, in a passage like the following from an "Ars antiqua" composition, (the motet "Ave virgo regia" [Coussemaker l. c. 48, 1, 1]),
considered from within, the C is really a passing note:

The question is whether there are any reasons for assuming that
this form of dissonance was thought especially gentle or mild, and
was therefore preferred to others, or whether its use was based
solely upon melodic motives. The truth is, probably, that all forms
were equally esteemed at first—or, more correctly, all were
equally unnoticed, being only the by-products of the collision between
the independently-conducted individual parts, where the melodic relations entirely absorbed the attention. When the feeling for tonal

combination developed after a time, there was a demand for clear harmonies upon the accented beats; but the unaccented also were gradually drawn into the vertical sphere of interest. The result was that, (with the exception of certain stereotyped ornamental forms), the passing-note was deemed the only worthy bearer of the unaccented dissonance. The oldest instance, known to the author, of the mention of anything like the passing dissonance, is found in the tract "Compendium de discantu mensurabile" of Petrus dictus Palma ociosa, which reads:

"Nota, quod quamvis in istis dissonantiis non debeamus diutius commorari, possumus tamen ascendere et descendere per eas breviter ad omnes alias species sive differentias discantus tam perfectas et medias quam etiam imperfectas."[1]

Perhaps the reference here does not concern veritable passing dissonances,—the omission of the word "gradatim" in connection with "ascendere" and "descendere" is probably of little significance, though rendering the interpretation of the passage less certain. In a similar, at all events very early, passage there is also the same lack of certainty. This is found in a tract called "Ars nova", a work by Philip de Vitry, (probably from a somewhat later part of the 14th century than the treatise by Petrus), and from which we quote:[2] "Et propter earum discordantiam ipsis non utimur in contrapuncto (note against note) sed bene eis utimur in cantu fractibile in minoribus notis, ut quando semibrevis vel tempus in pluribus notis dividitur id est in tribus partibus; tunc una illarum trium partium potest esse in specie discordanti."

The conjunct movement of the parts is not mentioned in this instance also, though in all probability it is implied. Not until the time of Tinctoris and Gafurius, the great 15th century theorists, was full light shed upon this subject. Tinctoris says:

"Ordinatio autem cujuslibet discordantiae haec est, ut tam ascendendo quam descendendo semper post aliquam concordantiarum et proximarum collocetur, ut secunda post unisonum aut tertiam, quarta post tertiam aut quintam, septima post quintam, aut octavam, et sic de

---

[1] Consult Johannes Wolf: "Ein Beitrag zur Diskantlehre des 14. Jahrhunderts". S. I M. XV p. 518.

[2] C. S. III p. 27.

aliis. Et hanc ipsam discordantiam, concordantia uno grado vel duobus tantum, quamvis hoc rarissime, distans ab ea immediate sequetur. Itaque si ab uno loco ascendatur vel descendatur per aliquam discordantiam ad eundem continuo non est revertendum, nisi ipsa discordantia adeo parva sit, ut vix exaudiatur".[1]

Tinctoris here enjoins that the dissonance must be approached by conjunct movement from the nearest consonance, and must be quitted by degrees or leaps of thirds, (in the latter case he was obviously thinking of certain ornamental phrases, which will later be discussed). To be sure, nothing is said about quitting the dissonance in the same direction from which it is approached, but as the last part of the quotation especially concerns the returning-note, (compare this treatise p. 105), we may take it for granted that the first part of the quotation concerns the regular passing dissonance.[2]

Gafurius, whose view exactly coincides with that of Tinctoris— quite naturally, since it is the rules of the same musical practice that both formulate—gives his observations in this form:

"Quae vero per syncopam et ipso rursus celeri transitu latet discordantia admittitur in contrapuncto".[3]

We have here a clear explanation of the motives for passing dissonance, in conjunction with a statement of the contemporary relation towards the whole dissonance problem, viz: dissonance signified something vehement and violent; as it was unavoidable, the point at issue was to conceal and muffle it as far as possible.

The methods of doing this were:

1. To place dissonance only on unaccented beats.
2. To allow dissonance only on comparatively small note-values.[4]

---

[1] Joannes Tinctoris: Tractatus de musica edidit E. de Coussemaker, Lille 1875, p. 378.

[2] It had already been remarked earlier in Tinctoris' work that dissonances of this kind could only be allowed upon unaccented beats.

[3] Practica musicae. Liber III, cap. 4.

[4] Prosdocimus de Beldemandis, Tractatus de contrapunctu (1412). C. S. III p. 197: Prima ergo regula haec est, quod discordantie superius nominate.... nullo modo in contrapuncto usitande sunt. .... Usitandum tamen in cantu fractibili, eo quod in ipso propter velocitatem vocum earum non sentinuntur dissonantie. Also Anonymus XI (C. S. III p. 363) attributes the use of the passing dissonance to the same motives:

3. To use dissonance only when introduced and continued in conjunct movement, or treated as suspension.[1]
4. To allow dissonance only when introduced in such a manner that the mutually dissonant voices do not simultaneously proceed to the discord. (Dissonance in note-against-note is consequently prohibited).

As the relation of Palestrina style to the first point has already been discussed, we may proceed to the second.

The question now is: upon what note-values is dissonance allowed?

It is interesting to turn here to the little historical sketch of dissonance treatment which Vicentino gives—though seen from a rather one-sided quantitative standpoint, it is still quite remarkable in a discipline which, in his time, very rarely adopted the historical point of view:—"The reader may know that, from time to time, some progress is made in music, and that one may see composers, in works that are not modern, place free dissonance (passing dissonance) as semibreves against a longa", (should probably be brevis), "and place the first upon the strong beat like consonance, and the second upon the weak beat like dissonance; later, however, feeling that this harshness lasted too long, they gave up this mode of composition, and in order not to offend the ear too severely, they substituted minims—the first consonant upon strong beats, and the second dissonant upon weak beats; and this arrangement also lasted for a time. In our own era we have given up

---

"Notandum de dissonantiis quod dissonantie in omni cantu ab omni auctore prohibite sunt, et dari non debent nisi in cantu figurativo scilicet in minima vel semiminima aut fusa, quibus artis dissonantia minus percipitur seu percipi potest ratione parve more seu velocitatis in pronunciando."

[1] Zarlino. Istitutioni (Opera I p. 240): Quando adunque tra molte Minime se ne ritrouasse alcuna, che non procedesse per grado; non sarà mai lecito, ch'ella sia dissonante, anzi l'una & altra de due figure, che faranno tal Grado, si debbono porre consonanti; Conciosia che se ben la Dissonanza è posta nella seconda minima nel mouimento di grado; tal mouimento & quel poco di uelocità, che si ritroua nel proferir simili figure, non lasciano udir cosa ueruna, che dispiaccia. Ma non è già cosi ne i Mouimenti di salto; percioche per tal separatione la Dissonanza si fà tanto manifesta, ch'apena si può tolerare; com'è manifesto à tutti quelli, c'hanno giudicio di cotal cosa."

the custom of employing the first minim consonant and the second
dissonant, seeing that the minims are now too perceptible—and not
alone these, but also the semiminims are heard too perceptibly if not
correctly placed, which is the reason that it is customary with us to
employ only semiminims and quavers as dissonances".[1]

Considered from a historical standpoint, this observation of Vicentino is a thoroughly reliable one. The "compositioni, che non sono
moderne" to which he refers must presumably have been works from
the Dunstable-Dufay period, where semibreves were occasionally used
as dissonant passing notes:

Dunstable: „Veni sancte spiritus" (Tr. I, 203, 3, 5).

[1] L'antica musica .... p. 32 v.: Lettore sappi che nella Musica si fà qualche
acquisto, di tempo in tempo, et si uede, che nelle compositioni che non sono moderne;
i compositori hanno composto le dissonanze sciolte, di semibreue in una longa: &
hanno fatto la prima buona nella batuta: & la seconda cattiua nel leuare: & di poi
per un tempo i posteri hanno sentito, ch'era troppo longa quella durezza, tal modo
fu abandonato, e per manco discordo à gl'orecchi usorno le minime; la prima buona
nel battere; et la seconda cattiua nel leuare e questo ordine ha durato un tempo.
Hora in questi nostri tempi habbiamo lasciato l'ordine di comporre le minime, una
buona & l'altra cattiua; & si hà considerato, che la minima è parte che à questi nostri
tempi si sente troppo, et non solamente quella, ma anchora la semiminima s'ode
quando non è ben posta; si che usiamo nelle compositioni far solamente le semiminime, et crome cattiue—"

Damett: Et in terra. Oldh. I, 22, 3,4.

Dufay: „Agnus Dei" (Tr. I, 155, 5, +4).

In the meanwhile it cannot be doubted that the semibreves were here of the same duration as the minims during the last decades of the 15th century and in the greater part of the 16th century ecclesiastical music. The minim is the shortest valued note that occurs in the compositions from which the above examples are cited. Crotchets were seldom used, and series of them only as rare exceptions, (not unlike quavers in the 16th century).

When we consider the history of the dissonance from the standpoint of the duration of dissonance, it is necessary first of all to settle the question of the time unit, of "tempus", in its changing significance in different eras. In the earliest mensural notation, "Ars antiqua", the breve was the unit. In the trecento this was changed, and the semibreve reckoned as the time unit. Towards the close of the 15th century the semibreve had to give place to the claims of the minim as the unit of time, which position it retained during the 16th century, so far as ecclesiastical music is concerned. In madrigals, on the other hand, crotchets were commonly used as time units.[1] The victory of the

---

[1] Refer to Georg Schünemann: "Geschichte des Dirigierens" p. 51.

crotchet was confirmed by the beginning of the 17th century, and to-day it is still the most commonly employed unit.

We thus see that the notation with respect to rhythm meant very different things in different periods. If therefore we wish to compare the duration of dissonances which do not proceed from the same period, it will be necessary to reduce them first to a common denomin-ator, to establish their relation (the rapidity of execution) towards a fixed time unit. This is rather difficult under the circumstances, partly because the conception of tempo in the various periods is not sharply defined, and partly because different conceptions may be comprised under the same notation, even in the same period. We have experi-ence upon this point in the practice of our own time. If we open one of the Protestant hymn-books now in use, for instance, we find that a melody may be written here in half-notes, while in another collection its notation may be in crotchets. Certainly we would not therefore play one transcription twice as fast as the other, but would determine the rate of execution by the musical context.

Compositions from the 16th century are often encountered in which the semibreve is the unit, while in others, (the majority from this cen-tury), the unit is the minim. And finally, as has been remarked earlier, the madrigal most frequently uses the crotchet analogously with the minim in sacred music.

In Palestrina style the minim is decidedly the standard unit of time, though there is no doubt that in certain situations, (for instance where 3 semibreves occur in each measure), these should be of the same time value as the 3 or 4 minims to the measure in other compositions.

Consequently the unit in this case is the semibreve. In the mass, "L'homme armé" (P. XII, 92, 1, + 3), in the following passage there cannot possibly be any doubt that we would give the composition twice as slow a tempo as intended, if the same duration is given to the minims here as is usually allowed in compositions with 4 minims to the measure, and which employs the alla breve sign:

We see this plainest in the dissonance treatment. To illustrate this point, it is necessary to touch here upon some subjects which will later be treated in detail. It must be noted, that in 15th and 16th century music it happens not infrequently in triple (for ex. $^3/_1$) time that, shortly before the concluding phrases, we find three measures of $^2/_1$ time inserted, instead of two $^3/_1$ measures. This occurs also in the above-cited examples, written in the black mensural notation, (the so-called hemiolæ); for the dissonance which falls upon the first beat, (a breach of the Franconian law!) plainly shows that the placing of the bar-line between the 2nd and 3rd measures is quite without *raison d'être*. If we remove this disturbing line, and divide the long measure formed by this elimination into 3 bars of $^2/_1$ time, we shall observe that the 2nd minim in the second of these measures of the upper voice dissonates with the 1st tenor. Such a treatment of minims, however, is a breach of the most elementary laws of Palestrina's style. When used with crotchets, on the contrary, it constitutes, under exactly these accessory circumstances, one of the favourite and best established effects of this style.[1] So it is unquestionable that the unit here is the semibreve, and that this passage, giving the minims "integer valor notarum", should be written thus:

---

[1] Refer to page 120.

A very interesting instance of semibreve time is furthermore to be found in the second volume of Palestrina's 4-part Lamentations, which was scored by Haberl from Palestrina's autograph composition, (Codex 59 in the Lateran archives), and is published in Vol. XXV. of the complete Collection.

That in which the interest centres is not immediately apparent in Haberl's edition, but is plainly evident if we correct this to conform with the information which Casimiri gives in his meritorious work, "Il codice 59" already mentioned. In this book Casimiri again brought to light the valuable manuscript, which seems to have disappeared for a number of years, and has substantiated numerous divergences between the original and Haberl's edition.

He remarks that the passage P. XXV, 54, 3, + 2 is not written, as Haberl gives it, with two semibreves, (C and D), but with one breve in the next to the upper voice, and should therefore appear:

So we find here two passing dissonances in the second measure upon the third minim, which would be absurd in Palestrina style, if we conceive the passage as being executed with the minim as the unit.

If, on the contrary, we adopt the semibreve as the bearer of the "integer valor notarum", there is nothing striking in the passage quoted; for in that case the minims are to be considered the equivalents of crotchets, and when 2 crotchets succeed an accented minim, (all 3 notes, as here, descending in conjunct movement), and with the minim as the unit, it is quite in order that the first of these crotchets is dissonant, (compare p. 125).

This, in connection with the circumstance that the passage quoted employs no notes of smaller value than the minim while the movement is essentially one of semibreves, gives added force to the assumption that the latter functions as the unit.[1]

If it is thus established that in Palestrina style the minim represents the longest duration of the passing-dissonance, it seems odd that Vicentino should declare at the time when Palestrina had just published his first works, that minim dissonance was antiquated: "usiamo nelle conpositioni far solamente le semiminime et crome cattiue". It did not agree with practice, at any rate; and other contemporary theorists, with Zarlino as their leader, held a different opinion.

Zarlino's view is expressed briefly in the form which Tigrini gives in his "Compendio della musica", (a successful attempt to popularize "L'istitutioni harmoniche"): ".... quando la Dissonanza serà posta nel mouimento congiunto nella seconda parte della Battuta, nella seconda Minima non apporterà disgusto alcuno all'orechie."[2]

In this the minim is accorded the right to dissonate upon the unaccented beat. By the "mouimento congiunto" he quite certainly means

---

[1] An interesting parallel to the case just mentioned is found in the madrigal, "Veramente in amore" (P. XXVIII, 81, 3, + 3). In this place, the first crotchet after the accented minim dissonates under the same circumstances as in the Lamentation; but here the time is 4/4, so the dissonant crotchet really represents a minim's value, and is therefore a breach of style. In the meantime the melodic and rhythmic character of the whole piece is such that there is a probability that it has been conceived and executed in minim time. A dissonance, like this arising out of imitation, might certainly be accounted for with earlier composers, but scarcely in the case of Palestrina.

[2] Il Compendio della Musica. 1588, p. 32.

conjunct movement as well in the approach as in quitting the dissonance, of which relation Zarlino says: "ma debbono procedere uerso il graue, ò uerso l'acuto per molti gradi continuati senz' alcun salto".[1] This represents essentially what the theorists of the 16th century, (and, for that matter, of the immediately succeeding centuries) have to say upon the subject of dissonance treatment. Still, a few additional observations should be made.

When Zarlino and other theorists of this period speak of minims, they always say the same thing, viz: that against 1 semibreve may be placed 2 minims, the second of which may dissonate. The only rhythmic possibility mentioned is that the dissonant minim can be introduced after a preceding consonant note of the same value,—all other contingencies were left out of consideration.

The same is the case with Fux's treatment of the question and the representations of the newer text-books based upon the Gradus ad Parnassum.

The result is that, having faithfully followed in the text-books' well defined pathway, and having finally reached freer fields, we really encounter here some possibilities that the previously given rules do not cover.

For example, we know from the exercise of the 2nd species that the dissonant minim must succeed an immediately preceding consonant ditto. Is it not perhaps possible that the last of these minims also can dissonate when the first note is not sounded, but tied over from the preceding measure, (and is thus a part of a larger note value)? This case belongs neither to the 2nd species (strict minim movement) or to the 4th species (strict syncopation), but is a result of a mixture of the two, and must therefore correctly be classified under the 5th species. But to my knowledge neither Fux, Bellermann, nor any later writer treats this relation, either in the rules of this species or elsewhere. Also its occurrence in musical examples, which are often more eloquent than the accompanying text, is rare.[2]

---

[1] L'Istitutioni Harmoniche (1589) p. 240.

[2] Only one single example is found in Fux, (Gradus 1742, Tab. XXXIV, Fig. 10). Compare also Bellermann: "Der Contrapunkt", 4. edition 1901, p. 190, the Ionian example lowest on the page.

It has full validity, however, in practice. I quote from Palestrina's motet, "Congratulamini" (P. V, 75, 4, + 3):

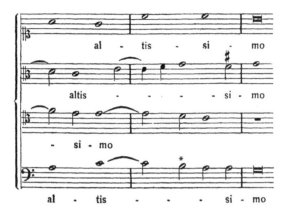

In this instance the value of a dotted semibreve precedes the dissonant minim. It makes no difference, of course, if the semibreve begins on 1 of the measure, as in the following example: P. V, 69, 1, 3. Motet: Salvator mundi,

nor if the preceding semibreve is not dotted:

P. XI, 34, +2. **Missa Inviolata.**

On the other hand, a note-value less than a minim may not immediately precede a dissonant minim in Palestrina style.

The movement itself may occur, but always in consonant minims only; for instance:

P. V, 84, 3, 1. **Motet: Quam pulchri sunt.**

Ultimately it must be remarked with respect to dissonant minims that they are encountered most frequently descending,—not so often as a link in progressions in the opposite direction.[1]

With crotchets we enter a field of great interest. The shorter duration of this note may well render a freer treatment possible—and does . to a certain extent,—the circumstances under which this freer treat-

---

[1] Most likely because they are more striking in ascending progression. Compare Leading Principle No. 3.

ment occurs forming the most enigmatical and attractive element of this matter.

Ordinarily it is said that of four crotchets placed in scale-like progression against a semibreve, the first and third must be concords, while the other two unaccented crotchets may be dissonant.[1]

In this way Fux explains this relation, though he adds that once in a while the third crotchet may be a discord, but (be it noted) only when the second and fourth notes are consonant, and the dissonant tone fills out the interval of a third. (The meaning of this is probably that the dissonance, [presuming a shifting of the accent], would be correctly treated in this way, which would not be the case if another dissonance either preceded or succeeded it).

To this rule both Bellermann[2] and Haller[3] subscribe, the latter, however, without mentioning the requirement with regard to the flanking concords. Franz Nekes, in his reviews of Haller's "Kompositionslehre", was the first to maintain in convincing manner that the rule of Fux was by no means the guiding one in Palestrina's time. The third of the 4 crotchets, it is true, may be also used here as a discord, but under quite other conditions. If we examine, for instance, a case like the following,

P. V, 107, 2, 2. Motet: Veni sponsa Christi.

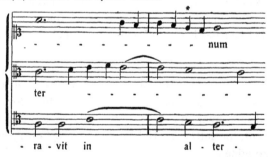

---

[1] Zarlino: "Opere" I p. 239: "Quando poi si uorrà porre nel Contrapunto quattro Semiminime equiualenti à tal Semibreue, allora si osseruerà che quelle Semiminime, che cascherano sopra'l battere, & sopra il leuare della Battuta siano consonanti. Per il che sarà di bisogno, che tali siano la Prima & la Terza semiminima; l'altre poi (com'è la Seconda & la Quarta) non è necessario, che siano in tal numero; ancora che quando occorresse, che si ponessero consonanti tornerebbe meglio."

[2] "Der Contrapunkt", 4. edition, Berlin 1901, p. 161.

[3] "Kompositionslehre", Regensburg 1891, p. 44.

we shall notice that the note upon the second as well as the third crotchet of the second bar stands in dissonant relation to both of the lower voices. As this is not any rare exception, but on the contrary quite a typical mode of expression, it may be taken for granted that the exaction of concords on each side of the discord is not historically founded.

What, then, are the rules, if Fux's statements do not agree with the facts?

Nekes gives his opinion on the subject as follows:[1]

"Von vier stufenweise abwärtsgehenden Viertelnoten, deren erstes Paar auf dem Aufschlag des geraden Taktes steht, darf die dritte in folgender Weise als durchgehende Dissonanz gesetzt werden:

Wie wir sehen, bereitet die eine Stimme eine Dissonanz vor, und zu der Vorbereitungsnote bildet die dritte Note der anderen Stimme einen Sekunden- oder Septimendurchgang. Es sei ausdrücklich bemerkt, dass in unserem Falle das zweite Viertel nicht notwendig konsonieren mus.... Abweichungen von der obigen Regel finden sich selten und dürfen dem Schüler des Kontrapunktes zur Nachahmung nicht empfohlen werden."

According to this the standard should, consequently, be that the dissonance upon the relatively unaccented third crotchet can only be employed when all four crotchets move in scale-like descending progression, and moreover one of the other voices forms a syncopated dissonance with the latter. To Nekes' (l. c.) exceptions,[2] the following examples are added:

---

[1] Gregorius-Blatt 1892.
[2] P. X, 118, 1, + 2. P. XVII, 67, 3, 4; 73, 2, + 3. P. XV, 21, 3, + 3; 84, 1, 3; 88, 3, 4; 103, 2, 3; 103, 2, + 2.

a) P. XII, 59, **2**, 3. Missa brevis.

b) P. XIV, 34, 2, + 1. Missa: Panis quem ego dabo.

c) P. XV, 109, 3, + 2. Missa: Dilexi quoniam.

d) P. XIX, 84, 3, 1. Missa: O virgo simul et mater.

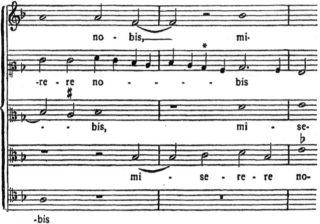

e) P. XX, 114, 2, + 2. Missa: Alma Redemptoris.

f) P. XXIII, 71, 3, + 4[1]). Missa: O sacrum convivium.

Nekes considers suspension the essential condition for the employment of dissonance upon the 3rd crotchet. In reality it represents
quite a constant proportion, (more than 99 out of a hundred cases
where Palestrina employs this form of dissonance being in conjunction
with suspension). Of the examples given by Nekes, P. X, 118, 1, + 2
and P. XVII, 67, 3, 4, and of the ones cited here, b, c, and e might
reasonably be reckoned as suspensions, latent even if undeveloped,
and at any rate consolidating the situation. The possibility of lengthening the stationary note, (meaning the note with which the third crotchet dissonates, and which at all events is retained during the 3rd and
4th crotchets), exists theoretically, for the stationary note is followed
here by its second below, and in case of syncopation would be correctly resolved.[2] (Refer to page 227).

This is not applicable to P. XV, 84, 1, 3 and 103, 2, 3 and + 2 quoted
by Nekes, where the stationary note after the collision makes a leap of
a fourth upward, nor to the instance in P. XVII, 73, 2, + 3, where
the stationary note in the upper voice (after a rest) is followed by its
fourth below. Neither does it apply to the quotations a and d, where
the syncopation would give poor suspensions, (a fourth in the lower

---

[1] See also P. XXVI, 102, 1, 3 etc. P. XXVII, 206, 2, + 3. P. XXXI, 60, 3, 1 (d.). P.
XXXIII, 3, 3, 4.

[2] The difficulty about accepting Nekes hypothesis with respect to the constituent
significance of suspension is the circumstance that very often 2 stationary notes

voice, and a second which resolves into the unison), nor to the example *f,* where the stationary note (already being a syncope) does not
admit of a further postponement of its resolution.

However, there is, in this connection, a certain factor which is *even
more constant than that of suspension.* If we go through the examples
given here, we shall observe that the dissonant crotchets in every
instance, (also in those given by Nekes, which are not printed in notes
here for want of space), are introduced as parts of a figure written
thus:

After a descending progression of 4 notes, the voice moves up a
second. As it is a universally acknowledged rule that whatever is
common to different variants of one and the same form is regarded as
the essential feature of the form, in which the psychological foundation is to be found, it is likely that the way to the inner causes of the
phenomenon leads not so much through suspension, as through the
just mentioned melodic phrase.

The thread is hard to find, however, and we must seek assistance
where it may presumably best be found. It is quite natural to turn to

occur coincidentally one of which only is syncopated. The following example shows
a very common and altogether quite legitimate phrase in Palestrina style:

As we see, the note B in the tenor is dissonant in relation to A in the upper and
F in the lower voice, while only the note in the upper voice remains stationary and
forms the syncopation. But a rule which suffers such frequent transgression rests upon
rather a weak foundation.

the theorists of Palestrina style, and hear their opinions on this subject.

As always when we desire an explanation concerning 16th century musical conceptions, it is Zarlino to whom we look first of all. In this instance, however, we shall be disappointed: for while he treats crotchet dissonance rather exhaustively, he does not mention the special instances where the third crotchet is dissonant. In reality he says no more than Vicentino, who expresses himself less circumstantially in these words:

"—si che usiamo nelle compositioni far solamente le semiminime, et crome cattiue, (facendo però) la 1. buona, e la 2. cattiua, e la 3. buona, e la 4, cattiua, battendo à ragione di quattro semiminime per battuta, che le buone saranno nel battere, & nel leuare, seguendo quattro semiminime, uno doppò l'altra; et quando sono due, apresso una semibreue sincopata, ouero una minima, & che discendino: la seconda deue esser buona & non la prima; & per il contrario quando saranno ascendenti la prima sarà buona, & la seconda cattiua."[1]

Briefly, this signifies that when 4 crotchets (of which the first is accented) immediately succeed each other, the rule already quoted from "l'Istitutioni" holds good. If, on the contrary, 2 crotchets succeed a preceding minim, whether tied over from the preceding measure or not, the first of these crotchets can, ("deue" is not to be taken too categorically, as is practically evident), be dissonant in conjunct descending movement; but if the progression ascends, only the second crotchet may eventually be dissonant, thus:

but never

To these rulings of Vicentino and Zarlino, Artusi adds:

---

[1] l. c. p. 32 v.

"Sogliono questi practici fare che per grado due semiminime siano dissonanti & fa molto buono effetto",[1]

and Tigrini remarks:

"Sogliono ancora i Musici quando vogliono venire à qualche cadenza col mezo di quattro semiminime, porle in questo mode, cioè, che la Terza semiminima sia dissonante,"[2] (adding an example similar to Artusi's).[3]

Thus we get but little information from these observations, merely that phrases of this kind were commonly used, and that Artusi looked upon the occurrence of the two adjacent dissonances as the noticeable feature of the relation. Tigrini furthermore gives the interesting information that this form of treatment of dissonant crotchets is employed principally in concluding phrases.

The Danish musical theorist, Hans Mikkelsen Ravn (Corvinus)[4] seems rather to agree with Artusi: "Ex Semiminimis hunc in modum progredientibus prima et ultima plerumq; consonent." (The musical illustrations added agree exactly with Artusi's, but more probably are taken from the treatise "Compositionsregeln Herrn M. Johan Peterssen Sweling", in which the same examples are accompanied by the following remark: "Also mag mann die 2 mittelsten Semiminimen beyde bös machen, aber die erste und letzte muss gut seyn."[5] Probably the

---

[1] l. c. p. 56.

[2] l. c. p. 33.

[3] Consult Adriano Banchieri: Altri documenti musicali. In Venetia. Apresso Giacomo Vincenti. M. D. C. XIII p. 103. This passage from Banchieri is, for the rest, cited in Zacconi's "Prattica di musica" (Vol. II. 1622, p. 229).

[4] "Heptachordum danicum" (Copenhagen 1646), p. 152. Hans Mikkelsen Ravn, (head master of the grammar school in Slagelse, Denmark, 1640—52, died while rector of Ørslev in 1663), a clever man, endowed with a marked sense of order and a practical grasp of things, yet lacking independence—like the majority of the musical theorists of his time. Compare with Angul Hammerich: Musikken ved Christian den Fjerdes Hof (Copenhagen 1892), p. 144.

[5] Refer to J. P. Sweelinck Werken. Deel X (Leipzig, 1901), p. 27. Sweelinck (1562—

roots of this formulation, which apparently rests upon rather superficial reasons, are to be found as far back as Pietro Aron's "Toscanello
in musica", 1523; the relation between consonance and dissonance was
determined here in the queer manner, that the first and last of the 4
notes into which a breve or semibreve could be resolved should be
concords, while the intermediate notes might be discords.[1] The quotations given up to this point have really not thrown much light upon
the subject, except in establishing the fact that the theorists seem to
have agreed that the third (accented) crotchet could occasionally be
employed as a dissonance in cadences; but otherwise they have not
devoted much thought to the rules governing the conditions of this
relation.

It is here that Cerone's quick eye for details is again manifest. He
writes in his "Melopeo" (p. 650):

"Solamente quando el canto abaxa con quatro Semiminimas de
grado, con las quales va à formar Clausula, se suele hazer que la
primera y quarta sean Consonantes, y la segunda y tercera Dissonantes — — — Aduertiendo que en semejante occasion es necessario que
las dichas Semiminimas abaxen gradatim; de mas desto, conuiene que
despues de la postrera figura de Semiminima, la primera que sigue
suba, segun podemos ver en estos exemples; de otra manera el dicho
passo no se concede":

1621) was at any rate indirectly the pupil of Zarlino; his "Compositionsregeln" consist mostly of a direct translation of "L'istitutioni", with a few additional excerpts
from other theoretical works.

[1] Toscanello (Venice, 1562), p. 16: "Et avertisci a i diminuiti, che sempre la prima
nota et ultima in uno discorso diminuito, vuole esser concordante, et i mezzi diversi
alquanto con dissonanze come il discorso naturale comporta, nel qual per la velocità,
che in se hanno le voci diminuite, essendo in essa alcune dissonanze, non sono in-
commode all'udito del cantore. Et questo è il modo et ordine al presente osservato,
come esaminando i canti de i moderni, potrai facilmente il tutto intendere."
Compare R. M. p. 351.

This is all that can be said, from a practical standpoint, on the subject: descending conjunct movement of all 4 crotchets, after which the
last crotchet moves up a degree. On the other hand, Cerone seems
not to hold the syncopated dissonance to be an integral part of the
whole. Like Tigrini, he merely says that the said dissonance form with
crotchets is only employed in cadences; the first of his examples shows
plainly enough that he was not thinking expressly of suspension alone
as a means of conclusion. As will be evident, all that Cerone writes
agrees exactly with the observations regarding the practice of Palestrina previously given in this treatise. However, the problem is not
yet solved, but enters its most interesting phase just at this point. The
question now is: why can the dissonance on the 3rd crotchet, (which
we will term in the future the relatively accented passing dissonance),
only be used in connection with these stereotyped melodic figures?
The purely musico-technical side of the problem is hereby transformed
into a musico-psychologic one: the question as to how these phrases
were understood by the listener, so that their employment was acceptable, while in other—seemingly similar—cases it was considered
unsuitable.

Why could not Palestrina write like this, for instance?

P. XXII, 50, 3, 5. Missa: Hodie Christus natus est.

And why is it that any one who is conversant with the spirit of the Palestrina style, and who to a certain degree has made the ancient mode of listening his own, is immediately aware that something is not quite right here? This feeling is justified by a closer examination of the place, for the crotchet E, (the 4th note in the bass, 2nd measure, which follows the relatively accented passing dissonance), moves further down to D, instead of going up to F. To modern ears, so little sensitive towards dissonance, such a progression sounds quite probable, even if we adjust our manner of hearing to the stricter, older fashion; but in Palestrina's time these dissonances seemed unduly harsh. It is not surprising therefore that a comparison with the original edition, from 1601, reveals that this place is the result of a misprint, and that according to this edition it should be written:

And we have just as little reason to wonder at the instance P. XV, 21, 3, + 3, which Franz Nekes knew and took quite seriously, (considering it illustrative of the motto: "One swallow does not make a summer"), as it also is due to a misinterpretation on the part of Haberl, who renders it in the complete edition as:

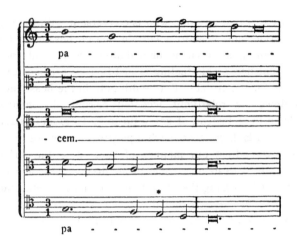

The time here is $^3/_1$, therefore the minims must be understood as being equivalent to crotchets in normal time, (p. 112), which makes the last crotchet after the relatively accented passing dissonance continue downwards, (like the former example), instead of moving upwards. According to the edition of 1596, the next to the upper voice should be corrected as follows:

in which form the relatively accented passing dissonance is replaced by a consonance. The last two examples are the only instances, to my knowledge, in Palestrina's authentic works, which conflict with the requirement of moving upwards after the 4th crotchet, and both are due to faulty renderings in the later editions.[1]

The rule seems valid to an unusual extent. The problem of the underlying motives herewith becomes acute—yet how solve this question?

When we encounter a similar difficulty of linguistic-psychologic nature, it generally repays the trouble to delve into history and, seeking here anterior forms of the linguistic feature in which we are especially interested, to work our way through its genetic course into the centre of vitality. The result here, however, is rather negative.

If we go back as far as the earliest time in which the phrase appears in its classic form, we shall notice that freer, co-ordinate forms are encountered simultaneously with other strictly treated ones; these at that time were considered equally legitimate, though later it was deemed expedient to root out the freer forms entirely. Here there is no question of a gradual development,—the different forms existed simultaneously in the notation of the period, and only gradually have the conditions underlying the sole recognition of the classical form evolved. We meet with the earliest examples of "correctly" treated relatively accented passing dissonance in works of the composers of the so-called Second Netherland School; for instance in Okeghem, (d. 1495):

---

[1] The phrase P. XXVII, 187, 3, 2, which has a certain resemblance to an irregularly treated rel. acc. passing dissonance, makes such a doubtful impression in every way that I venture, (without having had an opportunity to check the accuracy of my conviction more closely), to declare a priori that this also is a misinterpretation in the later edition. The rather similar case P. XXI, 14, 2, 1 is due, according to comparison with the 1601 edition, to a misunderstanding on the part of Haberl. The error lies in the upper voice, and should be corrected by changing the 2nd note in measure 1, + 1 to a dotted minim, which is followed by the crotchet D. In measure 2, 1 the first note should be eliminated, and the 6th crotchet replaced by a minim. Finally we have the very irregular case; P. XIV, 82, 2, + 4, which agrees at all events with the 1590 ed. of the 5th volume of masses. Yet it is pretty certain that the question here is of a misprint in the original edition, the second note in Tenor II. being probably B flat, and not G. Likewise the rel. acc. passing dissonance (in crotchets), P. XVIII, 111, 1, 1, is a misprint; this place, according to the orig. ed. (1599), should be changed so that the 2nd crotchet in Cantus II. is omitted, and the next to the last crotchet in the measure is replaced by a minim of the same pitch.

Okeghem: Je ne pas jeulx. Ambr. V, 14, 3, + 3[1]).

Similar instances are Obr. I, 35, 2, + 1. Obr. II, 5, 2, +2; 64, 1, + 1; 71, 2, + 1; 79, 4, 3; 81, 3, 1; 121, 2, 2; 143, 1, 1; 143, 1, + 1; 144, 2, + 2; 153, 4, + 1; 154, 3, 1; 154, 4, 2; 162, 2, 3. Obr. III, 21, 3, 3; 80, 1, + 2; 174, 3, + 1. Obr. IV, 231, 3, 1 etc.

From Heinrich Isaac. Is. I, 13, 5, 3; 83, 4, + 2; 152, 1, 4; 193, 1. 2. Is. II, 10, 1, + 2 etc.

Josquin des Prés, Ambr. V, 101, 2, 1; 108, 3, + 1; 130, 2, 2 etc.

However, as just mentioned, we find that synchronously with forms correctly constructed according to Palestrina's standard, there were other forms which a later period would not tolerate. For instance, there was nothing objectionable, according to the opinion of the Netherland School, in allowing the 4th crotchet succeeding the rel. acc. passing dissonance to continue the descent in conjunct movement:

Is. I, 105, 1, 2. Alleluia: Magnus Dominus.

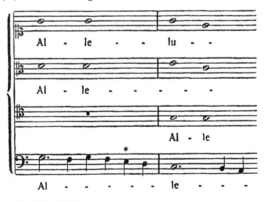

Refer also to the following:

---

[1] This example must be understood as being counted in semibreves.

Obr. I, 1, 1, + 2; 8, 1, 1. Obr. III, 12, 2, + 2; 160, 2, 2; 186, 4, 3; 214, 1, 1. Obr. IV, 101, 4, + 1; 119, 4, + 1; 121, 4, + 3. Obr. V, 2, 1, + 2; 62, 2, + 2 etc. Is. I, 11, 1, 4; 105, 3, + 3; 213, 1, + 1; 230, 3, 1. Is. II, 5, 3, + 1; 9, 5, + 3; 10, 1, 4; 33, 3, 2; 33, 4, + 2; 47, 2, 2; 124, 3, + 4 etc.

Compare furthermore: Ambr. V, 168, 2, + 2 and 178, 1, 1 (Brumel), as well as Josquin des Prés, Missa l'homme armé sexti toni. Et resurrexit, bar 16.

This movement may also ascend:

Obr. I, 29, 4, + 1. Missa: Je ne demande. (Compare Josquin des Prés. Missa: Una musque de Biscaya. Pleni, bar 50.)

The Oxford History of Music. Vol. II, p. 351, 2, + 2. Robert Whyte (ca. 1540—1574) Anthem: O prayse God in his holiness[1]).

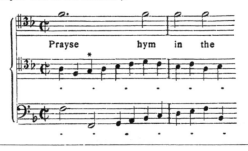

---

[1] This composition belongs to a comparatively late period. In Italy the younger generation of that time had long ago abandoned the archaic form of the rel. acc. passing dissonance. In England and also in Germany, such phrases were by no means rare, (e. g. the song by David Köler. Ambr. V, 366, 3, 2—3), in the period from 1550—70; but in these countries, at this era, musical thought found expression mostly in a rather rude, old-fashioned form, and was freed but slowly from the unpolished

Consult also Obr. I, 35, 3, 3; 182, 2, + 2. Obr. II, 70, 3, + 2; 81, 4, 1. Obr. IV, 36, 2, + 2; 90, 3, 1. Is. I, 47, 1, 3. Is. II, 25, 3, 4; 67, 1, + 1; 75, 6, + 4; 97, 3, 4; 102, 1, + 1; 102, 4, + 5; 103, 3, + 1; 119, 1, + 4; 120, 4, 2; 120, 5, 5; 120, 5, + 1; 120, 6, 5 etc. Josquin des Prés, Missa: Una musque de Biscaya, Benedictus (5th measure from the end), and Missa: Da pacem, Credo, bar 19.

It has previously been mentioned (p. 125) that when two crotchets in descending conjunct movement succeed an accented minim, the first crotchet may be dissonant in Palestrina style.[1] In older music this frequently occurs, also when the movement is of an ascending character:

Josquin des Prés: Missa: Malheur me bat. Gloria, bar 76. (Compare also Obr. III. 10, 3, 3 and Pierre de la Rue; Gauda cara. Maldeghem: Trésor musical. 1882, 11, 1, 1.

See also Ambr. V, 15, 1, + 2; 16, 2, 1 (Okeghem). Obr. I, 13, 1, 1; 13, 2, 1; 24, 2, 1; 32, 1, + 3; 37, 2, 1; 51, 1, + 1; 73, 4, + 2; 89, 2, 2; 90, 1, + 2; 111, 4, + 1; 112, 4, 2; 154, 4, 1; 194, 4, 1. Obr. III, 13, 3, 3; 72, 3, + 1; 80, 2, + 1; 106, 2, 2; 155, 3, + 2; 163, 2, 1; 228, 3, + 1 etc. Is. I, 132, 4, 2; 156, 2, 2; 159, 4, + 3; 165, 1, + 3; 180, 5, + 4; 245, 1, 1. Is. II, 5, 2, 2; 6, 4, 2; 29, 1, + 1; 96, 3, 3; 117, 6, 5. Is. III, 27, 5, 5; 38, 2, 2; 72, 1, + 1; 104, 2, 3; 124, 5, + 3; 173, 4, 3; 204, 2, + 1. Josquin des Prés, Missa: Una musque de Biscaya, Christe, bar 2. Missa super: Lami Baudichon, Agnus II, bar 15; Missa: Malheur me bat, Gloria, bar 14;

usages of the Second Netherland School. To these antiquated usages may be attributed many of the styliform phrases which are frequently, though incorrectly, considered national characteristics.

[1] An isolated instance of an ascending dissonance of this order may be observed in P. XXXI, 168, 2, + 2—an exception which only seems to prove the rule.

Missa: Didadi, Kyrie I, bar 2; Missa: Ad fugam, Christe, bar 30; Requiem Sec. pars, bar 6; Fuit homo, bar 68, etc.

On the whole great uncertainty prevailed with regard to this relation throughout the era of the Second Netherland School. That the Italians had not been able to put an end to this arbitrariness in a short time is obvious, for instance, from the following phrases in compositions by Costanzo Festa, (d. 1545), the greatest of Palestrina's Italian predecessors:

Regem archangelorum. Torchi: L'arte musicale in Italia. I, 50,2, 2.

Missa: Amis des que. Christe, (in the Papal archives).

However, Palestrina, in contrast to his predecessors, conformed most strictly to the rules. Now the problem is to account clearly for the cause of these rules.

The form of dissonance treatment in Palestrina which most nearly resembles the relatively accented passing dissonance, is the figure already mentioned—the accented minim succeeded by 2 crotchets (in descending conjunct movement), of which the first is dissonant. The similarity of these forms is immediately apparent, both having the dissonance upon the 3rd crotchet, both introducing the dissonance by degrees from above, and then moving down to the second. It is not until the note which succeeds the dissonance is considered with regard to its further progression, that the dissimilarities become evident.[1] While this note, as already stated, must necessarily move upwards by degrees on account of the relatively accented passing dissonance, the corresponding note of the analogous form has greater freedom of movement. It may, and often does, move upward by steps.

P. V, 3, 2,4. Motet: Dies sanctificatus.

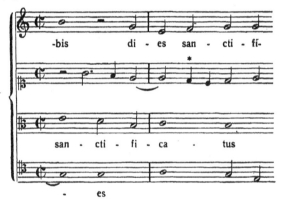

But just as often it may move downward in conjunct movement:

---

[1] It is curious that the English composer and theorist, Thomas Morley (1557—1603), denounces this form of dissonance treatment, (which was practised by the masters of the "purest" Palestrina style), in his work: "A Plaine and Easie Introduction to Practicall Musicke" 1771 [1597] p. 91: ".... it is impossible to ascend and descend in continual deduction, without a discord: but the less offence you give in the discord, the better it is; and the shorter while you stay upon the discord, the lesse offence you give. Therefore, if you had set a dott after the minime, and made your two crotchets, two quavers, it had been better". Though Morley expresses unmistakable purist tendencies, he is by no means over-sensitive with respect to the dissonance; moreover he is not very consistent, using the above phrases, that he had condemned, in the practical examples in his book, (e. g. p. 105).

P. XII, 114, 2, 3. Missa: Repleatur os meum laude.

Furthermore it may leap upward the interval of a third or fourth, for instance:

P. XV, 55, 3, 1. Missa: Sine nomine.

P. XXVII, 28, 3, + 2. Magnificat sexti toni.

Also it is possible to leap upward the interval of a fifth under these circumstances:

P. XVI, 22, 2, + 1. Missa: Sanctorum meritis.

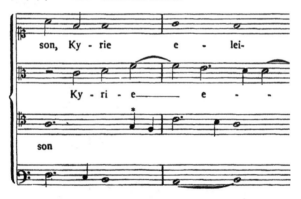

and even up to the octave in rare instances:

P. XXIII, 127, 1, + 1. Missa. Veni Creator Spiritus. (Also P. XXX, 142, 3, 2).

The reason why the further progress of *the last* of the four crotchets in connection with the rel. acc. passing dissonance is based upon this sole condition, may therefore be found in the fact that 2 crotchets, (and not a minim) precede the dissonance. If now we seek the inner causes of this, trying to find its psychological reason, the best procedure would be to choose for the first examination *the form with a preceding minim,*—this being the simplest and most usual of the two forms. The placing of the dissonance depends mainly upon the perception of the time unit.

Just as truly as the following would not be written in Palestrina style,

so also it may not (unconditionally) be used thus:

Nor is this form allowed:

while strangely enough
the following is legiti-
mate:

The reason why the analogy does not hold good here, is doubtless
that the last instance is perceived as minim tempo, whereby the dissonance falls on the unaccented part of the measure. In the case where
the dissonance follows 2 preceding crotchets, it is usually perceived
as crotchet tempo, whereby dissonance and accent fall together. However, it is by no means our intention to say here that a dissonance
succeeding an accented minim is solely to be understood as a passing
dissonance. On the contrary, it will more probably be perceived as
a relatively accented ornamentation of a succeeding principal note.
For when the dissonance is introduced in conjunct movement after a
preceeding accented minim, it is naturally expected that the dissonant
note, (analogously to the preceding instance), should be equivalent
to the minim in value. But if it be resolved into a concord after the
duration of only a crotchet, it makes such a striking effect that the
attention is especially concentrated on the 2 crotchets, and the dissonance thereby enters into a more marked accentual relationship to
the succeeding crotchets than to the preceding minim. The effect
produced is similar in character to what is called, in recent musico-
theoretical terms, a dissonant "Grace-note". By this, as is generally
known, is meant a dissonant note introduced upon the accented beat
which is explained by its relation as a second to the following con-

sonance, the relation to which becomes clear only when considered as an ornamentation or an immaterial embellishment of the principal consonant note.

Behind these notes

is really heard the following:

That the character of this relation is not perceptible to modern ears alone, is apparent from the usage in various editions and manuscripts of the same compositions from the beginning of the 16th century, where the two phrases are alternately substituted for each other. If we compare, for instance, "Petrucci, Misse Obrecht, 1503", with the Mus. Ms. 3154 in the State Library at Munich, we shall find, (according to the revision by Johannes Wolf of "Obrechts Werken"), the following characteristic discrepancies between the two:

Obr. I, 36, 3, + 2.   Munich Ms. 3154.

ibid. 36, 4, 2.   ibid.

ibid. 34, 4, +2.   ibid.

ibid. 40, 4, 2.   ibid.

Also a comparison between Egenolff's edition of Josquin des Prés' "In meinem Sinn hab ich mir auserkoren", (1534) and the form of the same composition in the Ms. 124a, in the City Library at Augsburg, yields information of value with respect to variants of this order.[1] That the discord is accidentally used in this manner, suggests that it was considered something inessential, while the succeeding consonance was looked upon as the essential feature of the relation. Another fact which also goes to prove that in the 16th century this kind of dissonance was used more like Grace-notes than as real dissonance, is that the Palestrina style was not afraid to give emphasis to this dissonance through its employment in note-against-note. Moreover it seems to attain its clearest and most characteristic form in this mode of treatment; for example:

P. V, 40, 3,+2. Motet: Fuit homo.

It is therefore principally employed in this manner, while note-against-note is seldom used in conjunction with the passing dissonance, the very essence of which is obscurity. However, it was only to a certain degree found appropriate to give prominence to the dissonance just mentioned, as is manifest by its being employed solely upon the place of the unaccented minims in Palestrina music. While it is considered quite proper to emphasize the dissonance in relation to the succeeding consonance, (whereby the "Grace-note" character becomes even more evident), it is desirable to secure at the same time the possibility of the perception of it in a larger context as unaccented—for by this means its non-essential character becomes most pronounced. Palestrina style therefore does not sanction the dissonance on the 1st and 3rd minims, while the Second Netherland School is less careful in

---

[1] S. Eitner: Publikationen älterer Musikwerke. Vol. VI.

its attitude in this regard, though mainly where the dissonance is of crotchet value and preceded by a crotchet:

Josquin des Prés, Missa: Una musque de Biscaya. Credo, bar 37.

Obr. II, 81, 3, + 2. Missa super Maria zart[1]).

Instances of this kind, though rare, may still be encountered in works of somewhat later composers, for example in motets of Richafort (a pupil of Josquin, died about 1550):

Maldeghem: Trésor musical. 1881, 31, 5, 2. Motet: Tulerunt —

---

[1] A most suggestive illustration of the fact that in Pre-Palestrinian music the "correctly" treated and the archaic forms of the dissonance could occur, in the literal sense of the word, in one and the same breath.

A similar figure occurs in a composition by Ludwig Senfl, (d. about 1555), and may be observed in "Senfls Werke" I, 58, 3, 3 (Denkmäler deutscher Tonkunst, zweite Folge, 3. Jahrg. Bd. II, Leipzig 1903). For completeness' sake, we mention that the only instance in Palestrina's works of this kind is the following:

P. XII, 118, 3,+1. Missa: Repleatur os meum laude.

which must be corrected to agree with the original edition of the 3rd volume of masses (Doricus, Rome 1570) in the following manner.

and consequently is not to be taken seriously in Haberl's edition. Phrases like the following are, however, trustworthy:

P. V, 28, 1 + 1. Motet: O rex gloriae. (Similar instances: i. a. P. XV, 35, 1, 3 and
65, 1, 4, P. XIX, 41, 1, 4. P. XXI, 67, 1, 2.

This might seem to be an example showing that the rel. acc. passing
dissonance may, as an exception, be placed upon the accented minim.
But in reality the dissonance here must be otherwise understood, because the last 3 notes in the first measure of the upper voice may be
replaced by a semibreve on A without at all altering the significance
of the passage. If a like substitution were undertaken with the rel. acc.
passing dissonance in its usual position, the phrase would thereby
only appear still less regular than before. The present instance therefore only represents quite a normal treatment of suspension, (refer to
p. 227), wherein one of the 2 notes that is dissonant with the syncope
is embellished by a returning-note of an altogether unimportant nature.
It is not necessary that the phrase, (as in the above example), should
assume the same melodic form as the phrase introducing the rel. acc.
passing dissonance, which is illustrated by the following:

P. XXI, 130, 3, 1. Missa: Viri Galilaei.

P. XXII, 20, 4, 3. Missa: Laudate Dominum.

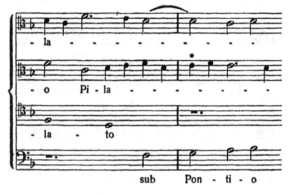

These 2 examples plainly show that the ornamentation is not
bound by any decided melodic conditions, but on general principles
is allowed wherever the correctly treated tied dissonance occurs. Passages like P. V, 28, 1, + 1, and others similar, have nothing to do
with the rel. acc. passing dissonance, since in these instances it is
not really the crotchet, but the syncope, (as always where there is
syncopated dissonance), which is dissonant and must be resolved.

Before proceeding to a more direct consideration of the rel. acc.
passing dissonance, there is one particular relation which must be
mentioned briefly. This dissonance form, besides the kinds already
treated, has another related form which is very commonly employed
in Palestrina style as a terminal phrase:

P. XX, 4, 4, + 1. Missa Descendit angelus.

As will be observed, the melodic contents of both forms are identical, the sole difference being of a rhythmic nature. The dissonance in the last quoted example is removed from the 3rd to the 4th crotchet, whereby it is moreover reduced to a quaver. With this reservation, the two forms exactly agree—in both, the syncope dissonance and the turning to the upper second are observed. In the last mentioned form, however, neither of these two features is a *conditio sine qua non,* though both are most often present. The absence of suspension is comparatively frequent; for instance:

P. II, 102, 2, 4. Motet: Beata Barbara.

It may also happen that the requirement of the upper second to the last of the two quavers is not taken into account; for instance:

P. XIX, 106, 1, 2. Missa: Quinti toni.

These examples seem to prove that the exaction concerning the upper second, depends greatly upon the 3rd crotchet being a veritable dissonance.

Assuming now that the dissonant crotchet following *the accented minim* functions as a kind of dissonant Grace-note, (as previously stated), and is legitimate as such, it is natural to inquire why the corresponding dissonance following *a crotchet* may not be explained in the same way.

The answer to this query must be that, while the dissonance in the first case is to be understood as unaccented in relation to the preceding minim and at the same time as accented in relation to the succeeding crotchet, such a two-fold perception is not applicable to the second case, where crotchet accentuation predominates; consequently the dissonance is exclusively perceived as accented.

But upon unequivocal accented beats we generally only encounter (excepting suspension dissonance) notes which exist independently and need no explanation through a succeeding consonance. Therefore in cases of this kind there is an inclination, when no other factors intrude, to apprehend the dissonance as an independent feature, and consequently a breach of style, instead of considering it a Grace-note before the next succeeding crotchet.

Yet the moment that the figure ends with an ascending second move, it is considered appropriate. Why?

The answer most likely is that the figure, thus enlarged, is understood as a cambiata phrase which is filled out:

The cambiata,[1] which has previously been briefly mentioned here, can best be defined as a melodic phrase which in its classical form usually appears in the following rhythmic figure:

---

[1] p. 70, cf. furthermore p. 210.

Its characteristic function is to divide the descending interval of the 4th into two intervals of a 2nd and a 3rd respectively. It may be employed either as consonance or dissonance, which in the latter case would allow the 2nd note to be dissonant, and thus violates the rule concerning quitting the dissonance by conjunct movement. That the cambiata notwithstanding is acceptable in this style, is due to the fact that the violation of this rule is only an ostensible one, since the 4th note of the figure was understood as a resolution of the dissonance, which—though belated—finally appears and clears up the situation. The cambiata, as well as the relatively accented passing dissonance, is first encountered in works (i. e. in compositions from the First Netherland School) where its classical form occurs simultaneously with freer forms. It has, consequently, not been gradually developed and refined; but after the establishment of the rule about conjunct movement in dissonance treatment, the classical form was the only one, out of many similar types, which conformed to the requirements of the new era. The same holds good with reference to the rel. acc. passing dissonance. The melodic form in which it is normally introduced signifies, like the cambiata, a standardized phrase used both in consonance and dissonance. The fact that this figure may also be employed dissonantly in Palestrina, is explained by the following circumstances. An extremely popular conclusion about the year 1500 was:

However, it was quite customary to embellish this figure by interposing a third crotchet after the two crotchets in the tenor. A case of this kind may be observed in Heinrich Isaac's Chanson, "Helogierons nous", where, (according to Johannes Wolf's report in the "Denkmäler der Tonkunst in Österreich", XIV, 1), some sources give bar 43 thus:

while in other places, (for example in Petrucci's Odhecaton 1501) it
is written:

The fuller form was consequently considered an embellishment of
the simpler. Both were accepted in Palestrina,—the simpler, because
it only apparently conflicted with the rule concerning conjunct dissonant progression—the more elaborate, because of its familiarity as
a variant of the simpler form. But regarding it as such, one found it
natural to count it in minims like the primary form, and consequently
the dissonance assumed the character of a Grace-note or ornament—
in brief, became dependent. The phrase:

was thus heard as:

just as this phrase:

was understood as:

We now clearly see why the rel. acc. passing dissonance is always employed in connection with the second above the fourth crotchet; for it is not until the appearance of this note, which corresponds to the most important of the cambiata's notes—the note of resolution—that the phrase is comprehended as the filling out of the cambiata figure, and is thereby included under the form: "crotchet dissonance succeeding a minim". For the same reasons, both come within the legitimate field of the style.

It still remains to explain the typical occurrence of syncopated dissonance in connection with the rel. acc. passing dissonance. Yet this relation is amply accounted for in the circumstance that syncope dissonance seemingly imparts a welcome underlining of the minim time, and thereby of the dependent character of the rel. acc. passing dissonance.

Apart from the exceptional cases just mentioned, the rules for the treatment of dissonant crotchets correspond exactly to those governing the employment of minims. What has been said (page 116 sqq.) with respect to minims, applies equally with respect to crotchets. They too may not be introduced dissonantly after smaller note-values, while on the other hand a crotchet, free or tied, or a greater note-value, (provided the usual rhythmic requirements are otherwise complied with), may quite well precede the crotchet dissonance.[1] With regard

---

[1] Regarding this dissonance form, which in the preceding pages has been designated "crotchet dissonance succeeding accented minims", it likewise holds good that

to the relationship of minims and crotchets, it is noticeable that minim dissonance is rarely employed in Palestrina style when another voice simultaneously is moving with crotchets.

Rare exceptions are places like:

P. V, 134, 4, +3. Motet: Ad te levavi. 2. P.

Compare also: P. VIII, 50, 1, + 1. P. XI, 120, 1, 3. P. III, 39, 2, + 2. P. IV, 60, 1, + 4. P. IX, 206, 3, + 3. P. XXII, 22, 2, + 3. P. XXIV, 43, 3, + 3.

That such cases are encountered so seldom is doubtless due to the confusion arising out of the simultaneous occurrence of crotchet and minim time accentuation. In order to perceive the minim as passing dissonance, it is necessary that an accented crotchet should not be heard upon the same beat where the minim is unaccented. When this happens, it renders the relationship vague and incomprehensible. On the other hand, another voice may employ 2 crotchets preceding the dissonance, (but only when a crotchet does not fall upon the latter); as for example:

---

greater note-values than the minim, (for example, the semibreve with or without the dot), may precede the dissonance.

P. XI, 13, 3, 4. Missa: De beata Virgine.

and it is not uncommon for two crotchets to occur simultaneously with the dissonance if the dissonance is not preceded in another voice by a crotchet; for instance:

P. XI, 71, 2, 4. Missa: Aspice Domine.

which goes to show that phrases like

were heard as minim tempo, while on the contrary places exclusively having crotchets were perceived as being in crotchet tempo.

With the quaver we finally reach the smallest note-value employed in Palestrinian music, though in $^4/_4$ time madrigals, of course, the semi-quaver (16th note) is employed, (representing quavers here). It is com-

paratively rare that more than 2 quavers in succession are encountered; however, once in a while as many as 4 are used in a series. In
the latter case they fall under the same rule as the minim and crotchet,
and instances may occur where the 3rd quaver is treated as a rel. acc.
passing dissonance; for example:

P. V, 129, 2, 1. Motet: Ecce nunc.

Consult also P. IV, 9, 3, 2 and P. IX, 138, 2, 3.
Instances of this kind, but without the suspension also occur:

P. VIII, 8, 1, 1. Hymnus: Christe redemptor.

On the whole, quavers are treated more freely than greater note-
values, on account of their shorter duration. Crotchets, for instance,
could not be used in the following connection:

P. XXVIII, 15, 3, 1. Madrigal: Nessun visse.

and also this form of dissonance treatment,

P. V, 131, 4, +4. Motet: Ad te levavi.

while quite common with quavers, is inconceivable with crotchets, where anything similar could only be employed in descending movement. This is the gist of what there is to say about dissonance treatment from a quantitative point of view.

There still remains the question of the employment of dissonance in note-against-note. The attitude of the theorists was quite simple; almost without exception, from the time of "Ars nova" up to Fux and Bellermann, they forbade every form of dissonance in this order of counterpoint.[1] The practical musicians, though well understanding the necessity of discretion here, generally are hardly so strict; consequently it is rather surprising that an excellent practician like Cerone here joins his theoretical colleagues.

With regard to minim dissonance in note-against-note, he writes:

"Dixe que una parte ha de estar firme y sin tocar nuevo punto,

---

[1] For instance: Tinctoris: "In ipso autem simplici contrapuncto discordantiae simpliciter et absolute prohibentur". (Tractatus p. 352).

aunque sea la misma posicion, porque tocando dos vezes la nota que
recibe el golpe de la dissonancia, offende mucho el oydo, y por esto
no se permite si no en las composiciones duras, asperas y lamentab-
les"[1]:

Cerone gives as his opinion that it is best to avoid minim dissonance in note-against-note, even if treated in the cautious way that
one voice in conjunct movement progresses towards the point of dissonance while the other repeats its preceding note, thus causing the
dissonant relation. This is the only possibility mentioned here, and
even this is said to be employed solely in compositions of a sad and
plaintive character.

This agrees, on the whole, with the custom of the latter part of the
16th century. However, there was not such a sensitive feeling concerning the effect of dissonance in the beginning of the cinquecento, and
consequently at that period we may relatively often encounter such
harsh phrases as the following:

Obr. I, 199, 4 + 1. Missa: Salve diva parens. Also Obr. III, 184, 4, + 2 and Josquin des Prés, Missa: Dung aultre amer, Agnus, 8 measures before the end.

A significant light is thrown upon Palestrina's attitude in this respect through the following passage, taken from the first volume of
the 4-part motets (1563):

---

[1] "Melopeo" p. 621.

P. V, 107, 1, + 3. Motet: Veni sponsa Christi.

How very urgently he felt the necessity of shunning dissonant note-against-note here, is shown by the circumstance that he does not even flinch from a break in the imitation when needed to avoid that undesirable effect. In this instance he therefore alters the 2nd note of the 3rd measure in the soprano, (which really should be *D*), to an *E*, in order to avoid the collision with *E* in the tenor. This is all the more significant since the theme is liturgical, being borrowed from the Gregorian melody, "Veni sponsa", in which the corresponding passage, (Vatican edition of the Antiphonale, 1912,) reads:

Nor do we in fact anywhere in Palestrina's works meet with such an unmitigated case of note-against-note treatment as would have resulted here from a strict execution of the imitation. The few instances of this kind in Palestrina's compositions are of a decidedly milder character, for example:

P. V, 57, 4, 1. Motet: Quae est ista. P. XVIII, 112, 3, + 2. P. XI, 135, 3, 4; 136, 1, + 2.

It is worthy of notice that in every one of these instances a very mild dissonance is used, namely the diminished fifth, which vibrates between consonance and dissonance; this interval is also used in other instances where, according to strict rules, only consonance was allowed,[1] as for example:

P. XIV, 37, 3, 1[2]). Missa: Panis quem ego dabo.

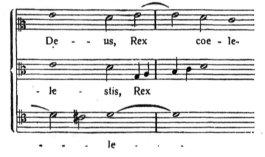

The fourth in the lower voice is resolved here into the diminished fifth, thus moving from one dissonance to another, which would conflict with the most fundamental rules for the treatment of suspension.

---

[1] This relation was fully approved by the theorists. Compare for ex. Artusi, l. c. page 50.

[2] Cf. Victoria: Opera, I, 50, 1, + 1 and 2, 4.

This use is conceivable only because the diminished fifth was perceived as halfway a consonance. Outside of these instances, in which the less pronounced character of the dissonance makes the freer treatment of it possible, I know of only very few passages in Palestrina's works which might be mentioned in this connection:

P. I, 3, 2, 4. Motet: O admirabile commercium. (Refer also to P. XXIX, 189, 2, 2.)

These are both of a less striking kind, being phrases of such common occurrence in Palestrina style as to pass nearly unnoticed; it is scarcely noticed therefore, whether the stationary note (as here) is divided into smaller notes or remains intact, as in the great majority of cases, (compare P. V, 69, 1, 3, cited in the foregoing, p. 117). Also the dissonant *crotchet* in note-against-note did not find favour in the eyes of Cerone, who declared its use as in the following example inadmissible[1]:

---

[1] l. c. p. 658.

Nevertheless, a similar employment occurs comparatively often in Palestrina's works:

P. V, 29, 4, + 1. Motet: Loquebantur. (Also see: P. XIX, 114, 2, 5.)

Compare also: P. X, 16, 2, 3; 37, 4, 1; 67, 1, + 1; 70, 3, + 1; 70, 4, + 4; 88, 2, 2. P. V, 132, 2, + 2; 170, 4, 3. P. VIII, 133, 3, + 3 etc.

There is, however, a form of dissonant note-against-note which, though really harsher than those just mentioned, (since *both* voices here progress towards the dissonant collision), yet is very commonly employed both in Netherland music and Palestrina's style. It may be encountered in crotchets, even though Artusi energetically maintains that this note-value should only be used consonantly in note-against-note:

"E quando il Compositore pigliasse per soggietto una parte che fosse di canto diminuito all'hora si osseruera di ponere tali semiminime che siano consonanti, secondo la dispositione, si della parte del soggietto, come quella del contraponto".[1]

However, the musicians of the 16th century constantly wrote passages like the following, without bothering about what the theorists thought:

---

[1] "L'arte del contraponto", p. 56.

Obr. I, 116, 2, + 2. Missa: Fortuna desperata.

Is. III, 171, 1, + 4. De sancto Martino, sequence.

Pierre de la Rue: "Gaude cara", Maldeghem 1882, 10, 3, + 3.

Costanzo Festa, Motet: Quam pulchra es. M. I. 17,2,1.

P. XIV, 50, 4, 2. Missa: Panis quem ego dabo.

P. VIII, 143, 1, + 2. Hymnus: Laudibus summis.

In all the dissonance forms hitherto mentioned in this treatise, there was no doubt about which note was the dissonance. The dissonance was always placed against a greater note value; the shortest of the notes which met in this dissonant relation was always understood as the dissonance, and it lay with the voice introducing the latter to provide for its correct continuation. Also in that part of the note-against-note examples given in the foregoing, in which only one voice progresses towards the point of dissonance, while the other is stationary, there can be no doubt about the position of the dissonance.

But here it is different—for which note should be considered the dissonance in the last cited example from Palestrina, the *D* in the alto, or the *C* in the tenor? Or are they both to be regarded as such, with the consequent obligations?

The latter supposition is plainly contradicted by the case in question; for while the tenor's attitude is correct with respect to this assumption, the alto would have a dissonance upon the 3rd crotchet in ascending progression, which (as we know) is foreign to Palestrina style. Meanwhile it will be observed that the irregularity of the phrase disappears as soon as the alto and tenor are not compared with each other, but each is considered in relation to the bass. In this way the dissonance in the tenor still conforms to the rules, and the dissonance on the 3rd crotchet in the alto is eliminated. Was the truth, perhaps, that in note-against-note with crotchets, it made not the slightest difference about the relations between the crotchets, which could be consonant or dissonant at pleasure, provided their relation to the bass was right? Much conduces to the belief that this assumption is correct. There are, first of all, the circumstances concerning the perfect fourth, and the diminished and augmented fifth and fourth. We are aware that in the 16th and the greater part of the 15th centuries, musicians considered the fourth as a dissonance. While the musico-theoretical world waged a bitter fight for and against this "*infelicissima consonantiarum omnium*"— as Descartes called it—whether it should be reckoned as consonance or dissonance, practical musicians were almost unanimous in considering it solely as a dissonance. This was also Palestrina's standpoint. However, it must not be supposed that fourths were treated with the same severity as the harsher dissonant seconds and sevenths. For instance, the perfect fourth could be treated quite like consonance, (which applies also to the less aggressive dissonances, the diminished and augmented fifth and fourth), though only when its notes pertained to intermediate and upper parts, and not to the bass. In 16th century theory I have found nothing that indicates a reason for this fact; however, Fux gives the following opinion about the appended musical example[1]:

"Wer siehet nicht, dass in diesem Exempel keineswegs die Quarte, sondern die Quinte und die Octave stecket? denn die Intervallen sind nach ihrem Grundton, nicht nach ihren mittlern Theilen abzumessen."

Thus the consonant employment of the fourth, in the example cited, is explained by Fux here as being due to the fact that neither of the notes that form the fourth dissonates with the bass. The free employment of the diminished and augmented fifths and fourths between upper and intermediate voices in Palestrina music is explained in the same way. The use of the augmented fifth makes possible the chord called in modern terms "the augmented triad in its first inversion". As the occurrence of this chord in pure style is seldom mentioned, and as it is rather commonly supposed that it suddenly descended from the skies expressly for Wagner's "Tristan",[2] examples are appended here, taken from Palestrina's works, showing that the 6th chord, (to continue in modern terms), was understood as a full consonance:

---

[1] Gradus (Mizler) p. 38.

[2] It cannot be denied that a splendid "psychological precipitation" took place here in Wagner's use of a tonal combination which had been known for centuries, yet under a form of less intensive animation.

P. XI, 115, 3, 3. Missa: Salvum me fac.

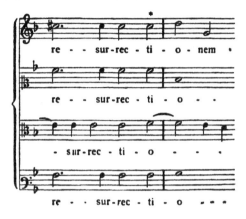

Further examples: P. XI, 101, 2, 1. P. III, 4, 2, 5. P. XIII, 45, 4, + 2;
60, 2, + 1; 82, 3, + 4. P. VIII, 8, 4, + 3. P. XIV, 33, 1, 1; 72, 1, 2.
P. XVIII, 80, 3, 2; 86, 2, + 3. P. XXI, 48, 3, 2; 50, 2, + 1; 56, 2, 4.
P. XXV, 26, 2, + 1; 64, 3, 4. P. XXVI, 25, 3, + 3; 38, 4, + 2. P. XXVII,
43, 2, + 2. P. XXVIII, 131, 1, 1. P. XXIX, 102, 1, 3; 168, 2, + 2 etc.

Now, however, it might perhaps be supposed that Palestrina style,
notwithstanding all this discourse upon polyphony and tonal combinations as functions of the simultaneous linear progressions, nevertheless
had certain perceptions of chords in the same signification as a later
period; also that the triad in its root position and its 1st inversion were
perceived as consonant units, and not as the sum of consonances,
while with the $^6/_4$ chord this standpoint was not attained, for reasons
rather difficult to explain. This meant, in other words, that the 4th
might very well pass as consonant when it was a link in one of the
above-mentioned accord forms, but only as such; it should consequently be treated as a dissonance in case it had other notes below it than
its deepest note's fifth or third. However, this supposition seems to
be contradicted by examples like the following:

P. X, 97, 1. 3¹). Missa: Gabriel Archangelus.

P. XII, 17, 2, 4. Missa: Spem in alium.

On that account there is reason to presume that dissonances really, as Fux says, were as a rule especially noticed with respect to their relations towards the bass; and, reciprocally, the weaker dissonances were disregarded, provided they were not dissonant with this part. Is it possibly the correct relation to this voice which explains and excuses the dissonant collision of the short notes in crotchet note-

---

¹ This phrase is rare, however, with Palestrina, while it is so frequently used by Isaac as almost to assume the character of a peculiarity of his personal style.—See Is. I, 76, 3, 4; 101, 4, 1; 102, 2, 3; 106, 2, 1; 118, 3, 4; 127, 1, 2; 144, 5, 2; 157, 1, 4; 168, 4, 3; 176, 4, 1; 211, 5, 3; 215, 3, + 3; 216, 4, 1; 221, 3, 3; 244, 1, + 1. Is. II, 10, 3, 3. Is. III, 22, 6, 5; 96, 3, 3; 105, 5, + 2; 110, 6, + 3; 122, 1, 3; 193, 3, 5. Refer also to Ambr. V, 382, 2, 1 (Arnoldus van Bruck).

against-note? As previously stated, I have found nothing in the theoretical literature of the 16th century, which was accessible to me, from which sure conclusions concerning these matters may be drawn. Efforts to find information pertinent to this subject in more recent literature were also unavailing. The only author who, to my knowledge, seems to have weighed these problems more seriously, is W. S. Rockstro, who in his treatise, "The Rules of Counterpoint", (London 1882, p. 102), remarks with regard to some Palestrina examples, (one of which is the following):

P. XI, 148, 3, 4. Missa: Papae Marcelli.

"These notes (crotchets) must always be irreproachable, in their relation to the Bass; but notwithstanding this, they frequently make frightful collisions with each other. Now, of these collisions, the greatest of the Great Masters took no notice whatever. Provided their Florid Parts moved well with the Bass, they cared nothing for the crashes which took place between them."

Whence Rockstro had his rule is unknown to me, perhaps he made it himself; but, strictly speaking, it need not be the consequence of passages like the above or others similar, cited by Rockstro. If the rule had been worded thus: "In crotchet note-against-note the dissonance may be employed, provided the colliding parts, considered individually, are each correctly treated", then it would have met the requirements of Rockstro's given instances. Thus, in P. XI, 148, 3, 4, the dissonant *B* in the upper voice (second note) is fully legitimate as a passing note, while the crotchet *C* in the lower voice, regarded under the view-point of cambiata, is likewise unrestrictedly justified. Both voices are quite correct if we conceive the dissonance as introduced over a stationary note. Perhaps it might be presumed that it was not considered necessary then, in the case of such short notes, to make a difference between this manner of treatment and note-against-note, and that it was only exacted that each of the implicated parts should keep strictly to the style with reference to dissonance treatment. That this presumption does not hold true altogether, is shown in places like the following:

P. V, 85, 1, 2. Motet: Quam pulchri sunt.

Victoria: Opera I, 38, 2, + 1. Motet: Duo Seraphim.

If we examine the above example from Palestrina, we shall observe that while the upper voice is correct, the lower voice, when it also is called to account for its dissonance, could not fulfil the requirements of Palestrina style; for, when considered in this way, it is responsible for an ascending dissonant progression on the third crotchet. It is the same thing with regard to the example from Victoria; the upper voice is quite correct, yet if we consider the second note in the lower voice as a dissonance, there appears a thoroughly irregular treatment of the cambiata, which is not native to the ecclesiastical musical art of the latter part of the 16th century. All these difficulties disappear if we consider (with Rockstro) that only the upper voice is dissonant, and accept everything else, provided that this part be correctly treated. However, examples of this kind are so rare, that it seems rather hazardous to form any theory based upon them. Even the Greatest of the Great may sometimes express himself less clearly and completely, and we ought not to put more into these expressions than really lies in them. The fact of the extremely rare occurrence of phrases of this kind—except when the note-against-note parts are used in connection with one or more stationary notes—seems to indicate that places like those cited were felt as being unclear, and were preferably avoided. On the other hand, when greater note-values in other voices were employed simultaneously with crotchet note-against-note, all indistinctness disappeared.

This relation may be observed in examples like the following:

a) P. XII, 61, 5, 2. Missa: Brevis.

b) P. VIII, 147, 3, + 2. Hymnus: En gratulemur hodie. (Also P. V, 134, 1, + 3. P. XV, 151, 2, 4. P. II, 109, 3, + 3. P. XXVI, 110, 1, + 3. P. XXIII, 138, 3, 5.)

In Ex. *a* the upper part is correctly treated with respect to the dissonance. But if we consider the second note in the next to the upper part as a dissonance, we should find, on the contrary, that the dissonance treatment in this part, (with a leap of a third to the dissonance which is then quitted by a sixth), is quite impossible in Palestrina style. The consonant relation of the 2nd note in this part towards both the deeper parts gives preponderance, however, to the conception of this note as dissonance, and makes it clearly understood that not it, but the 2nd note of the upper part, is the real bearer of the dissonance. Something like this applies, with reference to the conception of the dissonance, to most of the other examples of this kind.[1] Of especial interest here is Ex. *b,* in which the 3rd note of the alto, if considered as a dissonance, would represent an altogether falsely placed cambiata dissonance. Its relation to the extreme parts, however, characterizes it strongly enough as a consonance, at the same time as the real dissonance—the 2nd note in the tenor—is unveiled.

If therefore we would try to reconstruct the rule which was valid —consciously or unconsciously—for the composers of the 16th century with respect to these matters, it would be about as follows: Dissonance in note-against-note—provided the notes that stand in mutually dissonant relationship have the same value, and none of these are repetitions of immediately preceding notes—may only occur when the notes in question are crotchets. In cases where note-against-note parts occur coincidentally with greater note-values in other voices, the parts that progress in crotchets can either be consonant or dissonant as it may chance, provided each of these parts (when compared with each individual part that has greater note-values than crotchets), is correctly treated with regard to dissonance. If all the parts at a given musical moment are used in note-against-note, each and every single part must progress rightly with respect to every other part, so far as the dissonance is concerned. That the practical consequences of the bass-hypothesis which Rockstro incidentally advances, was not sufficient to insure against breaches of style, is shown in the following phrase, which, though agreeing with Rockstro's rule, yet is inconceivable in Palestrina music:

---

[1] Consult P. II, 109, 3, + 3. P. XXIII, 138, 3, 5.

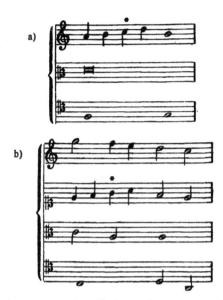

In both of these examples all the parts are correct in relation to the bass. The circumstances that the upper voice in Ex. *a* is incorrect when compared with the middle voice, and that the result of a comparison of the intermediate voices in Ex. *b* exposes quite an impossible dissonance treatment, suffice to exclude these examples from Palestrina style. For the exaction here is, as stated before, that each individual part is "correct", not alone in relation to the bass but also to every other part. The only exception is found where note-against-note parts, through mutual comparison, show a free treatment of the dissonance, but their relation to the stationary notes at the same time is irreproachable. Compare the following places, which further illustrate the attitude of Palestrina towards dissonance in note-against-note: P. X, 22, 2, 3; 24, 3, + 1; 44, 2, 3; 65, 5, + 1; 69, 1, 3; 73, 2, + 4; 125, 1, + 2; 125, 2, 1; 125, 2, 3; 125, 2, 4. P. V, 5, 3, + 2; 49, 1, 1; 79, 4, 2. P. XI, 111, 2, 1; 150, 2, 2. P. XII, 63, 2, +3; 76, 3, 1. P. III, 43, 3, 2. P. XXIX, 81, 1, 1. P. XIII, 1, 4, 4. P. IV, 133, 2, + 2. P. VIII, 156, 3, 1; 166, 2, + 2. P. XIV, 118, 1. 4. P. IX, 113, 2, + 3; 117, 2, + 3; 175, 3, 4—5. P. XV, 106, 1, + 1; 142, 4, + 3. P. XVI, 6, 3, 2. P. XVIII, 29, 4, + 2. P. XX, 4, 1, + 1; 28, 2, + 4; 35, 4, 1; 81, 2, + 2; 92, 4, 1; 117, 1, + 3. P. XXI, 49, 2, 3; 67, 3, 1; 117, 3, 1; 136, 1, 2. P. XXIII, 127, 1, +1.

It is evident that the treatment of note-against-note in Palestrina's music denoted an extraordinary advance with respect to the subdual of the dissonance. For instance, it is not unusual to encounter dissonance in minim against minim still in compositions from Josquin's generation:

Josquin des Prés. Missa: Dung aultre amer. Gloria. 8 bars from the end. (Compare also Josquin des Prés, Missa: Ad fugam, Qui tollis, bar 59.)

Obr. III, 84, 3, + 2. Missa: O quam suavis est. (See Obr. I, 240, 2, 1 and Is. III, 139 2 + 1).

Also in crotchet note-against-note we meet with instances of a harshness that is foreign to Palestrina style:

Obr. III, 44, 4, + 1. Missa: Si dedero. (Compare Obr. III, 228, 4, + 2.)

Costanzo Festa. Motet: Regem archangelorum. Torchi: "L'arte musicale in Italia" I, p. 49, 2, + 2.

A characteristic circumstance about note-against-note is that it was permissible for a voice to continue its course, even though it treated its dissonance freely with regard to a certain other voice, provided its more prominent coincident relations to other voices were correct. Akin to this phenomenon is one which has not yet been observed in recent research, which might very reasonably be called "parasitic dissonance". In this case too it appears that a voice, which in itself is "incorrect", through its correct (or more frequently, identical) relation to a more prominent voice and under cover of the latter, may be tolerated. To my knowledge, Cerone is the only musical theorist who was clear about these relations. He expresses himself thus[1]:

"Advierto mas que en Composicion de cinco bozes, se suele hazer Onzena al alzar del Compas con la parte mas alta ò con otra de medio,

----

[1] Melopeo p. 660.

subintrando à cantar despues de pausa: verdad es que esta Onzena (ò Quarta) ha de ser Unisonus con una de las partes, la qual ha de suplir al precepto musical, segun las reglas declaradas:

In both of these examples it will be noticed that a fourth in relation to the bass is freely introduced; but as they are each in unison with, or at the interval of an octave from, the correctly treated fourth in one of the other voices,[1] they are thus covered.[2]

---

[1] "Sponging", as it were, upon these.

[2] In the second example, the 4th in the next to the upper voice is a so-called "consonant fourth", a dissonant form which was sanctioned by Palestrina. (Compare p. 234).

Exactly similar relations are not to be found in Palestrina's works, so far as I know; altogether they are not of very frequent occurrence, but may occasionally be met with, as in

M. D. II, p. 484, 1, +3. Andrea Gabrieli: Motet, Sacerdos et pontifex.

This license is, however, not restricted to the one situation which Cerone points out, but seems to have been based upon a principle of general validity:

Victoria, Opera: I, 17, 2, 4. Motet: Senex puerum.

In this example, the 4th tone, B, in the tenor, collides harshly with A in the upper voice; as it is both introduced and continued by leaps, its employment here would be out of the question were it not for its octave relation to the B in the bass; which, on its part—being quite correctly related to the upper voice—covers the illegitimacy of the tenor's progression.

M. D. I, 179, 2, 1. Andrea Gabrieli. Missa: Brevis.

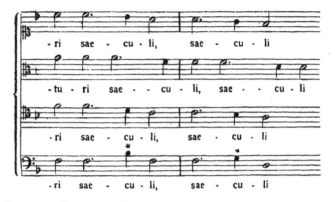

- ri sae - cu - li, sae - cu - li
-tu - ri sae - - cu - li, sae - - cu - li
- ri sae - cu - li, sae - cu - li
- ri sae - cu - li, sae - cu - li

In the preceding example it is the upper voice which undertakes to palliate the very irregularly treated dissonance in the bass.

P. XXXI, 158, 3, + 2. Canticum: Nunc dimittis. (Compare 159, 2, + 2.)

Cant. - nem gen - - -
Alt. - nem gen - - -
Ten. I. - nem gen - - -
Ten. II. - nem gen - - -
Bas. - nem gen - - -

Here in the 1st tenor the really incorrect leap from D (dissonating with C in the upper voice) to G is made possible by the circumstance that the G of the tenor is in unison with the G of the bass, which latter note is quite correct in relation to the upper voice.

Compare, with respect to this, the following:

P. I, 27, 1, + 2; 125, 3, + 2; 151, 1, + 3. P. III, 160, 2, 4. P. V, 59, 3, + 4. P. XI, 110, 2, + 3; 138, 1, 5; 147, 1, + 2. P. XII, 163, 3, + 1. P. XIII, 43, 3, 5; 69, 3, + 2. P. XV, 88, 2, + 2; 105, 3, + 2. P. XVII, 67, 1, + 2. P. XXI, 44, 2, 4. P. XXIII, 95, 1, + 3. P. XXIV, 84, 2, + 3; 114, 3, 1; 137, 1, 2; 140, 3, + 1. P. XXV, 143, 2, + 1. P. XXVI, 119, 3, + 3 (d.); 134, 4, + 2 (d.). P. XXVIII, 240, 2, + 4; 242, 1, 4. P. XXIX, 112, 1, 1; 125, 3, + 2; 181, 2, 2. P. XXXI, 76, 1, 2; 87, 2, 1; 168, 1, + 4. P. XXXII, 168, 1, + 2. P. XXXIII, 83, 1, + 3.

A couple of instances may be added:

P. XVII, 40, 2, + 3. Missa: O admirabile Commercium.

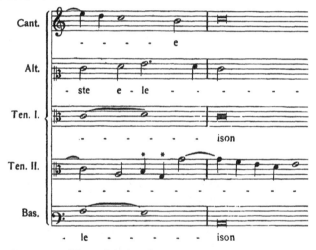

P. XX, 86, 2, 1. Missa: Octavi toni.

Examples like that last cited are extremely rare in 16th century music, while on the other hand they belonged to the ordinary musical vernacular of the Bach-Händel period. It should be noted that the examples latterly cited here all belong to the category, "parasitic dissonance". Whether this is accidental, or whether similar conditions are possible, as Bellermann[1] seemed to think, also without the consolidating influence of the stationary note, is a problem that I must leave unanswered, owing to the small amount of material at my disposal in the few instances with which I am acquainted.

The liberties that have been pointed out with reference to dissonance in note-against-note, as well as the idea: "parasitic dissonance", afford interesting evidence of the predominantly horizontal direction of volition in the 16th century. Although the harmonic element also claimed its rights, which were often granted to a remarkable degree, the chief aim was the melodic beauty of the individual parts. In situations where the vertical control of the horizontal caused difficulties, the occasion was often unscrupulously utilized to promote the freest possible development of melody.

b). Ornamental Dissonance

Nearly allied to passing dissonance are numerous forms of dissonance treatment which are attributable to the mode of singing and to ornamentation. These forms, as well as the passing dissonance, are due exclusively to horizontal motives—the melodic form being of primary importance, and the incidental consonance or dissonance of less significance. Ornamental dissonance may be divided into two groups:

1. The dissonant auxiliary-note.
2. Dissonance due to more developed forms of ornamentation.

We understand by the first group a dissonance which is itself placed upon an unaccented beat, and which is related as a second to an accented consonant note, either preceding or succeeding, or preceding as well as succeeding. The most commonly employed form of this

---

[1] Refer to "Contrapunkt", p. 234. Bellermann expressly states that he knows of no instances of this kind in Palestrina's works. The examples he gives in this connection are only constructions.

family is the dissonant returning-note. Palestrina's works teem with examples of this kind—we may open them anywhere and find numbers of instances. Theorists of the classical vocal polyphonic school did not write much concerning this dissonance form, seldom honouring it to the extent of a bare mention—and even then most frequently merely to forbid its employment.

Artusi says concerning the following example:

that it is best that the highest and lowest notes should be in accord and not, as many think proper, dissonant.[1] It is also noticeable that Bellermann's attitude is one of rejection: "Die Komponisten des 16 Jahrhunderts kannten zwar diese Art der Dissonanz auch, wandten sie indes nur bei schnelleren Notengattungen, Vierteln und Achteln, und selbst hier nur selten an".[2]

But "selten" is certainly not the fitting expression in this connection.

From a profusion of examples, I choose indiscriminately,

P. V, 64, 1, 1, Motet: Nativitas tua.

---

[1] "Arte del contraponto" p. 55: "Sarrà buono e ben fatto, che li fondi, & le cime siano consonanti & non come molti fanno dissonanti."

[2] "Contrapunkt" p. 154.

The returning-note descends here—as most often in this form. Ascending is less frequent, though by no means rare.

P. XI, 67, 3, 4. Missa: Ad fugam.

P. XII, 60, 5, 3. Missa: Brevis.

Compare with these, also: P. X, 3, 1, 3; 14, 2, + 3; 27, 3, 4; 32, 2, + 2; 88, 4, + 1; 126, 3, + 1; 127, 5, 3; 145, 2, + 1; 169, 1, 1; 170, 4, + 1. P. V, 15, 3, 1; 26, 3, + 2 and + 1; 34, 2, 4; 107, 2, 1; 144, 1, 5 sqq. P. XI, 142, 2, + 4 and + 3. P. I, 10, 1, 4; 34, 3, + 2; 71, 3, 2. P. XII, 37, 3, + 3; 71, 1, 1; 71, 1, + 2; 71, 2, 1; 71, 1, 4 (coincidentally ascending and descending returning-note = 71, 2, + 2). P. XIII, 49, 1, + 2; 80, 1, + 1; 82, 1, + 4.

The reason why the ascending dissonance (like the minim dissonance) must be used with greater discretion than the descending form, is probably that the effect of the higher note is more striking than the lower, (see p. 52), and that consequently the dissonance introduced after a preceding lower note is more obvious than when the introduction comes from above.

The returning-note is used almost exclusively with crotchets or quavers in Palestrina. Instances with minims are very rare:

P. XI, 120, 2, 3. Missa: Salvum me fac.

P. VIII, 106, 4 + 2. Hymnus: Deus tuorum militum.

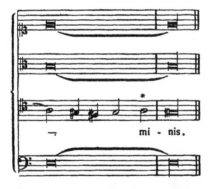

Examples like the last quoted occur, according to my observation, only in concluding cadences, (see P. VIII, 32, 4, + 2; 172, 1, + 2. P. X, 13, 4, + 2. Casimiri: "Codice 59", Musical Supplement 10, 4, + 2. P. XVIII, 139, 1, + 1. P. XXV, 208, 1, + 3. P. XXX, 74, 1, + 2 (d.); 87, 3, + 2 (d.). P. XXXI, 98, 4, + 2; 127, 3, 2; 130, 2, 5. However, they are still oftener found in this form:

P. XVIII, 10, 4, + 2. Missa: Ave regina coelorum.

The minim dissonance is replaced here by a crotchet. Compare furthermore:

P. II, 62, 3, + 2; 84, 2, + 2; 88, 1, + 2; 101, 1, + 2. P. III, 31, 3, + 1. P. XIII, 54, 1, + 2; 139, 3, + 2. P. XXV, 3, 1, + 2; 18, 3, 3; 78, 4, + 2. P. VIII, 100, 2, + 2. P. XIX, 116, 2, + 2; 131, 3, + 2. P. XXI, 110, 3, + 2. P. XXV, 111, 3, + 4. P. XXXII, 5, 2, + 2; 9, 3, + 2.

In all these instances the returning-note is introduced as a link of the same melodic phrase: the ordinary, ornamented, concluding formula with suspension before the 3rd of the dominant triad, which is further embellished by an ascending returning-note. The conditions for the employment of the returning-note are, as already mentioned, that it must come from a consonant note and return to the same, in conjunction with the stipulation that it can only be placed upon unaccented beats. These conditions were maintained almost without exception by Palestrina. I know of but two places where he has dissonance on both the returning-note and the preceding crotchets:

P. X, 4, 4, + 2. Missa: Ecce sacerdos magnus.

P. X, 54, 3, + 2. Missa: O regem coeli.

It is surely not by chance that both these instances are found in the 1st volume of masses, (Palestrina's Opus I.), in which there is a variety of things which, judged from his later standpoint in style, seem antiquated.

The accented returning-note is only encountered in Palestrina's works in quavers, (in $^3/_1$ time also in crotchets, of course, which correspond to quavers in normal notation).[1] We further find the crotchet returning-note accented in compositions from the Second Netherland School, though as a rule it is only placed upon the unaccented minim:

Josquin des Prés: Missa Lomme armé sexti toni, Christe, bar 8.

---

[1] The passage P. XIII, 83, 1, + 3, only apparently forms an exception to this rule, the last 2 notes of the upper voice being, not crotchets, as Haberl's edition has it, but according to the original edition of the 4th volume of masses (Gardano, Venice, 1582), quavers.

See also: Obr. I, 3, 5, + 2; 22, 4, 4; 30, 2, + 2; 30, 3, + 3; 31, 3, 1; 37, 3, 2; 37, 4, 3; 44, 1, 3; 76, 2, + 3; 100, 4, 3; 118, 4, 1; 177, 1, 3; 214, 4, + 1. Obr. III, 22, 2, + 2; 130, 4, 1. Obr. IV, 7, 4, + 2; 11, 4, + 1; 14, 2, + 2; 16, 1, 1; 44, 3, + 2; 93, 2, + 1; 121, 3, 1; 122, 3, 3; 142, 1, 1; 142, 3, 1; 142, 3, + 2; 214, 1, 1. Obr. V, 4, 1, 2; 5, 4, 1; 12, 4, 1. Obr. VI, 27, 3, + 2; 38, 2, + 2; 66, 2, 1; 77, 4, + 2; 84, 1, 3; 84, 2, 3; 139, 4, 3. Obr. VII, 31, 1, 1. Is. II, 45, 3, + 2; 45, 4, 3; 121, 2, + 1. Josquin des Prés: Missa, Ave maris stella, Kyrie I, bar 6; ibid., Et incarnatus, bar 11; ibid., Agnus I, bar 6; Missa, Malheur me bat, Credo, bar 60; ibid., Credo, bar 80; ibid. Credo, bar 181; Missa, Una musque de Biscaya, Qui tollis, bar 2, etc.

In all the cases cited here, the returning-note is treated with descending seconds. Ascending movement is considerably rarer in this form of treatment, but may occur:

Josquin des Prés. Missa: De beata Virgine. Gloria, bar 111, (compare Richafort Motet: Emendemus. Maldeghem 1881, 28, 2. l.)

Compare also: Obr. VI, 103, 4, 3; 106, 3, 3; 128, 2, + 2; 144, 4, + 2. Cipriano de Rore, Motet: Da pacem. Maldeghem 1876, 20, 2, + 1. Josquin des Prés, Motet: In principium erat verbum, bar 29.

A very customary form of musical embellishment also was the Portamento note. By Palestrina it was most frequently employed immediately before a syncope and in descending movement:

P. XXIII, 3, 2, + 1. Missa: In majoribus duplicibus.

though the syncope is not an invariable condition:

P. XVIII, 32, 1, 3. Missa: Veni sponsa Christi, (Consult P. XV, 131, 1, + 2).

The treatment of the Portamento dissonance by the Netherlanders differs in many ways from that of Palestrina. The latter, for instance, never uses this form of dissonance treatment ascending, while it may be observed in the works of earlier masters, though not very often.

Josquin des Prés, Motet: Factum est autem. Jos. III, 78,2,3.

Consult furthermore: Obr. VI, 144, 4, + 3. Is. I, 217, 3, 1. Is. III, 10, 6, + 3. Ambr. V, 215, 4, 2; 215, 4, + 2 (Carpentras). The Italian Frottolists in particular made extensive use of the ascending Portamento dissonance.[1]

Marcus Cara, Frottole: In eterno. Kiesewetter, "Schicksale und Beschaffenheit des weltlichen Gesanges", Beilage, p. 15, 2, + 4.

Compare also Torchi I, 5, 1, + 1 (Demophon); 21, 3, 1, and parallel instances (Tromboncino). In the last case cited, the dissonance is a minim. This is never admitted by Palestrina (if the count is in minims); but this form was employed by masters of the Second Netherland School, even with the Portamento dissonance ascending:

---

[1] Rudolf Schwartz: Die Frottole im 15. Jahrhundert. V. f. M. 1886, p. 454. Cf. furthermore my edition: "Die mehrstimmige italienische Laude um 1500", Leipzig and Copenhagen 1935, p. XLI.

Pierre de la Ru : O salutaris hostia. Ambr. V, 145, 1, + 2.[1])

By Palestrina, only the second below is used in Portamento dissonance. Other intervals were employed in this manner, however, by composers of the previous epoch. For instance, Josquin des Prés was so fond of the Portamento down to the 3rd below, that he may almost be recognized alone by the lavish use of this embellishment. I quote from the beginning of his famous "Stabat Mater":

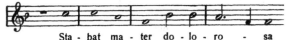

Sta - bat ma - ter do - lo - ro - sa

However, he used this figure too in a dissonant connection, and with minims into the bargain!

Missa: Ad fugam. Osanna, bar 17.

---

[1] If we compare this place with Obr. VI, 11, 1, 2, for instance, we scarcely understand the need of the interrogation point which the distinguished editor of Ambr. V, Otto Kade, placed upon the Portamento dissonance, (which he took for a misprint, proposing to change the note therefore to a C).

Likewise Josquin des Prés very often made use of the Portamento of the 5th, as in this characteristic phrase[1]:

This figure too was employed in dissonant form by the musicians of that day:

Pierre de la Rue. Motet: Gaude virgo. Maldeghem 1882, 7, 2, +2. (Compare Obr. I, 223, 4, 2).

Josquin des Prés. Missa: Malheur me bat. Qui tollis, bar 57.

---

[1] Missa "Ave maris stella". Qui venit, bar 12.

While the returning-note and the Portamento dissonance (under the conditions named) were indisputably legitimate for Palestrina, a number of other forms that occasionally appear in Palestrina music must be regarded as rudimentary or archaic relics of the Netherland era. In these archaic forms the dissonance is certainly conjunctly introduced, but its continuation is disjunct. These phrases were great favourites, from a melodic view, in this era; they were only employed, however, in consonant conjunction. Treated in this manner they may commonly be observed in Palestrina's works also, for example with the leap of a 3rd upwards[1]:

P. IX, 109, 3, +3. Offertorium: Benedicam Dominum.

while their use in connection with the dissonant auxiliary-note is extremely rare, and principally found in the composer's earlier works:

P. XII, 71, 2, 2. Missa: De Feria. (Compare P. XII, 123, 1, +2 etc. p. 197.)

---

[1] Consult figure 42 p. 70.

Of similar dissonantly constructed phrases in Palestrina's works, I have found the following: P. V, 101, 3, + 3. P. X, 95, 3, + 4; 125, 3, 4. P. XIII, 112, 3, + 1. P. XVII, 43, 1, + 2 and P. XXVII, 143, 3, 1 (d.); 189, 2, 5 (d.). P. XXX, 158, 1, + 2 (d.).[1]

In works of Josquin's generation, however, such phrases were everywhere current:

Obr. I, 13, 3,+3. Missa: Je ne demande. (See: Is, I, 85, 3, 1 and Maldeghem 1881, 27, 3,+4.)

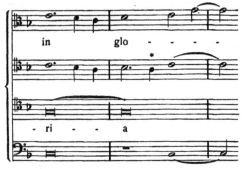

Compare also: Obr. I, 7; 2, + 3; 35, 1, 1; 37, 2, 2; 43, 3, 4; 52, 1, 4; 53, 1, + 1; 68, 2, 2; 70, 1, + 3; 102, 2, 2; 132, 2, 3; 155, 4, 1; 172, 4, 3; 187, 1, 1; 193, 1, 1; 195, 1, + 2; 205, 1, + 1; 205, 3, + 2; 207, 2, 3; 218, 1, + 1; 227, 3, 1; 235, 3, 1. Obr. II, 9, 1, + 1; 14, 3, 2; 48, 1, 3; 56, 5, + 2; 62, 4, + 2; 68, 4, 3; 149, 2, 2. Obr. III, 7, 1, + 1; 8, 2, + 1; 49, 2, 3; 114, 2, + 2; 117, 1, 1; 147, 3, 1—2; 185, 2, 2; 190, 2, + 1; 201, 4, 3; 226, 3, 3 etc. Is. I, 11, 2, + 3; 90, 4, + 4; 92, 2, 4; 95, 1, + 2; 105, 3, + 2; 114, 4, 4; 156, 5, 1; 161, 1, 1; 186, 3, + 3; 196, 3, 1; 202, 2, + 1; 202, 3, 2; 214, 3, + 4; 225, 3, 3 etc. Josquin des Prés: Missa, La sol fa re mi, Gloria, bar 35; ibid. Agnus I, bar 21; Missa: Gaudeamus, Kyrie II, bar 14; ibid. "Et incarnatus", bar 51; ibid. "Et unam sanctam", bar 6; ibid. "In nomine", bar 20—21; Missa: Fortuna desperata, "Pleni sunt", bar 34—35; ibid. "Pleni", bar 50; ibid. "Pleni", bar 57; Missa: Dung aultre

---

[1] The phrase P. XVIII, 27, 3, + 2, where a leap occurs from a dissonant minim to the 3rd above, agrees at all events with the original edition of the 9th volume of masses (Scotus, Venice, 1599), but is unquestionably due to a misprint in the orig. ed., the second note in the bass, (according to Palestrina music's ordinary usage), should doubtless be an A.

amer, Kyrie II, bar 11; Missa: Malheur me bat, Christe, bar 29; ibid. Gloria, bar 64; ibid. "Qui tollis", bar 27; Missa: Didadi, Christe, bar 11; ibid. Christe, bar 21; Missa: De beata Virgine, Gloria, bar 16—19 etc.

While this form is otherwise encountered in Palestrina's music only in crotchet values, (with one exception, P. XIII, 112, 3, + 1, where the time is $^3/_1$), it is sometimes found employed by the Netherlanders as a minim dissonance:

Josquin des Prés, Missa: Faysant regres, Gloria, bar 23. (Compare Obr. I, 177, 2, + 2.)

Is. I, 142, 5, 2. Introitus: Omnis terra.

The fact that the upper voice in the last example, (which agrees with the original edition of the "Choralis Constantinus"), is written thus in Codex 63 in the Munich State Library,

lau · · di

and furthermore that Obrecht gives the following variants,

Misse Obreht 1503. (Obr. I, 13, 3, + 3.)   Munich Ms: 3154.

projects a keen light onto the historical origin of this dissonance form, and upon its pronouncedly ornamental character. In this connection we must also consider the concluding formula, so widely used especially in the Dufay period, which interposed the second below the leading note just before the final note. Endeavours have been made to explain the leap of the third up to the tonic in this figure as a conscious evasion of the half-tone step in conclusion, being dictated by the well-known avoidance of the leading-note in plainsong.[1] The fact that these two forms very often alternate, so that no fundamental distinction between them could have been felt, makes against such an assumption.

If for instance we compare the two versions of the same mass, "O Rosa bella", communicated in "Denkmäler der Tonkunst in Österreich" XI, 1, we find that the passage written in the Tridentine Codex[2] thus,

is put down in the Modenese Codex as:

On the other hand, the passage in the Modenese Codex (Tr. II, 33, 4, + 2):

---

[1] Consult Peter Wagner: Elemente des gregorianischen Gesanges. Regensburg 1917, p. 143.

[2] Tr. II, 28, 3, 1.

is given in the Tridentine Codex:

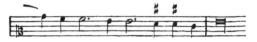

The character of the 3rd below as a Grace-note before the leading note is perhaps still more apparent in divergences like:

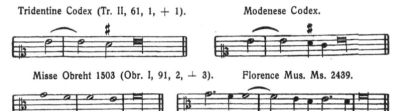

Tridentine Codex (Tr. II, 61, 1, + 1).   Modenese Codex.

Misse Obreht 1503 (Obr. I, 91, 2, ⊥ 3).   Florence Mus. Ms. 2439.

The explanation of this concluding formula is more likely to be found, not so much in the fear of the leading note effect, as in the general tendency towards a fuller ornamental development, which was a typical phenomenon in the formation of final cadences.

The established form most frequently used during the florescence of this embellishment, (ca. 1460), was:

Tr. I, 122, 2, 1. Dufay, Missa: "Se la face ay pale".

As is evident, the next to the last note is dissonant, which often occurred as long as the phrase was generally used.

As early as the first decades of the 16th century, however, there was a visible decrease in its employment, and in Palestrinian music its role was quite played out. From now on its existence, in many ways interesting, was but a shadowy one. For example, it occurs here in the upper voice only when the leap is filled out:

P. XV. 46, 4, 3. Missa: Sine nomine.

by interposing the quaver passing-note, which, however, eliminates the most characteristic feature of the phrase—the interval of the 3rd between the next to the last and the final note. In the *original* form it was only employed in an intermediate voice concealed by the other voices. Moreover its function had altogether changed character, since from its first independent office and purely melodic character, it was now degraded to an auxiliary of exclusively vertical nature.

In practically every instance where this phrase occurs in Palestrina's compositions, it is used in the following conjunction:

P. V, 57, 2, 3. Motet: Quae est ista.

Compare also: P. X, 4, 2, 4; 119, 1, + 1. P. V, 60, 4, 2; 86, 1, 2. P. XI, 37, 4, 1; 39, 1, + 1; 39, 3, 2[1]; 101, 3, + 2; 120, 1, + 1. P. XII, 106, 1, + 3.[2] P. I, 6, 3, + 1; 9, 2, + 3; 19, 2, 1; 44, 2, + 2; 45, 3, + 1; 49, 3, 1; 127, 1, 3. P. XII, 105, 3, 4; 118, 1, + 2; 123, 1, 4; 140, 2, + 2; 162, 1, 4; 186, 3, + 3; 187, 3, 1. P. II, 21, 1, + 4; 30, 3, 3; 61, 2, + 3; 73, 1, + 4 (Rodolfo); 106, 1, + 2. P. III, 42, 3, + 3; 122, 1, 1. P. XXIX, 6, 1, + 3. P. XIII, 84, 2, 3; 98, 4, 4; 117, 2, 4; 120, 2, + 3; 120, 3, 4; 139, 2, + 3. P. IV, 41, 1, + 3; 51, 3, + 4; 148, 2, 1. P. VIII, 13, 4, 1; 17, 1, + 3; 23, 4, 2; 56, 1, + 2; 75, 2, 4; 77, 1, 4; 95, 4, + 3; 140, 1, 2; 150, 3, + 2; 162, 3, + 1; 175, 4, 3. P. XIV, 74, 3, + 1; 117, 3, 2. P. IX, 50, 1, 3. P. XV, 60, 3, 1; 63, 1, + 1; 80, 2, + 1; 92, 3, 4; 112, 2, + 1. P. XVI, 19, 3, + 1. P. XXIX, 108, 1, 1; 159, 2, + 3; 160, 1, 1. P. XVII, 79, 2, 4; 97, 3, 2. P. XVIII, 1, 2, 3; 65, 2, + 2. P. XIX, 12, 4, + 2; 45, 3, 1; 54, 2, + 3; 86, 1, + 3. P. XX, 3, 3, + 1; 9, 2, + 2; 16, 2, + 4; 27, 1, + 1; 81, 3, + 2; 104, 1, + 4; 111, 2, 2. P. XXI, 12, 5, + 2; 15, 1, + 4; 98, 1, 2. P. XXII, 93, 1, + 3; 130, 1, + 1. P. XXIII, 4, 2, + 3; 11, 4, 3; 31, 2, 3; 72, 1, + 4; 80, 2, + 1; 80, 3, + 2; 91, 1, + 2; 91, 3, 3, and + 3; 124, 3, + 4. P. XXIV, 78, 2, 3. Also see Casimiri: "Il codice 59". Musical Supplement 5, 2, 3 and P. XXX, 133, 3, 4; 141, 4, 1; 166, 4, + 3. P. XXXI, 87, 3, + 2. P. XXXII, 40, 2, + 3; 139, 3, + 2. P. XXXIII, 4, 1, + 1; 11, 2, 2.

It doubtless here signifies an amplification of the following,

---

[1] According to the 1598 edition, (Gardano, Venice), the 3rd and 4th notes in the tenor should be changed to G and F (instead of F and E), by which alteration this place is brought into consideration here.

[2] Compare note 7 on p. 75 of this treatise.

and was, apparently, employed in order to evade the unusually ill-sounding fifths which are produced between the tenor and alto by the similar motion in the 3 upper voices. That this is the real state of the case, and that the melodic requirements here are not predominant, is apparent moreover from the circumstance that the phrase, (excepting a few individual cases still to be treated), occurs exclusively in situations where there is danger of irregularities of this kind, as in passages like the succeeding example:

P. XX, 19, 1, + 3. Missa: Descendit Angelus Domini. (Refer to Victoria, Opera I, 7, 2, 1.)

The few exceptions in Palestrina's works with which I am acquainted, are the following:

a) P. XVIII, 9, 1, 2. Missa: Ave Regina Coelorum.

b) P. XII, 106, 1, 1. Missa: Repleatur os meum laude. (Refer also to ibid. 118,2,1.)

c) P. XII, 123, 1, + 2. Missa: Repleatur os meum laude.

Even if we replace the 2 last crotchets of the alto in the first example with a minim on F, it would not produce fifths, but only two consecutive fourths. That this passage is nevertheless used in this instance, is due probably to its customary employment—provided the relationship of the intermediate voices is altered by moving the upper of these voices an octave higher:

P. XV, 112, 2, + 2. Missa: Dilexi quoniam.

Compare with the following: P. I, 44, 2, + 2. P. XII, 162, 1, 4. P. IV, 51, 3, + 4. P. XXIII, 80, 2, + 1 etc. Considering the fact that this phrase always occurs in one and the same vertical situation, it need scarcely excite surprise if, in a solitary instance where the harmonic circumstances are deceptively similar to the normal, it intrudes sometimes where its presence, strictly speaking, is not required.

The instances b, c, and P. XII, 118, 2, 1 seem rather irregular. It is noteworthy that all three appear in the same composition—namely, the mass "Repleatur os meum laude", from the 3rd volume of masses 1570. It is applicable to all three that they occur in connection with strictly conduced canons, (the middle voice, in example c, thus succeeds the next to the lowest voice in the canon in the 4th above). Though such circumstances seemingly played no role with Palestrina, who scarcely, even in the most difficult situations, relaxes the rules, yet it is not unlikely that the "obbligo" of the situation had some influence here; it is striking, under any circumstances, that these exceptions should all be found subject to identical conditions. It is moreover significant that the Grace-note in the last quoted example (c) is dissonant, giving rise to a leap of the third from a dissonance,—the only instance of its kind that I have encountered in Palestrinian works.

That the archaic cadence formula had retained but little of its original significance in Palestrina is further confirmed by its frequent use where it does not represent a real leading-note conclusion, for example:

P. XI, 101, 3, + 2. Missa: Salvum me fac.

Raising the C to C sharp in this place would entail something as contrary to Palestrina style as the augmented $^6/_5$ chord (in modern terms). On the whole, the conclusive character of the phrase was no longer taken into special account; therefore it also did not denote a stopping with regard to the melody, but the horizontal development was continued irrespective of its presence.

P. VIII, 140, 1, 3. Hymnus: Magne pater Augustine.

The history of this archaic cadence formula illustrates in an interesting manner an instance of the shifting of motives in music: that an effect which originally had only a purely melodic function was now employed solely for harmonic ends. We have here a case of the transference from one Dimension to the other, a transposition of effect.

The opposite of the case which has just been treated—viz., that form in which the *descending* second is embellished by an ascending auxiliary-note—is of much less frequent occurrence. On comparing the two "O Rosa bella" masses in Tr. II., we very often encounter discrepancies which plainly indicate the ornamental character of the phrase, (Tr. II, 46, 1, 4):

Modenese Codex

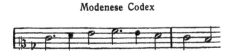

Tridentine Codex.

It does not conform to Palestrina's style if the auxiliary-note is dissonant; in the works of the Great Master, I have only found it in a single instance:[1]

P. XXVII, 27, 4, + 4. Magnificat, Sexti toni.

Also with the Netherlanders in the beginning of the 16th century it is not very common—decidedly less so than the corresponding form with descending auxiliary-note. A few cases may be quoted here:

Josquin des Prés, Missa: Ave maris stella. Agnus III, bar 23.

---

[1] Still another example is in the Canzone "Voi mi poneste" (P. XXX, 104, 4, 3), which is, however, hardly an authentic work. Even in its consonant form, the phrase is comparatively rare with Palestrina. Refer to p. 70. Ornament 47; refer also to p. 80.

Brumel, Christe. Maldeghem 1874, 36, 4, 1. (Compare also Maldeghem 1876, 15, 3, +1.)

Consult further for instance: Obr. I, 86, 3, + 1; 149, 1, + 2 (minim) 201, 4, 1; 224, 4, + 2; 231, 1, + 3. Is. I, 15, 2, 3; 102, 5, 3; 162, 1, 2; 179, 2, 2.

About 1500, a highly popular cadence was:

which is characterized by the upward leap of the 4th from a conjunctly introduced auxiliary-note. It belongs to those phrases of which Palestrina made very sparing use, mostly in his earlier works:[1]

---

[1] To the arguments which have previously been used in quite a convincing manner by Michel Brenet, (refer to "Claude Goudimel, Essai biobibliographique") to disprove the assumption that Goudimel had been Palestrina's teacher, may be added the great predilection shown by the French master for this dissonance form. In one mass alone, "Audi filia" (Goudimel: Missae tres. Paris, Adrien le Roy et Robert Ballard, 1558), I have counted this phrase 13 times, which signifies that in this one composition it occurs about as often as in Palestrina's entire authentic production, (more than 100 masses, ca. 400 motets, offertorias, lamentations, etc.). Incidentally I take occasion to remark, that the noted "Missa brevis" by Palestrina is not composed as a "parody" upon "Audi filia", as Baini, Ambros, Harberl and several later authors supposed. A certain resemblance between the two works is of a less constitutive than occasional nature, and need not imply Palestrina's acquaintance with "Audi filia".

P. XII, 107, **3,** + **3.** Missa: Repleatur os meum laude.

Compare also: P. X, 120, 3, 1; 120, 3, 4; 167, 3, + 2. P. V, 15, 4, 1; 35, 2, 2; 54, 3, 4. P. I, 160, 1, 3. P. XIII, 12, 2, 3; 13, 1, + 2. P. VIII, 73, 4, 1. P. XIV, 11, 3, 1; 34, 1, + 3. P. IX, 146, 3, + 1. P. XV, 38, 3, + 3; 81, 2, + 4; 136, 1, 5. P. XX, 6, 2, 4. P. XXI, 8, 4, 1. P. XXIV, 88, 2, + 2. P. XXXI, 175, 2, + 2 (d.). P. III, 16, 3, + 4. P. XXIV, 29, 2, + 1. 49, 3, + 4. P. XXX, 68, 2, + 1 (d.); 84, 4, 1 (d.). P. XXXI, 51, 1, 2 (d.); 51, 3, + 4 (d.); P. XXXII, 16, 1, + 2; 134, 2, + 3 (d.).

This dissonance form, as noted earlier, flourished in the beginning of the 16th century. We find it amply represented in the works of Josquin des Prés, Obrecht and Isaac, the latter using it more frequently than perhaps any other master.[1]

If on the whole the infinitesimal number of examples found in Palestrina's works may form a basis of comparison, the difference between his mode of treating this dissonance form and that of the Netherlanders seems to lie in the fact that, while Palestrina only lets the dis-

---

[1] Refer to the following, in Isaac I. alone: 20, 1, 4; 21, 3, + 1; 22, 4, + 3; 29, 1, 3; 34, 3, 2; 40, 4, 1; 40, 2, + 1; 41, 4, + 4; 47, 1, 4; 54, 4, 1; 57, 2, + 4; 66, 4, + 2; 69, 2, 4; 69, 3, 4; 105, 1, + 2; 116, 3, 2; 122, 2, + 3; 135, 5, 3; 142, 2, 2; 149, 3, 2; 154, 3, 3; 159, 4, + 2; 159, 4, 3; 165, 4, + 4; 167, 2, 1; 167, 3, + 4 and + 2; 167, 4, 3; 173, 1, + 2; 179, 4, 1; 185, 3, 3; 186, 7, 2; 187, 6, + 3; 188, 1, 1; 188, 2, + 2; 197, 2, + 4; 200, 4, + 3; 203, 5, 1; 213, 5, + 3; 220, 4, + 1; 220, 5, 4; 225, 4, 2; 241, 5, + 4; 254, 1, 2.

sonant Grace-note leap up to a note held as a syncope,[1] the Netherlanders are also seen to use the following method:

Obr. I, 194, 3, 3. Missa: Salve diva parens. (Compare Is. I, 69, 2, + 4.)

Also, once in a while it may be so treated that the note to which
the leap is made (which Palestrina always conducts conjunctly downwards) is, instead, continued ascending:

Is. I, 241, 5, + 4. Introitus: Jubilate Deo.

Costanzo Festa, Motet: Sancta Maria, succure miseris. M. I. 20, 1,+1.

---

[1] The only exception of which I know is P. XXIV, 29, 2, + 1 and 49, 3, + 4.
It is not unlikely that there is a misprint here, (the original was inaccessible to me
for comparison); however, this phrase must be considered archaic any way, as the
compositions in which it appears is written altogether in a rather antiquated style.

In most of the cases quoted from Palestrina's works, the dissonance is fairly well concealed in an intermediate voice, and it is found only in isolated cases placed in the upper voice and never in the bass. But with the Netherlanders it can quite well be found thus:

Is, I. 225, 4, 2. Introitus: Domine, ne longe facias.

However, this phrase does not belong to the style of Palestrina—at any rate, not when it is dissonant. In its consonant form, on the other hand, it may often be observed in Palestrina compositions[1]; but in connections where the usual melodic form would entail dissonance, the step of the second is almost always changed into a descending leap of the third. For instance:

P. V. 36, 1, 5.Motet: Lauda Sion.

---

[1] See Ornament 43, p. 70.

If the ascending 4th leap succeeding a dissonant Grace-note from above be among those effects which Palestrina rejects, then this applies in still higher degree to the opposite form:

Josquin des Prés. Missa: Lami baudichon. Qui sedes, bar 51.

It is not employed at all by Palestrina, and is moreover rarely met with in compositions of the 2nd Netherland School. When it does sporadically appear, the Grace-note is most often a minim:

Josquin des Prés. Missa: Lomme armé sexti toni. Qui tollis, bar 64.[1]

The ascending 5th leap succeeding a dissonant Grace-note introduced from above also does not belong to Palestrina's style, while it may still be observed with the Netherlanders about the beginning of the 16th century:[2]

---

[1] Compare Josquin des Prés: Missa: "Lami baudichon", Et resurrexit, bar 66; Missa; "Hercules dux Ferrarie", Gloria, bar 15; Obr. I, 137, 4, + 4. Obr. III, 214, 1, 2.

[2] In its consonant form the phrase is, however, used quite often by Palestrina. Compare Ornament 44, p. 70.

Josquin des Prés. Missa: Da pacem. Sanctus, bar 24. (Compare Is. III, 91, 5, + 2.[1]))

Costanzo Festa, Motet: Felix Anna. M. I. 29, 4,+3.

The contrary form—the descending 5th leap from a dissonant Grace-note introduced from below[2]—is still more rare:

---

[1] Consult further: Is. I, 54, 3, 1; 92, 1, 1; 159, 2, + 4; 199, 4, 3. Is. II, 9, 5, 1; 23, 3, 2; 50, 2, 1; 63, 1, + 4; 79, 4, 2; 83, 2, 5; 86, 5, 3 and + 5; 108, 6, + 2; 109, 4, 5; 110, 3, + 1 etc. Obr. I, 3, 3, 3. Obr. III, 14, 1, 1; 77, 2, + 1; 176, 2, 1. Obr. VI, 45, 3, 1; 128, 1, 1 Obr. VII, 19, 4, + 3. Josquin des Prés: Missa "Gaudeamus", Et in spiritum, bar 5-6; Missa: "Lomme armé sexti toni", Christe, bar 21, ibid., Credo, bar 14, ibid., Et resurrexit, bar 7; Missa: "Ave maris stella", Pleni, bar 56; Missa: "Hercules", Credo, bar 14.

[2] Refer to Ornament 49, p. 70.

Clemens non Papa. Motet: Mane nobiscum. C. C. III, 24, 3, 2.

That anything so extraordinary, even in Netherland music, as the ascending 6th leap from the dissonance:

Is. II, 31, 1, + 3.[1]) Je ne puis vivre.

Josquin des Prés. Missa: Dung aultre amer, Sanctus, bar 13.

---

[1] Compare the Ornament 45, p. 70.

is not employed by Palestrina is so immediately obvious as scarcely to require mention. It may appear inconsistent that, notwithstanding, passages like the following occur:

P. XVII, 9, 2, + 3¹). Missa: Quem dicunt homines.

In the meanwhile it must be taken into account that the octave in Palestrinian music was scarcely regarded otherwise than as a kind of repetition of the note. While all the intervals up to the fifth may be freely used ascending or descending, as remarked in the foregoing, the minor 6th is only used ascending, and the major 6th and the 7th are almost never employed; it is not till we reach the octave that we again find an available interval which may be freely treated. This indicates that, with respect to the last mentioned interval, the identity of the note was regarded more than the extent of the interval. It may be that places like this should therefore be understood as Portamento dissonance, where the transposition to the octave is undertaken for the sake of sonority—that is, to enable the part in question to come out in bolder relief vocally than it would in the lower position, thus bringing the melody into greater prominence.

*　　　*

*

Of the more complicated forms of ornamentation, the cambiata has already been incidentally mentioned.² Its fundamental form is construc-

---

¹ See also: P. I, 99, 3, 2. P. XVII, 16, 4, + 3. P. XIX, 122, 2, + 3. P. XXIII, 26, 3, + 3. P. XXVI, 52, 3, + 2 sqq.

² Consult Bernhard Ziehn's Study, (for its time, quite an instructive one): "Über die Cambiata und andere altklassische, melodische Figuren". Allgemeine Musikzeitung 1898, p. 497 sqq.

ted from an ordinary Grace-note, an embellishment of the fourth leap (most often descending):

Obr. I, 2, 4, + 2. Missa: Je ne demande.

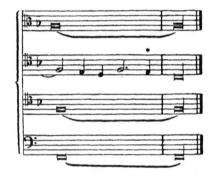

Tridentine Codex (Tr. II, 33, 1, 2.)   Modenese Codex.

The figure thus originally consisted of only 3 notes. The earlier Netherlanders considered this form satisfactorily conclusive as it was, but it is followed generally by a 4th note, which in Palestrina style is, almost without exception, the second above the preceding note. In the beginning of the 16th century, however, the attitude towards this relationship was more liberal:

Josquin des Prés. Missa: La sol fa re mi. Gloria, bar 20.

Josquin des Prés. Missa: ad Fugam. Sanctus, bar 11.

Josquin des Prés. Missa: Ave maris stella. Credo, bar 36.

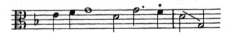

Josquin des Près. Missa: De beata Virgine. Et in spiritum, bar 13.

Simultaneously with these forms, appeared the one which was to supplant all the others, viz:

Dufay. Missa: Se la face ay pale. Tr. I, 129, 2 + 4.

In Palestrinian music this form is practically absolute. It is employed here almost exclusively in the 3 following rhythmic configurations:

a) P. XIV, 33, 3, + 4. Missa: Jam Christus astra ascenderat.

b) P. V, 106, 1, 2. Motet: Veni sponsa Christi.

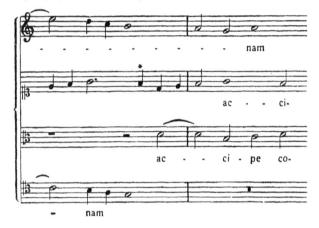

c) P VIII. 115. 3, 3. Hymnus: Sanctorum meritis.

Of these three forms, the one designated a) is most used; b) is by no means rare, though not so frequent as a), while c) comparatively is of rarer occurrence. It is worthy of note that, while the further progression of the fourth note (the tone of resolution) in form a) is freely conducted, like the following,

P. V, 39, 1, 2. Motet: Fuit homo.

in forms b) and c) there is introduced (almost without exception) as the fifth note: the second above the note of resolution.[1]

In all these forms, the cambiata in itself consists of only four notes; the fact that the fifth note in forms b) and c) seems to be related in a regularly established way to the preceding note, may doubtless be attributed to causes of a purely rhythmic-melodic nature. As has been remarked on page 78 sqq., Palestrina did not approve that the progression, after turning upon the second above, should return to the preceding note. For that reason the cambiata figure could not be continued thus:

In Palestrina the descending leap from a crotchet conjunctly introduced from below is also only reluctantly made, (see page 83); consequently such a continuation as:

---

[1] Nevertheless it is by no means admissible simply to decree, as Schenker does in his "Neue musikalische Theorien und Phantasien", (Vol. II, 1910, p. 308): "Diese Erscheinung (die Cambiata) bildet eine organische Einheit von fünf Tönen, deren Ablauf unabänderlich feststeht." For the classic form of the cambiata, as has been explained, consists merely of four notes, the fifth note only being conditional upon the continuation of the ascending movement in case the fourth note is a crotchet.

P. III, 134, 1, + 1. Motet: Surge illuminare.

is a unique occurrence;[1] that it is not well to leap further up after a preceding conjunct progression has already been pointed out, (p. 74); and therefore with crotchet progression in the cambiata figure, (in which sort of movement the collective conception is of an especially intimate kind), there remains, as the sole natural and acceptable possibility, the conjunct ascent of the fourth note of the figure.

Although the classic type of the cambiata is employed in the overwhelming majority of instances in Palestrina style, still it happens that we find, especially in the older works of the epoch, types that belong to the preceding musical period. For instance in Palestrina's 6-part mass, "Ave Maria", which must be classed unquestionably among its author's earliest compositions,[2] we observe the following phrase:

P. XV, 113, 2, 3.

---

[1] In Palestrina's works I have only observed one more analogous example: P. X, 18, 2, + 4.

[2] Refer to the preface of Vol. XV. of the complete collection of Palestrina's works.

Compare P. I, 147, 1 + 4. P. III, 121, 2, + 2. P. X, 80, 2, + 1; 86, 3, + 4; 123, 3, 1; 123, 3, + 3. P. XI, 149, 1, 2. P. XIX, 82, 4, + 1; 119, 2, 4. P. XX, 18, 1, 2. P. XXII, 65, 4, 3. P. XXVII, 114, 3, 2; P. XXVIII, 230, 1, + 3; P. XXXI, 51, 1, 2 (d.); 51, 3, + 4 (d.). P. XXXII, 137, 4, 3 and 4.[1] Victoria, Opera omnia 125, 2 + 1; 144, 1, + 2. "Orlando di Lasso Werke" III, 9, 4, + 3.

In the latter part of the 16th century, such phrases are very rare. Of somewhat more common occurrence though rather foreign to the style is the type which might be called the amplified cambiata. Its characteristic feature is the delay of the resolution by the introduction of an ascending leap of a third after the leap from the dissonance, which then is followed by a descending step of a second introducing the real note of resolution:

P. X, 66, 1, 1. Missa: Virtute magna.

Compare: P. X, 5, 4, 1; 20, 5, 1; 45, 4, 1 etc.; 47, 3, + 3; 65, 5, + 4; 65, 5, + 1; 80, 2, 5; 80, 3, 1; 80, 3, + 3; 80, 3, + 2; 90, 4, 3; 92, 3, + 2; 94, 1, + 4; 100, 4, + 1; 135, 1, 1 and + 4. P. V, 5, 3, + 2; 12, 4, + 2; 13, 1, 1; 13, 1, 4; 53, 3, + 3. P. VI, 42, 1, + 1. P. XI, 51, 1, 1 and 2; 51, 2, 1 sqq. P. XII, 35, 3, + 3. P. V, 119, 2, 3. P. XXV, 75, 3, + 2. P. VIII, 136, 3, 1. P. XIV, 41, 3, 1. P. XV, 113, 2, 6; 113, 3, 4; 140, 2, 2; 148, 1, + 1; 148, 1, 3; 148, 2, 2; 148, 2, + 2. P. XVI, 17, 4, + 1; 18, 1, + 1; 18, 2, 4. P. XX, 81, 2, + 2. P. XXIII, 44, 4 + 1 and + 2; 77, 3, 1; 140, 2, + 4. P. XXIV, 72, 2, 3; 73, 3, + 3; 85, 3, + 3; 85, 3, + 1; 86, 1, 2. P. XXVII, 161, 2, + 2; 255, 5, 5; 245, 4, + 2. P. XXX, 9, 2, 2. P. XXXI, 61, 1, 4 (d.). P. XXXII, 24, 3, + 4; 137, 4, 4.

---

[1] I have not quoted examples of this sort found in the mass, "Dominicalis" (Pal. Werke Bd. XXXIII), and in the motet, "Thomas unus ex duodecim" (ibid. Bd. XXXII, p. 134), these compositions being hardly authentic.

The amplified cambiata in Palestrina's time was a phrase which was undoubtedly becoming obsolete.[1] It will be noticed that it is only in P. X. (Palestrina's first published work), that it is encountered by any means frequently. To be sure a large number of instances may be found in P. XV and P. XXIV. However in P. XV, (the 6th volume of masses from 1594) all the cases come from the mass "Ave Maria", already mentioned as dating from Palestrina's youth; and in P. XXIV (consisting of masses handed down in manuscript form only) all the instances originate from the "Benedicta" mass, which seems to have been composed in as comparatively early a period of the composer's production as 1562.[2] A rather odd form of the cambiata may be seen in the motet "Hodie beata virgo Maria" (P. V, 19, 3, + 3)[3]

Here the third note of the cambiata figure goes down a step instead of moving up a second, as is the normal procedure. If we consider that the returning-note together with its two flanking notes is in reality only the embellishment of a longer stationary note, (see p. 145), it is

---

[1] Kitson reverses things when he remarks, in connection with the freely continued and extended cambiata in Byrd's and Willaert's compositions, ("Counterpoint" p. 55): "through constant use the real significance of the Nota Cambiata has been forgotten." These phrases do not denote here the result of a progressive development, but quite the contrary—the classic cambiata form being, not the starting-point, but the culmination in the evolution of this genus.

[2] Consult Otto Ursprung: "Jacobus de Kerle", München 1913, p. 12, and Bertha Wallner: "Musikalische Denkmäler der Steinätzkunst", München 1912, p. 171.

[3] Compare Ambr. V, 72, 2, 1 (Josquin des Prés) and ibid. 396, 2, 1 (Ludwig Senfl).

plain that the form before us must be understood as an ornamental extension of the following:

This rhythmic fundamental form is otherwise not encountered very often, but is permissible in principle:

P. VIII, 116, 3, 1. Hymnus: Sanctorum meritis. (Also P. XIV, 36, 4, 1; 122, 2, + 3 P. XXIII, 33, 1, + 1; 64, 1, + 4. P. XXIV, 63, 1, 4 etc.)

With regard to the ascending cambiata, Bellermann remarks:[1] "Im 15. und 16. Jahrhundert findet man die Wechselnote nur abwärtssteigend angewandt; in modernen Kompositionen ist sie aber auch recht gut aufwärtssteigend zu gebrauchen."

This is correct in so far as it never occurs in Palestrina.[2] In the 15th and the beginning of the 16th century, on the other hand, it is —even if not nearly so commonly used as the descending cambiata— yet sometimes to be encountered; for example:

---

[1] l. c. p. 164.

[2] Also as a melodic phrase without dissonance it is very rare. Refer to p. 70, Ornament 50.

Dunstable: Veni sancte spiritus. Tr. 1, 204, 4, + 2.

Cook: Et in terra. Oldh I, 32, 3,+3.

Josquin des Prés. Missa: Hercules. Qui tollis, bar 47 etc.

See further: Tr. I, 184, 1, + 3; 205, 1, + 3; 217, 1, 4; 263, 1, 4. Tr. II, 70, 4, 3; 95, 5, 4. Tr. III, 63, 2, + 1; 63, 3, + 3; 64, 4, + 2; 71, 1, 4; 71, 4, + 2; 73, 3, 3; 79, 1, 3. Obr. IV, 98, 2, 2. Obr. VI, 82, 1, 2. Josquin des Prés: Missa "La sol fa re mi", Agnus I, bar 5; Missa "Gaudeamus", Gloria, 3rd bar before the end. Missa "Lomme armé sexti toni". Credo, bar 15; ibid., Sanctus, bar 16; Missa "Ave Maris stella", Credo, bar 26; ibid., Agnus I, bar 12; ibid., Agnus II, bar 23; Missa "Didadi", Gloria, bar 7; ibid., Pleni, bar 30; ibid., Pleni, bar 22; Missa "De beata Virgine",

Gloria, bar 64; Missa "Sine nomine", Credo, bar 47; Canon "Ad nonam canitur", bar 12 etc.; Chanson "Adieu mes amours" (Obr. IV, 36, 4, 3; cf. Ambr. V, 131, 2, 3); Lied "In meinem Sinn hab ich mir auserkoren" (Eitners Publikationen Bd. VI, p. 116).

It will be noticed that in all these instances (excepting Tr. I, 184, 1, + 3 and Tr. II, 70, 4, 3), the form corresponds exactly to the descending classic cambiata, where the upward leap of the third is followed by a downward second step. The need of resolution was earlier perceived in the case of the ascending than the descending form, which is explicable through the circumstance of the dissonance being more obvious in ascending than in descending progressions, and therefore it requires a more cautious treatment in the former.

Two ornamental figures that were very popular in the 16th century are:[1]

The first of these has been used from the time of "Ars nova"[2] up to the classical period in the 18th century.[3] We find, with respect to the second figure, that it was used but little by the early Netherlanders, whose melodies, (through the lack of such phrases, and the use of scale-like ornamental ascensions and descensions instead), had a tendency to be stiff. This ornament, however, was highly esteemed about 1520-30, and was among those most often used in Palestrina style. Both figures may now and then be observed in dissonant conjunctions, also where the dissonance is entered by a leap of a third:

---

[1] Refer to p. 61, also to Niemann: Studien zur deutschen Musikgeschichte des XV. Jahrhunderts. Km. J. 1902, p. 5.

[2] Consult for instance Guillaume de Machault's Coronation mass, Wolf: "Geschichte der Mensuralnotation" III, p. 50. Especially the Credo abounds in phrases of this kind.

[3] Refer to the motet "In voce exultationis" by Pitoni (d. 1743). M. D. II, p. 215. However, this figure, as a periheletic phrase, began to decline, about 1530-40.

P. X. 18, 2, 2.[1]) Missa: Ecce sacerdos magnus.

P. XX, 17, 4, + 2.[2]) Missa: Descendit angelus. (Cf. P. XVIII, 27, 2, + 2.[3]))

Although it seems probable to me that these forms of dissonance in Palestrina should be regarded as archaisms, I do not think we are warranted in accepting this assumption as sure. In works from the 1st and 2nd Netherland Schools these dissonance forms are almost never

---

[1] See further: P. X, 48, 4, + 1. P. IX, 78, 1, 3. P. XVII, 20, 1, + 1. Unusually harsh are the two places: P. XIII, 74, 2, + 2 and 76, 3, 4, which Palestrina most probably adopted from a work of an earlier composer.

[2] Cf. also: P. XI, 38, 1, + 3. P. XIII, 139, 2, 4. P. IV, 41, 3, + 3; 42, 1, 1; 44, 2, + 3 and + 2; 54, 2, 1; 142, 3, + 4. P. XIV, 9, 3, 4. P. XVI, 18, 4, + 3. P. XXVII, 38, 5, + 3; 126, 2, 2; 174, 4, + 1. P. IX, 80, 2, 2. P. XVIII, 72, 1, + 2; 114, 2, + 1. P. XIX, 132, 4, 1. P. XXI, 14, 3, + 2. P. XXIII, 79, 3, 3; 96, 2, + 2. P. XXIV, 73, 2, 4; 93, 1, 3 and + 1. P. XXX, 61, 3, 2 (d.). P. XXXIII, 83, 2, + 2. Also M. D. I, 112, 3, 3 (Orlando di Lasso) and 167, 3, + 2 (Andrea Gabrieli).

[3] Consult P. X, 44, 2, 3. P. XI, 68, 2, 4.

encountered,[1] and unfortunately the immediately succeeding period (just prior to Palestrina's appearance) is so sparsely represented in new editions that it is impossible to judge these relations with sufficient surety. It is worth noticing, however, that Clemens non Papa —who together with Senfl represents the most gifted among the composers of that epoch, and who is the only one whose works are comparatively well represented in modern editions—employed these phrases very freely, also in dissonant forms.[2]

The final result of this inquiry, with regard to melodic dissonance, is that Palestrina—strictly speaking—only recognizes the conjunct method of dissonance treatment. Only the passing note, the returning-note, the cambiata (in its classic form), and the Portamento of the descending second are of general validity. Dissonances encountered besides these are mostly rudiments from a less thoroughly cultured past.

Dissonance as a Primary Phenomenon.

In the beginning of the 15th century a number of new impulses swept over the musical world like a fresh breath of Spring. This breeze came from the West—from the British Isles—bringing with it sunshine and warmth, fertility and growth. After this sudden, brilliant Spring-tide, musical conditions developed with marvellous, triumphant rapidity into the magnificent and bountiful Summer of Palestrina's time.

Tinctoris expresses his surprise in 1477, that music which dates from more than 40 years prior to his own time no longer finds favour

---

[1] Rare exceptions: Is. II, 125, 5, 4. Is. III, 30, 3, + 3; 223, 4, + 1. "Inviolata", Eitner 47, 2, + 3 as well as Obr. III, 187, 3, 3 and Josquin des Prés, Missa: Fortuna desperata. Sanctus, bar 64.

[2] Cf. for ex.: C. C. III, 7, 3, 1; 10, 4, + 3; 13, 1, + 1; 19, 2, + 1; 20, 3, + 3; 55, 1, 1 and + 1; 64, 2, + 3; 71, 2, + 1; 78, 2, + 1. C. C. V, 20, 3, + 2; 21, 1, 3; 21, 3, 2; 21, 3, 3; 22, 3, 4; 22, 3, + 3 and + 2; 35, 2, 2; 37, 4, 1; 38, 3, 1; 40, 1, 1. Furthermore: Willaert: "Da pacem", Maldeghem 1880, 42, 2, + 2. Crequillon: "Judea et Jerusalem", Maldeghem 1876, 35, 1, + 2. Senfl: "Salutatio tertia", Denkmäler der Tonkunst in Bayern III, 2, p. 111, 1, + 2. Richafort: "Emendemus", Maldeghem 1881, 25, 2, + 1.

with connoisseurs of music.[1] Judging from the signs, it seems that we
have here an utterance of a more far-seeing character, and otherwise
superior to those usually typical of every fertile period which enter-
tains a traditional contempt for the time through which it has just
passed, and above which it feels itself immeasurably removed.

As far as can be discerned at present, there is a marked and very
significant boundary line, especially in a musico-technical respect, at
about the transition from the 14th to the 15th century. What happened
at that time may be characterized as a change in the conception of
consonance—the definite, practical recognition of the 3rd and 6th as
not only having privileges in musical art equal to the 4th, 5th and 8th,
but moreover as main consonants—tonal combinations decidedly preferred above all others, and regarded as fundamental factors in musical composition.

As we are aware, the vertical technique of "Ars antiqua" is principally based upon the 5th. However, various circumstances seem to indicate that British composers understood at a very early period the
eminent harmonic qualities of the 3rd. Thus Anonymus IV. recounts
in Coussemaker that both the major and minor third were much used
in England towards the end of the 13th century,[2] and Walter Odington,
an Englishman who lived in the same century, mentions the 6th as
something quite ordinary.[3]

A practical witness to the correctness of these assertions is the
little popular 2-part song, "Foweles in the frith"[4] which is dated ca.
1270 by the publisher, and which has a very striking end with consecutive 6ths. Likewise the 2-part hymn, "Nobilis humilis",[5] written in
the 12th century in honour of St. Magnus, Earl of the Orkney Islands,
which moves almost exclusively in consecutive 3rds, is most likely

---

[1] "Neque, quod admirari nequeo, quippiam compositum nisi citra annos quadra-
ginta extat, quod auditu dignum ab eruditis existimetur." Tractatus p. 201.

[2] Tamen apud organistas optimos et prout in quibusdam terris sicut in Anglia in
patria quae dicitur Westcuntre, optimae concordantiae dicuntur quoniam apud tales
magis sunt in usu. C. S. I, p. 358.

[3] C. S. I, p. 200.

[4] Stainer: "Early Bodleyan Music", London 1901, II, p. 10.

[5] Cited by the Norwegian musico-historian, Georg Reiss. See "Two norröne latin-
ske kvæde med melodiar fraa Codex Upsal. C. 233", av Oluf Kolsrud og Georg Reiss.
Kristiania 1913.

derived from very ancient Anglo-Saxon or Celtic music. Nevertheless, the two pieces mentioned remain isolated examples up to the present, and all the known polyphonic music of the 12th and 13th centuries seems to owe its character more to the auspices of the 4th and 5th. It was not until towards the close of the 14th century that certain episodes of consecutive 6th accords appear, like islands emerging from the sea, in compositions which sound anything but harmonious to modern ears. For instance the motet, "Petrus cephas ecclesie",[1] is most interesting, being evidently a transitional form between the old French motet and the new mode of composing. Its date is probably ca. 1375. Consecutive 5ths and 6ths here graze peacefully side by side, the 6th (or more correctly, the 6th chords) being decidedly in the majority. Phrases of this kind are, moreover, encountered in French and Italian works from about the year 1400;[2] it is noticeable, however, that they only occur here in conclusions, while in "Petrus cephas ec- clesie" they are woven into almost the entire texture of the composi- tion, forming Faux-bourdon episodes of not altogether brief duration. On the whole this composition, whose like has not yet come to light in researches into both French and Italian contemporary literature, strongly suggests that England is really the native home of the Faux- bourdon. It also shows that Guilelmus Monachus (ca. 1450), the very earliest writer who mentions Faux-bourdon, was not altogether wrong when he expressly calls this mode of writing "modus anglicorum".

It seems also that Faux-bourdon forms the universally perceptible technical basis of this school's polyphonic practice. It is the same with the musical works of the Dufay period; but there is no doubt that this period must be understood as genetically related to the musical contributions of the English, and that it was in the British Isles (which Tinctoris called "novae artis fons et origo")[3] that the musical flores- cence of the 15th and 16th centuries was inaugurated. The situation

---

[1] See Stainer, l. c. p. 25.

[2] Refer to Wolf: "Gesch. der Mensural-Notation" III, 79, 2, 3 (Johannes Ciconia); 84, 2, + 1 (P. Fontaine); 111, 3, + 2 (Bartolinus de Padua); 126, 1, 2 (Francesco Landino); 147, 5, + 4 (Gratiosus de Padua).

[3] Tractatus p. 403. Also the French poet, Martin le Franc, gave his opinion about his contemporaries of the Dufay generation in "Le champion des Dames" as follows: "Et ont prins de la contenance Angloise et ensuy Dunstable."

may most likely be explained by the circumstance that, while music on the continent was mostly treated horizontally, English composers quietly advanced towards the mastery of harmonic elements. Towards the end of the 14th century, this movement—which undoubtedly, as Adler asserts,[1] originated in folk-song—began to exert its influence upon the higher musical art, first at home and later, (through the leading and most gifted artists, like Dunstable), upon the musical development in France and Italy. We should scarcely be far wrong in regarding the new relations towards consonance as the focus of interest in this event.

While we have the feeling that the attitude of "Ars antiqua" was of a more intellectual nature, and was actually only manifested in the requirement of clearness, transparency and conformity upon all the more noticeable points of polyphonic composition,[2] the relation seems now to assume a more decided form. The tonal combinations in themselves become a more obvious factor, causing a state of tension between the two Dimensions, in which contest the vertical interests were temporarily predominant—a state of affairs that was gradually eliminated in the course of the 15th century, so that the ideal equilibrium of Palestrina could only be established through the renewed transmission of harmonic impulses, (again from folk-music: the Frottole). It is scarcely too daring to assert that it was not until the English appeared on the scene that there was any intenser relationship to consonance in musical art; it can hardly surprise us therefore that the contrasting relationship—that of the *real* dissonance—should simultaneously enter the ranks of musical effects.

It is true of all the forms of dissonance treatment which have been discussed up to this point, that the melodic phrase introducing the dissonance may just as often (and in most cases, oftener) be used in

---

[1] Guido Adler: "Studie zur Geschichte der Harmonie". Sitzungsberichte der kaiserl. Akad. der Wissenschaften. Philosoph.-histor. Klasse. Bd. 98. Wien 1881.

[2] In this domain we are left, at any rate temporarily, almost exclusively to the faculty of subjective perception. An indication of historic and more objective kind, which is of interest in this connection, however, may lie in the division which Anonymus V in Coussemaker (C. S. I, p. 366) makes of consonance, viz: "clarae" (5ths, and 12ths), "minus clarae" (3rds, 6ths and 10ths), and "clarissimae" (unisons, octaves, and double octaves).

consonant as in dissonant conjunction. Here for the first time we encounter a dissonance which is not the accidental result of a melodic progression, but which is used just because it is dissonance, and because it is desired that dissonance—and dissonance only—should be heard at the point where it is placed. I allude here to the syncope dissonance:

This form of dissonance treatment, consciously applied, first appeared in English compositions from the beginning of the 15th century. This fact accords with the circumstance that the first theorist who discussed it, Guilelmus Monachus, writes especially of the practice of this school of composers.[1] He says:[2]

"Octava regula talis est, quod quamquam posuerimus duodecim consonantias tam perfectas quam imperfectas, tam simplices quam compositas, non obstante, secundum usum modernum, consonantie dissonantes aliquoties nobis serviunt, sicut dissonantia secunde dat dulcedinem tertie basse; dissonantia vero septime dat dulcedinem sexte; dissonantia quarte dat dulcedinem tertie alte et illa tertia dat dulcedinem quinte et hoc secundum modernum."

To be sure, it is not said in so many words that it is the syncope dissonance to which the author alludes, nevertheless there can be no doubt upon this point. In the first place, the musical examples show that Guilelmus was thoroughly familiar with this form of dissonance treatment; and in the second place, the rules that he gives agree so perfectly with those governing the practice of the period that his meaning is in reality quite explicit. When Guilelmus for instance teaches that the 2nd resolves into the "low" 3rd, (this being most likely rather an awkward way of expressing that the dissonance should be placed in the lower voice), or that the 7th resolves into the 6th and the 4th into the "high" 3rd, (meaning that the dissonance should be in the upper voice), he herewith gives the very best and most commonly used resolutions possible to the syncope dissonance.

---

[1] The syncope itself had, however, been mentioned—without entering into the question of its possible employment as a dissonance—by theorists of the "Ars nova" See R. M. p. 294 sqq.

[2] C. S. III, p. 291.

Had it been the intention to imply that the reference was to the passing dissonance, such a detailed accounting for resolutions would have been superfluous; for the passing 2nd (for instance) may as well be resolved into the unison as into the 3rd, the 4th into the 5th as well as into the 3rd, etc.

The only difficult point in the interpretation lies in the allusion to the "high" 3rd as a dissonance requiring resolution into the 5th.[1] Hugo Riemann gets over this difficulty by assuming that in Coussemaker the word "tertia" has crept in instead of "tritonus".[2] However, but little is gained by this assumption, for the most natural and the usual interval of resolution of the augmented fourth was, and still remains, by means of syncopes, not the 5th, but the 3rd. Moreover, it is difficult to ignore the "illa" which, as it stands, indicates that "tertia" is correct. It is most probable that Coussemaker's wording is correct, and the case to which he alludes, of the following or a similar order:[3]

In this example, which is taken from the Guilelmus tract, (see Adler l. c. Musical Supplement p. XI), the syncopated upper 4th in the middle voice resolves into the 3rd, which is then followed by the 5th. This was a very current conclusion at that period, and the circumstance that the progression 3-5 so often follows 4-3 in practice, may explain that the latter accompanies the former into a representative relationship where, strictly speaking, it does not belong.

Great psychologic importance attaches to the expression which

---

[1] The 3rd is classified earlier in the treatise as an imperfect consonant, according to contemporary custom.

[2] R. M. p. 298. Coussemaker's edition agrees exactly with the very well-preserved and distinctly written original manuscript of Guilelmus, which accordance I had an opportunity to substantiate in St. Marks Library, Venice.

[3] Compare for instance Tr. I, 199, 2, 7.

Guilelmus uses to explain the underlying motive of syncope dissonance. He says that it adds sweetness to the succeeding consonance. This seems to indicate that the people of that day perceived syncope dissonance in the same way as we understand it—as a conscious presentation of dissonance in æsthetically accentuated contradistinction to consonance. It is thus, also, that Zarlino explains this relationship; for, after first trying to find a more traditional reason for its employment, (in its alleged less conspicuous character), he finally concludes:

"—nonsolamente tal Dissonanza non li dispiace, ma grandemente in lei si compiace; perche con maggior dolcezza & maggior soauità fa udire tal Consonanza. Et questo forse auiene; perche Ogni contrario maggiormente si scopre & si fà al sentimento più noto per la comparatione del suo Opposto."[1]

This expresses the inner meaning of the syncope dissonance. With respect to Palestrina's mode of treating it, the following fundamental rules apply to the dissonant tone:

1. It must be prepared through introduction upon the unaccented beat;
2. it must then remain stationary, whereby the dissonant relationship upon the next accented beat is formed;
3. and finally it must be resolved into consonance by the descending degree of a second upon the succeeding unaccented beat.

It is matter of course that these rules had only gradually acquired the fixedness which characterized them in the Palestrina period. For instance, the syncope might very well be introduced dissonantly in the 15th century:

Tr. I, 152, 5, 1. Dufay: Sanctus papale (Compare also Tr. I, 216, 1, 2).

[1] Opere I, p. 240.

Similar employment may be observed in the 15th and in the beginning of the 16th century:

Excetre: Et in terra. Oldh. I, 56, 2, 3.

Pierre de la Rue(?).Motet: Dulces exuviae. Maldeghem 1882, 18, 2, + 1.

Naturally Palestrina is generally superior to such, though extremely rare exceptions may be observed, even with the Great Master himself:

P. XXV, 65, 2, + 4, Lamentation.

P. XXIX, 49, 3, + 1. Madrigal: O cibo. (Compare also P. XXXI, 75, 1, + 1.)

The exact correspondence of the above examples will be noted. Both differ from the other instances, cited in this connection from works of earlier composers, in the circumstance that the accented part of the syncopation here is dissonant, but is introduced consonantly in relation to the voice which causes its dissonance. In all likelihood these examples should rather be regarded as instances of note-against-note in a somewhat careless treatment. In P. XXV, 65, 2, + 4 on the other hand, we find (besides the dissonance just mentioned), one of a more essential and aggressive character: the syncopated note A in the next to the upper voice is introduced dissonant with G in the next to the lowest voice, and then remains stationary in the same dissonant relation during the accented beat. Instances like this are rarely encountered in the Palestrinian epoch. In the beginning of the 16th century they are, however, rather commonly used, for example:

Is, I, 16, 4, 4.[1]) Prosa: Pater, Filius. (Also compare Josquin des Prés. Missa: Gaudeamus, Credo, conclusion.)

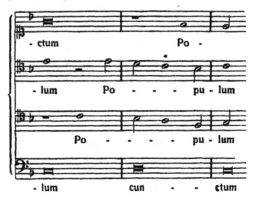

Costanzo Festa, Motet: Felix Anna. M. I. 31, 2,+3.

It may also appear in a more ornamental form:

---

[1] Further examples: Obr. I, 28, 2, 3; 31, 3, 3; 214, 4, + 2. Obr. II, 152, 3, 1. Obr. III, 7, 1, 2; 214, 1, 2. Obr. IV, 17, 1, 2; 29, 2, 2; 114, 3, 2; 198, 4, + 1; 236, 1, 2. Obr. V, 24, 4, + 2; 52, 4, + 2; 83, 3, + 3. Obr. VI, 86, 2, 1; 94, 3, 2; 130, 4, 3. Obr. VII, 9, 4, + 2. Is. II, 117, 2, 1; 117, 2, 5. Is. III, 12, 4, + 4; 62, 3, 1; 153, 4, 4; 212, 2, + 1. Josquin des Prés, Missa: "Gaudeamus", Agnus II, bar 37; Missa: "Lomme armé sexti toni", Osanna, next to last bar; Missa: "Da pacem", Gloria, bar 27; ibid. Pleni, bar 20; ibid. Benedictus, bar 24.

Obr. II, 125, 3, + 2. Missa: De sancto Martino.

Obr. IV, 206, 2, 1. (Octave transposition of portamento!) Missa: Caput. (Compare also Is. II, 49, 2, 4[1]).)

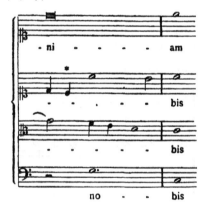

Dissonances like these are rare with Palestrina, and only occur in earlier works.

---

[1] Refer also to Obr. I, 27, 1, 2. Obr. II, 70, 3, + 1. Obr. IV, 88, 4, + 2. Obr. IV, 158, 3, 2; 181, 4, + 2. Obr. VI, 121, 3, 2. Is. III, 182, 1, + 2. Josquin des Prés: Missa "Gaudeamus", Et in Spiritum, bar 12; ibid. bar 14; Missa "Fortuna desperata", Agnus II, bar 14; Missa "Hercules", Benedictus, bar 7 (important!).

P. X, 18, 2, + 2¹). Missa: Ecce sacerdos magnus.

However, similar cases may often be observed if the dissonance introduced upon the unaccented beat forms a 4th with the bass, and then is afterwards replaced upon the accented beat by a harsher dissonance, (7th or 2nd); for example:

P. XXV, 18, 4, 2. Lamentation. (Cf. P. V, 145, 4, 4.)

Yet the last instance may be classed more correctly among the so-called "consonant 4ths."

As stated earlier, the 4th was treated as a dissonance by the practical musicians of Palestrina's time. Palestrina himself was most strict in his treatment of this interval, using it almost exclusively in syncopation or as a passing or ornamental dissonance. Isolated ex-

---

¹ Consult further: P. X, 11, 4, + 4. P. XI, 84, 4, 4 and P. XII, 75, 3, + 2; 99, 3, 1. P. XXV, 184, 2, + 2. P. XXX, 100, 4, 2. P. XXXI, 48, 2, 4 (d.). P. XXXII, 4, 2, 3 (d).

ceptions, belonging to the category "expressional" dissonance, will later be discussed; for the present, only the following deviations from the normal mode of treatment are quoted:

P. XXV, 59, 4, + 3. Lamentation.

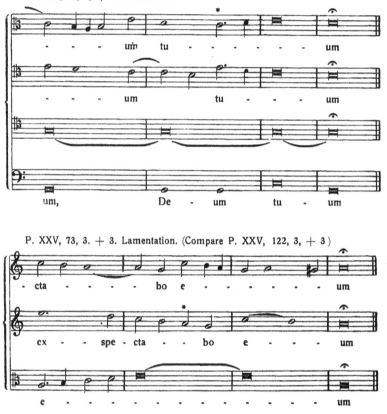

P. XXV, 73, 3. + 3. Lamentation. (Compare P. XXV, 122, 3, + 3)

These three instances, (as far as my knowledge goes, the only ones found in Palestrina's works), are met with in cadences, and it will be noticed that in them all the dissonance is introduced above a stationary note in the bass. It might therefore be justifiable to regard these forms as the first germs of pedal dissonance, which later reached

such a high state of development, though otherwise but rarely encountered in 16th century vocal polyphony.[1]

Akin to these forms is the so-called "consonant 4th", already mentioned. Bellermann, who gave it this name, defines it in the following
paragraph:[2]

"Wir haben die Quarte bis jetzt stets als eine Dissonanz zum tief-
sten Tone eines Zusammenklanges behandelt; hiervon kann man aber
eine Ausnahme machen, wenn sie stufenweise, sei es aufwärts- oder
abwärtssteigend, die unbetonte Taktzeit erreicht, der Bass schon vor-
her und noch ferner auf seinem Tone liegen bleibt und sie selbst auf
der folgenden guten Taktzeit zur wirklichen Dissonanz wird, und sich
so gleichsam selbst vorbereitet und sich dann auf der nächstfolgenden
Thesis auflöst".[3]

This mode of treating 4ths is encountered exceedingly often in
Palestrina's compositions. One instance, out of a great number of
analogous ones, is quoted here:

P. XII, 85. 1, + 4. Missa: L'homme armé.

---

[1] Compare with this statement: Leichtentritt, "Geschichte der Motette", 1908, p.
52 sqq.

[2] Fux had, however, already drawn attention to it. See his Gradus (Mizler), p. 103.

[3] "Der Contrapunkt", p. 220. Consult also: Heinrich Bellermann, "Einige Be-
merkungen über die konsonierende Quarte bei den Komponisten des 16. Jahrhunderts". Allg. musikalische Zeitung. Jahrg. 1870, Nr. 35.

I have been able to trace it back to the earliest masters of the 2nd Netherland School:

Tr. III, 59, 2, + 2. Okeghem, Missa: Caput.

However, it can hardly be much older than this.

That Bellermann insists that the fourth should be conjunctly treated in these phrases is quite rational, this being the typical mode of treatment in Palestrina's time. Exceptions occur, however, and not alone in works of the Netherlanders:

Obr. IV, 90, 4, 3. Missa: Carminum. (Compare also Obr. IV, 243, 1, 1 and Is. I, 152, 5, 1.)

but also in compositions of Palestrina himself:

P. XI, 66, 1, + 2. Missa: Ad fugam.

The designation "consonant 4th" is, after all, not very apt; for even though the treatment of the 4th in this instance should be such as is otherwise only accorded to consonance, it is not a given fact that the 4th has really been heard as consonance. It is more likely that the practicability of this dissonance is due to its less prominent character in this treatment. The circumstance that the bass remains stationary during the introduction of the 4th, (the introduction itself being most discreetly conducted), and that a harsher dissonance immediately afterwards draws attention to itself, causes the irregularity to pass comparatively unobserved. The presence of this harsher dissonance upon the accented beat is probably the factor which particularly le gitimizes this relation in Palestrina style. The phrase is, notwithstanding this, occasionally encountered without such a dissonance, for instance:

P. VIII, 107. 1, + 2. Hymnus: Deus tuorum militum.

P. XXIII, 141, 3, 4.[1]) Missa: Veni Creator Spiritus. (Cf. P. XII, 69. 4, + 4.)

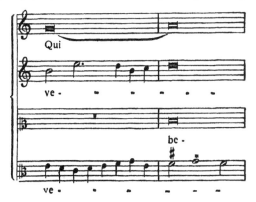

In the last example, the G forms a freely treated 4th with the lower as well as a second with the upper voice. Relations of this kind are not altogether uncommon. Also 4ths + 7ths occur:

P. XXV, 73, 1, + 2. Lamentation.

On the other hand, we never see 2-part examples of this category with Palestrina, while they are comparatively often encountered in Netherland compositions from ca. 1500:

---

[1] Refer also to P. XXX, 63, 1, 2; 98, 1, 4; P. XXXII, 136, 3, 2; 163, 1, + 2. P. XXXIII, 30, 3, + 3.

Obr. III, 51, 4. 3. Missa: Si dedero. (Cf. Josquin des Prés. Missa: Hercules, Qui venit, bar 7.)

With these composers we frequently find also a freer mode of introducing the dissonance than is normally approved in Palestrina style. For instance:

Obr. II, 59, 3, 2.[1]) Missa super Maria zart.

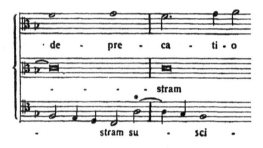

With respect to cases like the last example, "Compositions Regeln Herrn M. Johann Peterssen Sweling" writes: "Aber doch muss man per gradus auf die dissonantien oder ligaturen gehen, denn dieses folgende ist bei den alten nicht vor gut gehalten".[2]

[1] Consult: Obr. I, 100, 2, 1; 149, 1, + 1; 152, 3, 3; 183, 2, + 3. Obr. III, 199, 3, + 1. Obr. IV: 11, 4, 1; 21, 4, + 3. Is. III, 41, 1, 1.
[2] Sweelinck, Werke X, p. 23.

I know of but few similar instances in Palestrina.[1] On the whole,
the use of dissonantly introduced syncopation ("la sincopa tutta cat-
tiva", as the 16th century theorists called it), with the sole exception
of the "consonant 4th", was rapidly declining in Palestrinian music. It
had reached the culmination of its florescence towards the end of the
15th century; in the later part of the 16th, these forms were considered
archaic—especially the type with the semibreve syncope. The form
with minim syncopes still appeared not infrequently, mostly in madrigals, but also occasionally in the ecclesiastical compositions of
Palestrina's time:

P. XI, 131, 3, 1.[2]) Missa: Papae Marcelli. (Cf. i. a. Victoria: Opera I, 136, 2,
+ 1 and M. D. II, 353, 3, 1.)

It is to be noted that this form, like consonant 4ths, was mainly
used in terminal formations, though there are exceptions; for example:

---

[1] See P. XII, 69, 3, + 4; 190, 1, 1. P. XXX, 139, 1, 2 and + 1. P. XXXI, 20, 4, + 2.
P. XXXII, 70, 1, 3. 136, 3, + 3 (d.). P. XXXIII, 34, 2, 1 etc.

[2] See further: P. XXVIII, 45, 3, 3; 112, 4, 1. P. XI, 134, 2, + 3; 134, 3, 1. P. I, 115,
2, + 3. P. XII, 104, 3, + 4. P. V, 64, 3, + 2; 160, 1, + 4. P. IV, 7, 3, 4; 132, 2, 4;
134, 1, 1; 138, 1, 4; 167, 2, 1. P. XXVIII, 112, 4, 1. P. VIII, 75, 3, + 4. P. XV, 124,
3, + 1. P. XXIX, 108, 1, + 1; 165, 3, 1; 177, 2, 1; 179, 3, 2 and 1; 187, 2, 1. P. XVII,
92, 3, + 1; 131, 1, + 2. P. XXII, 22, 4, 4; 102, 2, 3. P. XXIII, 19, 1, 2. P. XXIV, 5, 3, 2;
39, 2, 3; 76, 2, + 2; 76, 3, 3; 79, 2, 4; 99, 3, 3; 99, 3, + 3. P. XVIII 111, 1, 1 (according to the original edition from 1599). P. XXVI, 71, 3, + 4; 72, 1, 2; 82, 1, 1 and
+ 2; 93, 1, 4; 108, 3, + 2; 111, 3, 4; 185, 2, + 1 (d.). P. XXVII, 70, 2, 2; 92, 4,
1; 174, 3, + 1; 254, 3, 4. P. XXXI, 31, 3, 4. P. XXXII, 173, 2, + 2 etc.;
175 etc.

P. XII, 50, 4, 1. Missa: Brevis.

It is noticeable, moreover, that in the great majority of instances the syncopated note forms the minor upper second of the note of resolution—in modern terms, the phrase in its typical form represents a turn with the tonic upon the 3rd of the dominant triad. But there are exceptions here also, (refer to P. XII, 69, 4, + 4). Finally it must be remarked that when the syncope forms either a second or a seventh with a stationary voice, it is almost without exception the major second or minor seventh. Altogether, these dissonant types must be understood as more or less nonchalant variants of terminal formations of this or a similar order:

With the gradually refined appreciation of the dissonance, these forms passed out of customary usage. The steady, legitimate employment in Palestrina of "consonant fourths" (which designation seems too well established to be changed now) while other, freer forms seem antiquated and sparingly used, must certainly, as already mentioned, be attributed to the circumstance that the dissonant character of the fourth (in itself weak), is still further effaced by contrast with the succeeding harsher dissonance.

The following at first sight rather astonishing tonal combination, must be regarded in connection with the dissonantly introduced suspension:

P. XII, 189, 1, 1.[1]) Missa: Ut re mi fa sol la.

It is undeniably surprising to come across the famous introductory chord from Mendelssohn's Wedding March in the middle of the 16th century. The psychologic background in the two instances is naturally of a widely different nature, the effect in Palestrina's case being scarcely as remarkable as it seems at first sight. This phrase really belongs to a series of tonal combinations which arise when the voices, which lie at the moment that the syncope is dissonantly introduced, change their notes simultaneously with the entrance of the dissonance. Places like the one just cited are to be understood as an amplification of the following:

Such phrases are met with rather commonly in compositions from ca. 1500:

---

[1] Peter Wagner was the first to call attention to this effect. Refer to "Gesch. der Messe", p. 440. Compare also P. XII, 189, 2, + 1; 190, 1, 1; 190, 2, 2.

Obr. III, 12, 4, + 2.¹) Missa: Si dedero.

Is I, 137, 1, + 1. Introitus: In excelso throno.²)

Exactly the same tonal combination as the example cited from Palestrina, (which expressed in modern terms would be: the chord with minor 3rd, diminished 5th, and minor 7th, in its first inversion), seems to have been rarely used in the earlier part of the 16th century. A place like the following from Clemens non Papa:

---

¹ Consult also Obr. III, 160, 4, 2. Obr. IV, 2, 3, + 1; 51, 4, 1. Obr. VI, 127, 4, 1; 138, 1, 1. Obr. VII, 28, 4, + 2; 38, 1, + 2.

² Compare further Is. I, 31, 4, 3; 62, 3, + 2; 79, 4, + 1; 250, 5, + 4; Is. II, 10, 4, + 2; 88, 4, 6. Is. III, 108, 5, + 2; 170, 3, 1. Torchi: "L'arte musicale in Italia" I, 48, 2, 3 (Spartaro) and M. f. M. 1874, p. 61 (Mahu).

Motet: Tristitia obsedit me. C. C. V, 25, 1, 3.[1])

resembles it very much, but does not correspond exactly unless we assume that the rule, "una nota super la semper est canendum fa", is valid with respect to the upper voice, which is not absolutely certain.

Besides in the places already cited, it may be found also in the second part of the motet, "Tribularer si nescirem" (P. II, 85, 2, + 3).[2] Two interesting cases of a similar order by contemporaries of Palestrina are appended:

Victoria: "Opera omnia". I, 144, 3, + 2. Motet: Pastores loquebantur.

[1] Refer also to C. C. V, 39, 3, 3 by the same composer.
[2] Cf. also: P. I, 161, 1, + 2; P. VIII, 165, 3, + 1 and P. XVI, 100, 3, + 1.

Francesco Soriano: Passio secundum Mathaeum. M. D. IV, 9, 3, + 2.

Finally a most extravagant variant of this form in keyboard-music may be cited:[1]

Andrea Antico da Montona: Frottole intabulate da sonare organi (1517), Nr. 16, Takt 12.

In this transcription of a frottole of Marchetto Cara we, apparently, meet with a phenomenon as alien to the sixteenth century as the second inversion of the chord of dominant seventh with augmented fifth. Really, however, it must be regarded as a combination of two returning-notes furnished with the ordinary chromatic alterations.

Considering the small quantity of available material (especially from the period just prior to Palestrina), too great significance need not be attached to the fact that I have not succeeded in definitely proving the presence in that period of similar forms to P. XII, 189, 1, 1. But on the other hand this makes it impossible to answer decisively the query concerning the archaism or modernism of this effect. How-

---

[1] Marchetto Cara: "Per dolor mi bagno el viso." Cf. my edition: "Die italienische Orgelmusik am Anfang des Cinquecento". Copenhagen 1943, p. 87.

ever, my opinion is that it should be classed under the former, partly because this form of dissonance had (as far as principle is concerned) been employed by Netherland composers before and much oftener than Palestrina ever did, and partly because the Palestrina compositions in which it occurs belong to the earlier works of the master.[1] Finally the words at this place give no especial occasion for employing dissonance; for Palestrina only (though rarely) uses a freer, "modern" type where the textual contents afford a motive for it. When dissonant effects of a harsher kind otherwise occur in his works, they may usually be regarded as reminiscences of the less cultured practices.

*   *

*

The applicability of the different dissonances in syncopation depends upon whether the syncope is dissonant in relation to the upper or lower voice. The most commonly used tie-dissonance in Palestrina's music, perhaps, is the 7th in the upper voice resolved into the 6th, (the normal resolution downward by a second). On the other hand, the 7th in the lower voice and its consequent resolution into the octave is never encountered in Palestrina's 2-part compositions, so far as I know. Also in the works of the Second Netherland School it is very rarely treated thus, though sometimes observed:

Obr. VI, 41, 1, + 2. Motet: Salve crux.

---

[1] The mass, "La sol fa re mi" and the motet "Tribularer" are both cantus firmus compositions. The mass, published in 1570, has been incorporated in Codex 39 of the papal chapel archives since 1562, (cf. Haberl's Catalogue, p. 18). The motet makes a very old-fashioned impression, owing to the independent text to the cantus firmus—a pronounced transalpine trait.

This resolution of the 7th, however, is occasionally found in Palestrina when the composition has more than 2 parts:

P. XII, 186, 4, + 2. Missa: Ut re mi fa sol la. (Cf. XXIV, 17, 1, + 2.)

Vicentino teaches that the fourth, (which he agrees with the ancient musical theorists in considering a consonant interval), should be succeeded by the third when it is used in syncopation; as nature likes variety, and as both fourths and fifths are perfect consonants, these are only reluctantly used immediately after each other—and in every case only where the composition is in several parts, so that other voices may relieve the monotony.[1]

This agrees precisely with Palestrina's practice, in which fourths are used without restriction as suspensions in the upper parts, while they are hardly ever employed in 2-part composition in the lower voice, (resolving into the fifth). However, in the beginning of the 16th century, composers very occasionally wrote as follows:

---

[1] La Quarta appresso i Filosophi si hà per consonanza che habbia in sè perfettione, et per tal ragione non fa diuersità alcuna, nel sentire quando ella è posta appresso una Quinta, ouer Ottaua perche la differenza dell'armonia, è quasi equale di perfettione; il Compositore dè pensare che la natura si nutrisce di uarietà, et non gode quando le consonanze non sono uariate; et miste, di perfettione; imperò che la Quarta si accompagnerà con la Terza — — — et quando sarà accompagnata con la Quinta à molte voci, la moltitudine delle uoci la cuoprirà, et si deue mettere nelle parti di mezzo, à cinque, & à piu che non sarà sentita. "L'antica musica" p. 30v.

Ambr. V, 211, 2, 1. Anton Fevin, Motet: Descende in hortum.

Is. III, 147, 3, 1. Sequens: Haec quae sibi — (Cf. Ambr. V, 254, 3, 2.)

which Palestrina extremely seldom does:

P. XXVII, 9, 1, 4.[1]) Magnificat.

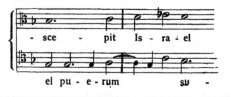

---

[1] Compare also P. XII, 100, 2, 1 and P. XXVII, 67, 2, 2. It will be noticed that the dissonant relations in these three examples (which are all that I know of in Palestrina's works), have only the duration of crotchets, which makes the dissonance less conspicuous than in the previously cited examples by the older composers. With regard to the rhythm, it should be noted that syncope dissonance in Palestrina music is most often of the duration of a minim. Sometimes, though rarely, it may happen that it lasts through the value of a semibreve (compare, for example, P. XXIII, 71, 3, + 4, this treatise, p. 123), and occasionally the value of a crotchet, (cf. this treatise, p. 264).

With more parts (without requiring, however, that there should be at least 5 voices, as Vicentino seems to think), Palestrina also resolves the 4th into the 5th quite often:

P. XIV, 16, 3, 4.[1]) Missa: Jam Christus astra ascenderat.

The resolution of the 4th into the diminished 5th is, however, even more common than into the perfect fifth. Concerning this, Zarlino remarks with reference to the following example, (Opere I, p. 242):

"Usaremo etiandio la Quarta sincopata, dopo la quale segua senz' alcun mezo la Semidiapente, & dopo questa immediatamente succeda la Terza maggiore; percioche la Semidiapente è posta in tal maniera, che fà buono effetto—".[2]

So far as I have observed, Palestrina does not employ this treatment in 2-part counterpoint, though his Netherland predecessors do:

---

[1] Consult also P. XI, 60, 2, + 3. P. XII, 68, 1, + 2. P. XIV, 64, 1, + 1; 71, 2, + 3. P. XVI, 85, 3, 2. P. XVIII, 59, 1, + 2.

[2] Refer also to Vicentino, l. c. p. 31 v.—Artusi, ("L'arte del contraponto", p. 50, who [like Zarlino] teaches that the 4th in the lower voice should resolve into the diminished 5th, after which the dissonant note should return to its starting-point— thus the 5th into the major 3rd), compares this relation with a military exercise— where the party which attacks then retires a step to meet the counter-attack, advancing again to the attack, so as not to be placed *hors de combat*.

Is. I, 231, 2, 4. Tractus: Deus meus. (Cf. Obr. IV, 93, 5, 2.)

Where there are more parts, it is quite a usual form with Palestrina also:

P. XVI, 45, 3, 4. Missa: Emendemus.

This manner of resolution may sometimes also be used with syncopes in the lower voice, by which procedure—and in spite of all the strict rules—it happens that a tied dissonance is resolved into another dissonance. The voluntary impulse towards the semitone step in cadence formation is so strong, however, that the harmonic incompleteness is tolerated on that account. For instance:

P. XII, 107, 2, 3. Missa: Repleatur os meum laude.

While the syncopated 2nd placed in the lower voice, and consequently resolved into the 3rd, is one of the greatest favourites of vocal polyphony, the suspended 2nd is only rarely used in the upper voice, where its resolution is into the unison. To be sure, Zarlino says:

"che Si potrà anco alle uolte (come costumano fare i buoni Musici, non senza suo gran commodo) dalla Seconda sincopata uenire all'Unisono, & ciò quando le parti sarano ordinate in tal maniera, che l'una faccia il mouimento di Tuono & l'altra di Semituono":[1]

Still its appearance in 2-part counterpoint seems the exception. At any rate, I know of but two examples of this kind:

Josquin des Prés, Missa: Da pacem. "Et iterum", bar 26,

P. XXV, 197, 1, + 4. Lamentation.

While it is true that the last example is taken from Palestrina's works, the authenticity of the collection of Lamentations in which it is found (Ms. in Section Ottobonia, Vatican Library) is not altogether certain. It is worthy of note that both examples tally exactly with the foregoing citation from Zarlino. In multipart counterpoint, the 2nd is more frequently resolved into the unison, by Palestrina also:

---

[1] Opere I, p. 242.

P. V, 15, 1, + 2.[1]) Motet: Tribus miraculis.

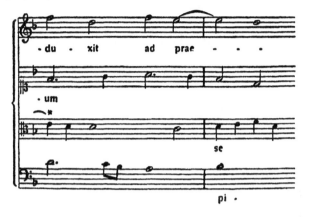

The same conditions apply to the employment of the 9th as to the 2nd, the 9th being normally only employed in the lower voice, and resolved into the 10th. It is only exceptionally used in the upper voice, with resolution into the octave. Zarlino remarks regarding this interval:[2] "Sogliono ancora i Prattici usar di porre la Nona, quando dopo essa si uiene all' Ottaua per contrarii Mouimenti, & l'una delle parti ascenda per Quarta, ò discenda per Quinta, & l'altre discenda per grado; come più oltra nell'essempio si uede".

Zarlino's requirement that the note which is dissonant in relation to the syncope should be introduced by an ascending 4th or a descending 5th leap, seems after all not to have been fully valid:

---

[1] Refer also to P. X, 36, 4, 4; 95, 1, + 2. P. V, 17, 4, 1; 32, 3, + 3; 36, 3, 4-5; 36, 4, 1; 37, 3, 1; 39, 4, 2; 50, 1, + 1; 59, 2, + 4. P. XI, 111, 4, 3. P. XII, 67, 3, + 2. P. XXIII, 49, 1, + 3.
[2] Opere I, p. 242.

Josquin des Prés. Missa: Gaudeamus. "Et in Spiritum", bar 18. (Cf. Is I, 135, 1, + 2 and Obr. III, 120, 2. 1.)

The resolution of the 9th into the octave is, incidentally, the exception with Palestrina in 2-part writing:

P. XII, 122, 2, + 3. Missa: Repleatur os meum laude.

An interesting circumstance is noted in this and the three similar cases which I have observed in Palestrina,[1] in the crotchet value of the dissonance (the note of resolution being embellished by a Portamento), and in the introduction of a third voice coincidentally with the entrance of the real tone of resolution, by which the bare effect of the octave is evaded. Altogether, we may assume that behind all the rules concerning the treatment of syncope dissonance, there lies in reality the craving for complete, satisfactory harmony after the dissonance.[2]

---

[1] P. V, 119, 1, + 2. P. XIX, 7, 3, 3 and P. XXIV, 88, 3, 1.

[2] Vicentino gives a rather palpable reason for this, typical of the period. His opinion was that Nature does not favour extremes, and that consequently a dissonance should not be immediately succeeded by a perfect, but preferably by an imperfect consonance. "L'antica musica" p. 30: Il Compositore sarà auuertito di non dare una dissonanza pessima, all'orecchi, & poi che subito segua una consonanza ottima, acciò la natura non si confonda, per cagione dell'una & dell'altra estremità, ma perche il Filosofo considera, che tra due estremi, si dà il mezzo, adunque, tra una dissonanza pessima & una consonanza ottima, si darà una piu proquinqua à quella, che sarà la consonanza imperfetta.

Therefore we observe how the placing of syncope dissonances which resulted in resolutions into 5ths, unisons or octaves began to fall out of use in compositions by Palestrina, (whose perception of sonorousness, in comparison with the Netherlanders, was more highly developed), or to be employed only in multipart counterpoint where other voices conceal the emptiness.

It is well to add, for the sake of being explicit, that the 9th in the upper voice is quite commonly used by Palestrina in cases where more than two parts are employed; for example:

P. V, 47, 4, 2. Motet: Surge propera.

It must be noted, finally, that augmented and diminished intervals are often found syncopated in Palestrina, though nearly always where there are more than two parts. Cf. for ex. P. XXV, 22, 4, + 3, (augmented 4th), P. V, 133, 2, 1 (diminished 4th); P. XXVI, 37, 1, 4, (augmented 2nd); P. XIX, 75, 4, + 2, (diminished 7th). The diminished 5th occurs practically only where the contrary part continues its progression simultaneously with the progress of the syncope dissonance to its resolution; however, in this case they may also be met with in 2-part composition. (Refer to P. XIV, 8, 4, 3). The augmented 5th, on the contrary, is used equally as little by Palestrina in syncopation as the remaining augmented and diminished intervals.

Quite a common occurrence in the music of the 15th and 16th centuries is the coincident appearance of several syncope dissonances. One of the oldest forms—perhaps the very oldest type of this kind of syncope dissonance—is the double suspension of the 4th and 7th:

Sturgeon: Sanctus. Oldh. III. 56, 3,+2.

Leonel: Sanctus. Oldh. III, 65, 4,+2.

Tr. I, 198, 4, 2. Dunstable, Motet: Sub tuam protectionem.

About 1420-50 it was very popular. In the course of a century, however, it had fallen into disuse, and in Palestrina we only find it employed as an exception.[1]

---

[1] See P. V, 58, 3, 2. P. XII, 72, 4, + 2; 107, 3, 4; 112, 3, 2. P. II, 8, 3, 5. P. VIII, 88, 1, 3; 110, 4, 1. P. XVIII, 88, 3, + 2.

Yet in so relatively late a composer as Costanzo Festa, the first great composer of the Roman school, it is still to be found:

Costanzo Festa, Motet: Regem Regum. M. I. 53, 4, 2.

Instead, the $^6/_4$ chord with double ties played a prominent role with Italian composers, while the Netherlanders seem not quite to have appreciated the tonal beauty of this effect:

P. V, 14, 3, + 4. Motet: Tribus miraculis.

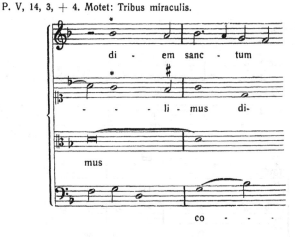

Also in cases where only the 4th was syncopated, the Italian treatment of the $^6/_4$ chord had its own typical character. A case like the following from Costanzo Festa is scarcely to be found in the works of earlier masters:

Motet: Hierusalem, quae occidis. (Jacob Modernus: 3. lib. motettorum 1538.)

whereas it might almost seem to be the preliminary, somewhat unfinished sketch of the following splendidly developed episode in Palestrina's motet:

P. V, 55, 2, + 4. Motet: Beatus Laurentius.

A few more quotations are given which are marked by a rather rude treatment of the double dissonance on Palestrina's part:

P. XI, 129, 1, + 1. Missa: Papae Marcelli.[1])

P. XII, 61, 4, 3. Missa: Brevis.

However, phrases of this order are rare with the Roman school, and the same applies to the triple dissonance:

[1] Refer to analogous cases in P. III, 66, 3, 4 and P. XXIX, 168, 2, 4.

P. XXXI, 93, 4. 3. Hymnus: Magnae Deus potentiae. (Cf. P. XXXI, 92, 2, 1; 96, 3. 3.)

though it had been used quite often by earlier composers. Compare, for instance,

Brumel, Motet: Laudate Dominum. Maldeghem 1875, 5, 3, + 3. (Cf. 1875, 6, 3, + 1. A. f. M.II258, 2, + 2 [Adam Rener].)

After this investigation of the introduction and nature of syncope dissonance, it now remains to observe its continuation. When vocal polyphony was at its height, this continuation was accomplished almost without exception by the descending step of a second. Deviations from this rule may be observed especially in the 15th century. Though the descending continuation was the usu.. one in this era also, yet we encounter cases where the resolution is brought about by an ascending progression:

Cook: Et in terra. Oldh. I, 33, 2, 3.

Tr. I, 198, 5, + 1. Dunstable. Motet: Sub tuam protectionem. (Cf. Tr. II, 23, 4, + 3.

Obr. I, 34, 2, 3. Missa: Je ne demande. (Cf. Obr. I, 119, 2, + 2.)

Josquin des Prés. ¹) Missa: De beata Virgine. Et in spiritum, bar 60. (Cf, Is. III, 166, 3, + 1).

Such a mode of treating the syncope dissonance does not come within the scope of Palestrina's style. It should be mentioned here that all instances in Palestrina's works where ascending syncope dissonance is employed as minims, are based upon faulty transcriptions or misprints. Thus Espagne misunderstood the following:

P. V, 98, 3, 4. Motet: Gaudent in coelis.

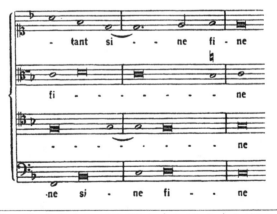

---

¹ See further: Obr. I, 40, 1, 2 and 3; 139, 1, + 1; 144, 1, + 2; 162, 1, + 1; 178, 2, + 1. Obr. II, 94, 1, 2; 128, 1, 2. Obr. III, 109, 4, + 1; 156, 2, + 2. Obr. IV, 55, 4, 2; 94, 2, 2. Obr. VI, 123, 1, + 1; 128, 1, 2. Obr. VII, 47, 5, 3; 89, 3, + 2 (Pipelare). Is. I, 24, 5, + 2. Is. III, 166, 4, 1; 220, 2, 2. Josquin des Prés: Missa "Didadi", Gloria, bar 37; Missa "Sine nomine", Pleni, bar 27.

In the soprano, which is given in the first volume of 4-part motets, (Soldus, Rome 1622), as

he mistook the stroke for a "punctum additionis" while it is really intended as a "punctum divisionis", which signifies that the semibreve F before the breve, (the time being "Perfect"), must be altered. This place then assumes quite a normal appearance:

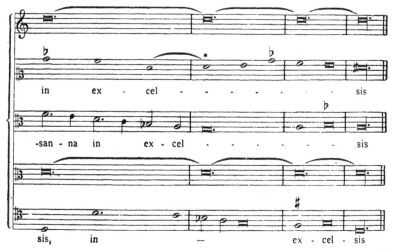

Likewise, the following is attributable to a faulty transcription:

P. XIII, 79, 2, + 4. Missa: Eripe me de inimicis meis.

Tenor I., (the middle voice) in the original edition, 4th vol. of masses (Gardano, Venice, 1582) is given thus:

As the notation in the black characters denotes "Perfect" mensuration, it should result in the following natural conclusion:[1]

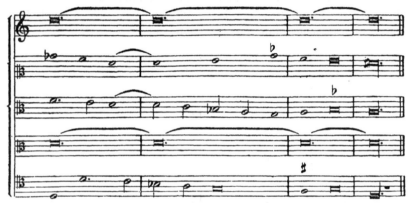

When the dissonant relationship has the duration of a crotchet's value, however, it quite often happens that Palestrina lets the syncope dissonance continue upward the degree of a second:

---

[1] Concerning misprints, in this connection, I do not think it necessary to go into much detail, but only point out the following cases. The second note in the upper voice in P. XI, 7, 2, + 1, according to the edition of the II. Vol. of Masses (Gardano, Venice 1598) should only be a minim, and not tied over to the next bar; the second note in 7, 3, 2 (in the same part) is consequently not a minim, but a semibreve—the notes lying between these two retaining the rhythmic form of Haberl's edition. Likewise the second note in the upper voice in P. XII, 161, 2, 3, to agree with the original edition of the III. Vol. of Masses, (Valerius and Doricus, Rome, 1570), should be a semibreve, while the third note, on the contrary, should only be a minim. Also the third note in the tenor in P. XIII, 1, 2, + 2 should, to agree with the orig. ed., IV. Vol. of Masses (Gardano, Venice, 1582), be a minim, and the fourth a semibreve; in like manner the first note of the tenor in P. III, 16, 3, 4 (by comparison with the orig. ed., III Vol. of 5, 7, and 8-part Motets, Scotus, Venice, 1575), should be a minim; the second note, however, must be a dotted semibreve; finally the first note in the upper part in P. XX, 15, 3, + 3 to agree with the orig. ed., (Scotus, Venice, 1600), should be a semibreve without dot, succeeded by a half-note pause. The apparent examples of ascending resolutions of the syncope dissonance are eliminated through the corrections in all these instances.

P. V, 38, 4, 2.[1]) Motet: Fuit homo. (Cf. P. XIII, 43, 1, + 3.)

It is curious that the dissonance in all these instances falls upon the relatively unaccented beat. Palestrina employs it solely in this manner (as a rare exception compare P. XIII, 7, 4, + 2), while, on the other hand, earlier Netherland and English composers are observed to have used it also on fully accented beats. For example:

Obr. I, 3, 3, 2. Missa: Je ne demande.

[1] Other instances: P. X, 4, 3, + 2; 4, 4, 4; 43, 1, 2; 55, 3, 1. P. V, 55, 3, + 4; 55, 3, + 3; 68, 1, 2. P. XI, 90, 4, + 1. P. I, 11, 3, + 2; 30, 3, 4; 34, 1, 4; 54, 3, 4; 91, 3, 1. P. XII, 25, 3, 1; 88, 1, 4; 103, 1, 1; 125, 3, + 2; 146, 2, 4. P. II, 14, 3, 1; 17, 1, + 1; 19, 1, 4; 95, 3, 4; 104, 1, + 2; 166, 1, 4. P. III, 57, 3, + 2. P. V, 136, 3, 4; 156, 3, 2. P. XIII, 114, 2, + 1. P. IV, 38, 1, 1. P. XXV, 41, 1, + 2; 73, 3, + 4; 74, 4, + 3; 76, 2, + 1. P. VIII, 49, 3, + 1; 77, 3, + 3; 140, 3, + 2; 153, 3, + 2. P. XIV, 34, 2, 4; 85, 3, 4; 95, 2, 3; 118, 1, 4. P. XXVII, 27, 1, + 2. P. IX, 68, 2, + 2; 188, 2, 4. P. XV, 134, 3, 3; 138, 4, 5. P. XVI, 31, 3, 1; 37, 3, + 4; 40, 1, 2; 86, 1, 2; 100, 2, + 3. P. XVII, 37, 3, + 2; 123, 2, 4. P. XVIII, 11, 3, + 2; 21, 2, + 1; 79, 3, 1; 109, 2, + 3; 122, 1, + 2. P. XIX, 9, 4, + 1; 49, 3, 3; 70, 3, 2. P. XX, 54, 1, 2. P. XXII, 107, 2, 4; 118, 4, + 1; 138, 4, 2. P. XXIV, 72, 3, + 3; 73, 1, + 4; 95, 5, 3.

Pierre de la Rue: Salve Regina. Maldeghem 1882, 4, 1, 3.

Christopher Tye, Missa[1]): Euge bone. The old English edition. X, 3, 2, 1.

In Palestrina music this form of treating the dissonance would only be used on the first and third minims of the measure when the continuation of the dissonance descends:

P. V, 97, 1. 2.[1]) Motet: Gaudent in coelis.

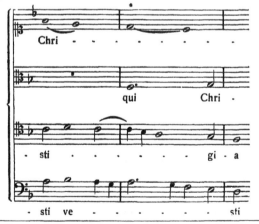

---

[1] This form is very frequent in works of 16th century English composers. It is such a particular favourite with Tye as to amount to a typical, styliform characteristic. (Refer to Morris, l. c. p. 68).

P. XV, 39, 2, 1[1].Missa: In te Domine speravi.

In the opposite case, placed upon the second and fourth minim, the resolution is accomplished equally as often through ascending as descending progression.[2]

It seems plausible therefore to assume that in Palestrinian music only the tie upon the first and third minim was understood as genuine suspension, the crotchet syncope upon the unaccented minim presumably not being felt as real syncope dissonance. Certainly it is dissonance, and if continued, its further progression consequently requires conjunct movement. But its continuation is in itself not obligatory, as it is in the case of the syncope dissonance. In the example P. V, 38, 4, 2 (p. 263) there would not be the slightest objection to allowing the soprano to lie stationary upon the *A*, while the part next to the upper, with its dissonant crotchet, is continuing. And what applies in this case is applicable to almost all the other similar cases in Palestrina. But if we suppose the example just mentioned placed upon accented minims and the note-values doubled, the syncope dissonance would require continuation, and would appear as a veritable, irregularly treated suspension.

---

[1] Compare also: P. XI, 20, 3, + 4. P. XIV, 31, 3, + 3.

[2] As examples of the last mentioned form, reference may be made also to the following: P. X, 95, 1, 4; 118, 3, + 3. P. V, 43, 1, + 2; 72, 2, + 2; 73, 4, + 2. P. XI, 5, 2, 2; 20, 3, + 4; 103, 2, 4; 112, 1, + 2; 119, 4, 4. P. XII, 23, 3, 4; 27, 1, + 1; 142, 3, + 1; 187, 4, 2; 193, 1, 4. P. II, 13, 3, 2; 73, 3, + 1; 152, 1, + 2. P. V, 119, 2, 3; 157, 4, 1; 181, 2, + 1. P. VIII, 148, 2, 3; 150, 2, 4. P. XIV, 6, 3, + 3; 69, 2, 3; 79, 3, 4;

Although the practice of conjunct continuation of the syncope dissonance is followed as an almost invariable rule by 15th and 16th
century composers, we find exceptions, even in the works of Palestrina:

P. V, 26, 1, 3.[1]) Motet: Jesus junxit. (Cf. P. XII, 146, 3, + 3.)

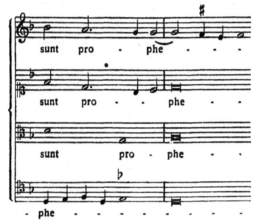

We have to do here with an ornamental amplification of the syncope dissonance, which undertakes (before proceeding to final resolution into its second below) a leap to the third below. It sometimes
happens with Palestrina and his contemporaries that the interposed
note is dissonant:

108, 2, + 3; 117, 2, + 4. P. IX, 148, 2, + 1. P. XV, 74, 4, 4. P. XVI, 82, 3, + 3.
P. XXIX, 122, 1, 1; 136, 2, + 2. P. XVII, 85, 2, + 3. P. XVIII, 135, 3, 2. P. XIX, 101,
2, 3; 118, 1, 1. P. XX, 75, 1, 3. P. XXI, 100, 2, 1. P. XXII, 57, 2, 4; 69, 3, 3; 73, 1, + 2.
P. XXIII, 4, 1, 3; 21, 4, + 1. P. XXIV, 43, 3, 4.—Dissonance in this rhythmic form is
not very often met with in Palestrina style, (nor is it of common occurrence in the
preceding epoch of style); the usual duration of the syncope dissonance here is,
as stated before, of minim value.

[1] See also: P. X, 49, 5, + 2; 126, 1, + 2; 128, 4, + 2; P. XXVIII, 19, 2, 3; 20, 2, 2;
P. XI, 27, 2, + 2; 38, 3, 1; 84, 4, + 2. P. I, 9, 3, 2; 16, 3, + 3; 116, 1, + 2. P. XII, 9, 3.
1; 30, 1, + 2; 39, 5, + 2; 51, 4, 3; 52, 2, 4; 54, 2, + 4; 58, 3, + 1. P. XIV, 124, 1, 1.
P. IX, 81, 1, 1; 99, 3, 4; 110, 1, 2. P. XVI, 10, 1, 2. P. XVII, 44, 3, + 2; 87, 1, + 4.
P. XIX, 127, 3, 4; 130, 3, + 3. P. XXII, 21, 1, + 1. P. XXIV, 92, 2, 4; 104, 1, 4 and
+ 2; 104, 2, 3.

P. XI, 68, 2, 1.¹) Missa: Ad fugam. (Compare the interesting variant P. XXIII 95, 1, + 3.)

Analogóus cases in Palestrina's own compositions are extremely seldom observed. On the whole, this kind of resolution of suspension dissonance is mainly encountered in works by masters of the First and Second Netherland Schools.² By the end of the 16th century it had become an antiquated form.

This remark is applicable to a still higher degree with regard to the figure which arises from the interposition of the 5th below the

---

¹ Similar examples: P. XXVIII, 50, 3, 3. P. XII, 6, 1, 1; 58, 4, 1. P. II, 68, 3, + 3 (Sylla). Examples where the inserted third below occurs on the unaccented minim are rare in Palestrina. However, consult the following: P. XI, 149, 2, + 2; 149, 3, 2. P. I, 34, 1, 4. P. XV, 75, 2, + 2. P. XXI, 81, 3, + 2.

² Additional examples: Tr. I, 81, 1, 6; 81, 3, 5; 85, 2, + 2; 95, 2, 9; 142, 3, 4; 169, 1, 6; 175, 1, 2; 175, 3, 3; 178, 4, 5; 180, 4, + 2; 181, 4, 6; 184, 3, + 3; 188, 1, 4; 190, 5, 5; 194, 4, + 2; 214, 4, + 2; 219, 4, 2; 220, 3, 4; 220, 4, 3; 223, 6, + 1; 224, 1, 5; 231, 1, 3; 235, 4, 4; 240, 1, 2; 248, 4, 3-6 and + 2; 261, 5, 2; 262, 3, 6-7; 270, 1, 3; 271, 2, + 2; 271, 5, 2. Tr. II, 1, 2, 4; 5, 1, + 1; 12, 2, 2; 16, 1, 3; 16, 2, 3; 17, 5, 1; 17, 5, + 2; 48, 4, + 1; 49, 4, + 3; 52, 2, 1; 57, 3, 1; 58, 3, + 2; 60, 1, 4; 76, 2, 3; 87, 5, 5; 88, 1, + 2; 94, 3, + 2; 95, 1, 1; 101, 3, 2; 105, 2, + 2; 108, 4, 3; 112, 4, + 1. Tr. III, 23, 4, + 3; 24, 2, + 3; 31, 3, 1; 43, 4, + 3; 44, 4, 3; 60, 1, 3; 60, 4, 1; 63, 4, + 4; 64, 1, + 2; 64, 2, + 3; 64, 3, 4; 64, 3, + 3; 68, 3, 1; 69, 1, + 1; 70, 4, 1; 70, 4, + 2; 71, 3, 2; 72, 1, 1; 74, 1, 3; 74, 4, 3; 77, 4, 2; 97, 2, 7; 98, 3, + 3; 101, 1, 2; 110, 1, 3; 121, 1, + 3; 126, 1, 4; 126, 3, + 3; 143, 2, + 2; 151, 4, 1; 172, 5, 2. Obr. III, 85, 1, 3. Obr. IV, 23, 1, 3; 92, 3, + 1; 99, 2, 1; 100, 2, 2; 102, 3, 2; 108, 1, + 1; 147, 3, + 1; 148, 4 3; 178, 4, 1; 215, 3, 2. Obr. V, 27, 4, 2; 45, 2, 1; 88, 2, 1-2; 88, 3, 2. Is. I, 11, 3, 3; 41, 4, + 3; 152, 2, 4; 152, 4, + 1; 192, 3, 2; 207, 4, 1; 207, 5, 1. Josquin des Prés: Missa "Fortuna desperata", Et incarnatus, bar 48; Missa "Hercules", Credo, bar 35; Missa "Lami baudichon", Gloria, bar 48; Missa "Faisant regres", Gloria, bar 6; ibid., Credo, bar 61; ibid., Osanna, bar 11 etc.

syncope dissonance between the dissonance and its resolution. As far as my own observation goes, this occurs but once in the whole collection of Palestrina's compositions:[1]

P. XIII, 1, 4, 1. Missa: Lauda Sion.

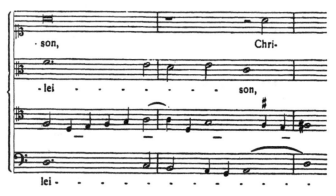

Yet it was comparatively often used by Netherland composers of the 15th and early 16th centuries.

Obr. III, 53, 3, + 1. Missa: Si dedero.[2])

---

[1] In consonant conjunction, however, it is often found, as a comparison with Ornament 29, (p. 62) shows. Incidentally, its dissonant form played a prominent role later in the music of the 17th and 18th centuries. The fact that Fux employs it to such an extent in his Gradus is probably due to his borrowing unconsciously from the musical dialect of his own time. It by no means belongs to Palestrina's style.

[2] Compare also: Obr. III, 34, 4, + 1. Obr. VI, 103, 2, + 2. Obr. VII, 87, 4, + 3 (Brumel). Is. 141, 5, 3. Josquin des Prés: Motet "Factum est" (Motetti C), bar 153. Crequillon: Motet "Ave virgo gloriosa" (Maldeghem 1876, 29, 1, + 3).

Its placing here, however, clearly indicates that the foremost consideration has been the melodic embellishment of the syncopated relationship, and that the question of consonance or dissonance was regarded as of secondary importance. Both the syncope and the intervening note are often dissonant:

Tr. I, 223, 4, 4.[1]) Johannes Martini: La martinella. (Josquin des Prés, Missa Da pacem. Benedictus, bar 47.)

It may also happen that the intervening note alone is dissonant:

Is. II, 8, 2, 3.[2]) Lied: Es het ein Baur ein Töchterlein. (Cf. Is. I, 10, 3, + 3.'

[1] See also: Obr. III, 169, 1, 2. Obr. IV, 127, 4, + 2 (Anonym). Is. I, 105, 4, + 3; 7, 3, 2; 164, 3, + 2; 208, 4, + 2. Is. II, 103, 4, + 2.

[2] Cf. Josquin des Prés: Motet "Propter peccata" ("Novum et insigne opus musicum", Nürnberg, Graphaeus 1537), bar 6. Is. I: 202, 3, 4. Is. II, 8, 2, 3.

Pre-Palestrinian composers had besides at their disposal other methods for the melodic embellishment of the syncope, and did not particularly concern themselves with regard to the resulting consonance or dissonance:

Obr. V, 90, 1, + 3. Missa: Lomme armé. (Cf. Obr, I, 202, 4, + 1 and Is. II. 48, 2, 4.)

Tr. I, 224, 2. + 2.[1]) Johannes Martini: La martinella.

And in the beginning of the 16th century it was not taken amiss that the resolution of syncope dissonance was delayed still more, or even wanting altogether; for example:

---

[1] Cf. Obr. I, 128, 4, 3; 129, 1, 1; 203, 1, 3. Obr. II, 124, 3, 1. Obr. IV, 152, 4, 3; 168, 4, + 2; 185, 4, 3. Obr. V, 7, 3, 2; 8, 4, 1; 85, 5, 1; 89, 1, + 1; 89, 2, + 1. Obr. VI, 39, 2, + 3. Is. I, 7, 3, + 1; 13, 3, 3; 144, 1, 1; 209, 5, + 1; 209, 5, 4; 223, 4, 4. Is. II, 24, 2, 3; 60, 1, 2; 117, 6, + 3. Is. III, 46, 3, 3; 143, 1, 2; 146, 1, 3; 148, 8, 3; 157, 2, 1; 217, 3, 4.

Constanzo Festa, Missa: de B. M. V. Agnus I, bar 12.

Josquin des Prés. Missa: Malheur me bat. Incarnatus, bar 64.[1])

With Netherland as with Italian composers, it happens quite frequently that the part counterpointing to the syncope dissonance progresses simultaneously with the movement of the dissonance towards
its resolution. There is really nothing remarkable in this fact, and no
special rules attach to this eventuality, except of course that it must
proceed to a note which is consonant with the note of resolution of the
dissonance. However, it may also happen that the part counterpointing
to the syncope continues, before the latter is resolved. In such an
eventuality, it is noticed that Palestrina either lets the part having
the most rapid movement turn upon the note,

---

[1] Cf. Artusi: "L'arte del Contraponto", p. 40.

P. XXIII, 73, 2, 2.[1]) Missa: O sacrum convivium.

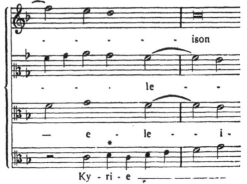

or else move either up or down two degrees, (counting from the dissonant collision with the syncope), in the same direction:

P. XVIII. 4. 4, + 2. Missa: Ave Regina coelorum. (Cf. P. XVI. 32, 4, + 3.)

P. V, 82, 2, + 1. Motet: Doctor bonus.

---

[1] Compare also P. XXI, 130, 3, 1 and P. XXII, 20, 4, 3, this treatise, p. 145—146.

273

P. V, 118, 2, 2. Motet: Domine quando veneris. (Cf. P. XIX, 88, 1, 5.)

rae tu -

- vul - tu   i - - rae

Concerning passing and ornamental dissonance the same rules apply in Palestrina's music to triple as to duple (even-numbered) time.[1]

With respect to the syncope dissonance, it appears that it occurs more frequently upon the second minim than—as it would be natural to expect—upon the first.[2] This is due to the syncope dissonance being most often used in forming conclusions; consequently in triple time, (in which the conclusion falls customarily upon the first note of the measure in cadences), it is desirable to hear the leading-note immediately before the end, (that is, on the third unit), and the result is that the suspension (preceding the leading-note) falls upon the second unit. Occasionally Palestrina placed the syncope dissonance upon the third unit in triple time. For instance:

---

[1] It must be remarked, however, that while in duple time the time unit (minim) may be employed as a passing dissonance, only the last half of the unit may be so employed in triple time, (for instance in $^3/_1$, the 2nd, 4th, and 6th minim). It is therefore not altogether correct that Fux teaches, (Fux-Mizler, p. 77), that the second minim in $^1/_2$ time may be dissonantly employed, or that Bellermann ("Contrapunkt", p. 172) and Haller ("Kompositionslehre", p. 42) would extend this privilege also to the third minim.

[2] Fr. Nekes was the first to draw attention to this circumstance. Cf. Gregoriusblatt 1892, p. 81.

P. XI, 66, 2, +1[1]) Missa: Ad fugam.

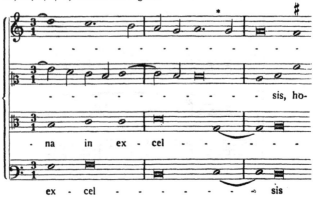

Still it is only possible for us to understand places like this as an accentual alteration, since it is the nature of suspension to be resolved upon unaccented beats. We therefore feel that the note of resolution is not accented, no matter how much the notation may substantiate the opposite. In this case we are obliged to reckon with a rhythmical change which would alter the notation, (if the bar lines in the foregoing example are to agree with the accents), in the following manner:

Instead of two bars of ³/₁, we get one bar with three breves, by which change, (the semibreve being still the unit), the syncope dis-

---

[1] Compare with this, the following: Obr. IV, 110, 1, + 2. Is. II, 37, 6, + 2; 39, 4, + 3; 42, 5, + 3. Is. III, 48, 1, 1. P. X, 24, 2, + 2; 24, 4, + 3; 50, 1, 3. P. V, 5, 1, 6; 5, 2, 5; 37, 4, 3. P. XI, 66, 4, + 3; 67, 1, + 3. P. XII, 43, 3, 3; 44, 1, + 4; 44, 3, 4; 92, 1, + 3. P. III, 38, 3, 4; 140, 4, + 4. P. VIII, 125, 3, + 1. P. XVII, 50, 4, 1. P. XXII, 153, 1, 1. P. XXIII, 16, 2, 3; 44, 5, + 3.

sonance in the soprano, as well as in the alto, falls upon an accented unit, and is prepared and resolved upon unaccented units. Such a transition into a larger time occurs especially in final cadences in triple time. There is certainly a psychological connection here with the "mora vocis" of plainsong and, as in the latter, also the desire for a convincing, broadly developed conclusive effect.

We can trace this feature back as far as to English 15th century composers. An example is

Anonym: "I Pray zow alle" (ca. 1450), Stainer: Early Bodleyan Music", p. 87.

Composers of the 16th century especially made extensive use of it, but also those of the 17th and 18th knew and employed it.[1]

The following very rarely used phrase should be classed, it seems to me, at any rate under change of accent:

P. XI, 99, 1, + 2.[2]) Missa: Salvum me fac.

---

[1] See Hugo Riemann: "Gedehnte Schlüsse im Tripeltakt der Altklassiker". Z. I. M. XV, p. 3, compare with this the critical remarks of Hermann Roth, ibid., p. 95.

[2] Refer to P. XXV, 61, 4, 1. (Cf. Casimiri, "Codice 59", p. 65). P. XXIX, 145, 3, + 2 and P. XXXII, 133, 2, + 3 (d.).

Rinaldo del Mel(?): Magnificat 4. Maldeghem 1875, 46, 3, 7–8.

It is more natural to assume a transition here to triple time, by which means the dissonance would fall upon the second unit, than to suppose the dissonance resolved upon the accented part of the measure; for the syncope dissonance is so heavy that it would surely assert itself even if immediately preceded by an accent. But precisely for this reason it is impossible, as already stated, to perceive the beat which succeeds the syncope otherwise than as unaccentuated.

Dissonance as a Means of Poetical Expression.

Franchinus Gafurius writes in the year 1496 in his "Practica musicae" (Chapter 14) about a certain kind of "contrapunctus falsus" which was the fashion in Milan at that time. It was constructed upon a liturgical melody, which was accompanied (Organum-like) by dissonances, (mostly seconds and fourths). It was used, as Franchinus tells us, according to the precepts of St. Ambrosius, in masses for the dead and vigils for martyrs, which disorder so vexed Fr. that he could scarcely bring himself to write of it.[1] This might appear to be the earliest evidence of dissonance as a means of interpreting the text (in the expression of sorrow or pain). But the phenomenon of which Gafu-

---

[1] Cf. J. Handschin: Zur Ambrosianischen Mehrstimmigkeit ("Aus der alten Musiktheorie" III, Acta 1943, p. 2 etc.) Compare also Ernst Th. Ferand: The "Howling in Seconds" of the Lombards. The Musical Quarterly. New York 1939, p. 313 etc.

rius writes is probably quite an isolated one, and at any rate his assertion is (to my knowledge) not substantiated by other writers nor
practically in musical works.[1] However this may be, it is not unlikely
that in a period where the "duritas" of the dissonance was clearly understood, and where precautions were observed in its use for this very
reason, there was no better known means, when the point at issue was
to interpret musically an oppressed or painful effect, than the amassing
of discords. The important fact here is that this music had nothing
to do with art—it was not considered seriously by the well informed
musicians of the period, and had no influence upon style. The freer
treatment of the dissonance in order to serve textual ends, which
scarcely goes back further than to the Italian madrigalists, differed
from the case just mentioned in being characterized by no infringement of the generally valid musical laws of the epoch, but only by
an occasional (and often very delicately shaded) extension of the exist-
ing regulations. When Palestrina in his madrigal, "Se amarissimo
fiele", (If the bitterest gall), seeks to express the text in the following
combination of notes, (P. XXIX, 129, 1):

---

[1] It is entirely incomprehensible to me that Ambros should write concerning Jhan
de Gero's Motet, "O Roche beatissime": "Die herben Wehelaute, absichtlich und
zum Teil überkühn eingeführte harte Dissonanzen, die unvermutheten Harmonie-
wendungen haben etwas Erschreckendes. Vielleicht hat Gero seine erste Anregung
von den alten dissonierenden Todtenlitaneien erhalten". (Ambr. III, 585). I have
scored Gero's composition from the "Symphonia quatuor modulata vocibus excell.
(vulgo nuncupati) Metre Jehan, quae alias Motecta nominantur. Venetiis apud Hie-
ronymus Scotum 1543", (the only edition which gives it). It is a beautiful and serious
composition, as good as the best of its time, but by no means exceptional with
especial respect to dissonance treatment. With regard to this point, it could just
as well have been written by either Obrecht or Josquin des Prés. Perhaps the brilliant
but at times rather too impulsive imagination of Ambros was aroused by a couple
of augmented triads, which Gero treats, however, quite correctly according to the
rules for syncope dissonance, which was employed quite frequently in this way
about the year 1540, without being to any degree subject to textual conditions.
(Refer, for instance, to Willaert's "Pater noster", Ambr. V, 539, 1, + 2.) There is
nothing here, however, of "überkühn eingeführten Dissonanzen", and still less of
tonal combinations which might lead one to think of the "barbarous", funereal music
of which Gafurius writes.

Se a-ma-ris-si-mo fie - - le e mor-tal

Se a ma--ris-si-mo fie-le e mor-

Se a - ma-ris-si-mo

Se a-ma-ris-si-mo fie-

Se a-

the manner of treating the dissonance, though of striking effect, is really a well-known one which, under ordinary circumstances, does not need any textual motive to explain its employment. That which gives the "amarissimo", however, is the increased harshness which the form receives through the employment of only 2 parts in the counterpoint, with the minor second and major seventh as dissonances, while otherwise it is mostly used with more parts and only with milder dissonances, (the major second and its inversion, the minor seventh).[1] The following likewise

---

[1] See p. 240.

P. V, 122, 1, + 3. Motet: Heu mihi Domine.

is a variant of the same form, (the dissonantly introduced syncope dissonance), where the circumstance of the $^6/_4$ chord lying immovable and inanimate, with not a single voice marking the accented part of the measure, seems to express the deep penitence and impotence of the words, "Quid faciam miser?" On the whole, it almost seems as if the $^6/_4$ chord with the double suspension, (without replacing the 4th on the accented beat by a stronger dissonance), was felt as an especially harsh effect in this period. Palestrina thus employs it mainly in conjunction with such sombre-coloured words as "aspri", (P. XXIX, 181, 1, 1), "l'empia" (P. XXVIII, 98, 3, 2), "crudelis" (P. XXV, 142, 1, 4; 203, 2, + 2).

It must be characterized as pronounced madrigalism (in the least favourable interpretation of the word: a mere play), when Palestrina symbolizes "fallo" (fault) by such an irregularly treated $^6/_4$ chord as in

P. XXIX, 24, 2 + 2. Madrigal: Vergine sola al mondo.

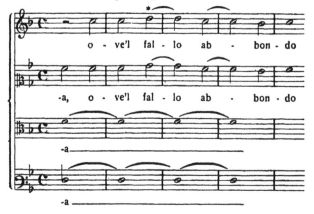

or when in the motet, "Peccavimus cum patribus nostris", (obviously influenced by the madrigal), he is instigated by the words "injuste egimus" (we have acted unjustly) to a breach of the laws of style, (as I believe, the only instance in his whole artistic career), by introducing the passing 4th in relation to the bass upon the accented beat.[1]

---

[1] This episode can hardly be accounted for, like P. XXV, 59, 4, + 4 sqq. and 73, 3, + 3, (compare p. 233 sqq.) as being due to pedal dissonance. This is partly because it is introduced while the composition in which it appears is still in full process of development; the two instances named both appear in cadences, (which is characteristic of pedal effects). In the second place, it is because the dissonance in the motet is introduced shortly after the stationary note's entrance. But the psychological explanation of pedal lies precisely in the fact that one voice, by retaining its position while the other voices continue, separates itself so distinctly from the latter that both are heard independently. However, the conditions for this mode of hearing require the stationary voice to manifest its will to appear independently of the others *before* tonal combinations are introduced which—if the stationary note is considered in connection with them—are incomprehensible. Therefore the dissonance upon "injuste" is not perceived as a pedal, while on the contrary the G in P. XXV, 59, 4, + 3 has already been placed so long before the offending C is introduced, that the correct impression is assured beforehand. With respect to P. XXV, 73, 3, + 3, where the dissonance (as in P. IV, 158, 2, 3) enters two minims after the entrance of the stationary note, the circumstance that the tonal combinations in the third bar from the end are exactly the same upon the first and third minim, probably, by a little vertical encroachment, causes the linear difference to be overheard—a not unusual example of musical mimicry.

P. IV, 158, 2, 3.

Padre Martini in his work, "Exemplare ossia saggio fondamentale pratico di contrappunto", (1774-75, Vol. II, p. 76), draws attention to a severely dissonant episode in Palestrina's Madrigal: "Alla riva del tebro". To such an inciting text as "Saziati, o cruda Dea, della mia acerba e rea", (Sate thyself, O cruel Goddess, in my bitter and outrageous [death]), Palestrina summons all the violent discords that he can possibly command, (P. XXVIII, 106, 1, + 1):

It is noteworthy, however, that none of these dissonance forms are treated in a revolutionary way. The dissonantly introduced ⁶/₄ chord at a) only represents, like b) and d), a freer treatment of the "consonant 4th", and the double passing dissonance at c) may often be met with in Palestrina's compositions in connection with quite indifferent words, (cf. for instance P. X, 118, 3, + 3).

The striking effect in this instance is partly to be attributed to the form of treatment which, usually only employed where the unit is the minim, is used here in conjunction with a crotchet unit, and is consequently more conspicuous. But this effect is also and especially due to the unusual concentration of dissonances which, in the short space of 9 bars, is found here.

A similar amassment of dissonances may be observed in the madrigal,

„Ecc'oscurati" (P. XXVIII, 55, 3, 1):

There is scarcely a doubt that in this case it is the text which gives rise to such an extraordinarily extensive use of dissonance. It is particularly interesting that all the dissonances in this quotation receive a perfectly regular treatment; it is not, therefore, the manner of treatment, but the number of dissonances which produces the marked effect.

From this circumstance the query arises whether other effects with Palestrina, beyond those apparent at the first glance, may not also be classed as expressional dissonance. If Palestrina in this case depicts "cruel death" merely by amassing dissonances in their most legitimate treatment, it is conceivable that upon other occasions (where the text invites it) he should have given his compositions a tragic colour solely by a fuller employment of dissonances than he otherwise affects, without utilizing any particularly free form of dissonance treatment. The query is: Did Palestrina use dissonance as a means of poetic expression apart from the instances of rarely used madrigalism, just discussed?

In order to clear up this question, I have undertaken a comparison between the "Crucifixus" and "Benedictus" of all the works in his 15 volumes of masses. These texts were chosen especially because they denote a very decided contrast of mood, and because they differ so widely in their musical treatment by later composers.[1] Judging from an ordinary musical standpoint, there seems to have been no very obvious difference with regard to the dissonance treatment in the

---

[1] While the "Benedictus" most often is a delicate idyl, the "Crucifixus" has generally dissonances of an intense, violent effect. It is only necessary to recall, in this connection, Lotti's 6-part "Crucifixus", or that in Bach's B minor Mass.

two fragments of the masses under consideration. For the purpose of eventually verifying this observation, I deemed it expedient to calculate the "dissonant percentage", meaning by this term the percentage of rhythmic units in all these fragments of Palestrina masses which are dissonant. For practical reasons I chose the crotchet as the rhythmic unit, the dissonance of a crotchet's duration counting as one point, the dissonance of minim value two points, etc. Where two or more dissonances occur simultaneously, each is counted separately. In the "Crucifixus" I examined the episode "Crucifixus etiam pro nobis", and an equal number of bars from the corresponding "Benedictus". The result is given in the following table:

Crucifixus

	In "Pierluigi da Palestrina's Werke"	Number bars exam.	Number syncope diss.	Number pass. diss.	Number orn. diss.	Total diss.
Missarum liber primus	Vol. X	118.0	96	70.5	26.5	193.0
Missarum liber secundus	Vol. XI	110.5	86	75.5	18.5	180.0
Missarum liber tertius..........	Vol. XII	131.0	114	86.5	13.5	214.0
Missarum liber quartus.........	Vol. XIII	99.0	69	61.0	25.5	155.5
Missarum liber quintus.........	Vol. XIV	100.0	75	57.0	24.0	156.0
Missarum liber sextus	Vol. XV	108.0	82	70.5	29.5	182.0
Missarum liber septimus	Vol. XVI	77.0	57	47.0	16.5	120.5
Missarum liber octavus.........	Vol. XVII	81.0	57	50.5	16.5	124.0
Missarum liber nonus	Vol. XVIII	101.0	89	77.0	16.5	182.5
Missarum liber decimus ....:.	Vol. XIX	99.5	76	59.0	16.5	151.5
Missarum liber undecimus	Vol. XX	88.0	106	68.0	22.0	196.0
Missarum liber duodecimus	Vol. XXI	93.0	50	78.5	26.0	154.5
Missarum liber tertiusdecimus ..	Vol. XXII	68.0	38	48.5	16.5	103.0
Missarum liber quartusdecimus .	Vol. XXIII	104.5	67	72.5	20.5	160.0
Missarum liber quintusdecimus .	Vol. XXIV	111.0	101	84.5	26.5	212.0
		1489.5	1163	1006.5	315.0	2484.5

Benedictus

	In "Pierluigi da Palestrina's Werke"	Number bars exam.	Number syncope diss.	Number pass. diss.	Number orn. diss.	Total diss.
Missarum liber primus	Vol. X	118.0	70	96.0	37.5	203.5
Missarum liber secundus	Vol. XI	110.5	58	129.5	34.5	221.5
Missarum liber tertius..........	Vol. XII	131.0	92	100.5	33.5	226.0
Missarum liber quartus	Vol. XIII	99.0	74	100.5	27.5	202.0
Missarum liber quintus	Vol. XIV	100.0	58	91.5	18.0	167.5
Missarum liber sextus	Vol. XV	108.0	56	115.0	39.0	210.0
Missarum liber septimus	Vol. XVI	77.0	46	64.0	21.0	131.0
Missarum liber octavus.........	Vol. XVII	81.0	57	98.0	35.5	190.5
Missarum liber nonus	Vol. XVIII	101.0	75	72.5	40.5	188.0
Missarum liber decimus	Vol. XIX	99.5	60	103.5	13.0	176.5
Missarum liber undecimus......	Vol. XX	88.0	57	77.5	23.0	157.5
Missarum liber duodecimus	Vol. XXI	93.0	74	105.0	33.0	212.0
Missarum liber tertiusdecimus ..	Vol. XXII	68.0	41	57.0	20.5	118.5
Missarum liber quartusdecimus .	Vol. XXIII	104.5	52	122.0	33.0	207.0
Missarum liber quintusdecimus .	Vol. XXIV	111.0	85	137.0	35.5	257.5
		1489.5	955	1469.5	445.0	2869.0

Reduction to Percentage

	Syncope dissonance.	Passing dissonance.	Ornamental dissonance.	Total
Crucifixus	9.76 %	8.45 %	2.64 %	20.85 %
Benedictus	8.01 %	12.34 %	3.73 %	24.08 %

With respect to the employment of dissonance, the result shows that Palestrina made but slight difference in the two texts, the difference in the percentage of the two—20.85 against 24.08—being so insignificant as in reality to be negligible.[1] It is particularly noteworthy that the "Benedictus" fragments especially—contrary to all expectations—show a higher dissonance percentage than the "Crucifixus". The reason for this is obviously the great number of passing and ornamental dissonances in the former, (12.34 % and 3.73 % as against 8.45 % and 2.64 % respectively). On the other hand, the "Crucifixus" has the majority of the syncope dissonances, (9.76 % against 8.01 %).

It is, however, a little risky to conclude from the latter circumstance that it was Palestrina's intention to depict the Passion of the Cross by a more intense use of the specially prominent syncope dissonances.[2] For, in the first place, it often happens that a larger number of syncope

---

[1] To prevent misunderstanding, I admit that I am not unaware of the very apparent drawbacks in forming conclusions by a numeric method. In order to apply it here, I am obliged to assume different factors as being of a common denomination, without any certain proof that this is really so. For instance, it is obvious that a long dissonance leaves a stronger dissonant impression than a shorter one, and that a double dissonance is felt more intensely than a single one. However, it can not for that reason be said that a dissonance of a minim's value makes exactly four times as strong an impression as a dissonance of a quaver's duration, or that the double dissonance has twice as dissonant an effect as a single dissonance of the same duration. There is likewise the inequality of the intensity of harshness in the different dissonant intervals, without the possibility of fixing the degree of difference, for instance between the dissonance of the 7th and the 4th. All these relations cannot, on the whole, be measured in this manner. Despite hindrances I believe nevertheless that this method may be used after all, partly because I have already acquired, by general analytic methods, the decided impression that there is no preference of any particular interval, rhythmic form or dissonant complex upon any side, and partly because the problem here is not absolutely numeric, but comparative—both objects being subjected to the same principles. The strength of the dissonant impression cannot be measured, and therefore I have only measured the area of the dissonance, (proceeding, it is true, from the assumption that the former is connected with the latter in a close, even though not quite identical relation).

[2] Notwithstanding that theorists like Zarlino (Opere I, p. 439), reckon the syncope dissonance among the expressional means suitable to interpret sorrow and similar emotions.

dissonances appear in the "Benedictus" than in the "Crucifixus" of the same mass,[1] and in the second place this relationship is quite naturally explicable in a liturgic-musical way. While the "Crucifixus" most often is merely a transitory episode in the lengthy epic of the "Credo", the "Benedictus" was treated as an independently developed polyphonic composition by the masters of the 15th and 16th centuries, as the order of Divine Services allows an opportunity at this place for devout meditation. Therefore the "Benedictus" most frequently is full of passing dissonances, which are a natural consequence of the character of the piece, with its ornamentation and skilful imitations. The intenser use of the syncope dissonance in the "Crucifixus" is doubtless especially due to the circumstance that note-against-note is usually written to this text, (probably out of regard for time—to prevent a still further lengthening of the already long "Credo"). But such note-against-note pieces are most frequently used with a strong admixture of suspension, which satisfies the natural call for a break in the rhythmic monotony through the syncope, and spices the too simple harmonies by dissonance.

The result of this examination is therefore that Palestrina, with the exception of the few instances influenced by the madrigal, employs the dissonance exclusively for musical ends; and furthermore, that even when he wishes to make a more intensely dissonant effect, he rarely departs far from his ordinary manner of expression.

Those who revere him most would probably have preferred that he had held himself aloof from the exaggeration and superficiality of the madrigalists. But he lived in a period of transition, which creates difficulties, even for the greatest and purest.

---

[1] For an example, see the mass, "Memor esto" (P. XVII, p. 74 and 80), in which the number of syncope dissonances in the "Crucifixus" is five, while the "Benedictus" has fifteen.

Conclusion

The German scholar, Hugo Riemann, whose work has greatly influenced modern musical science, has given utterance to some most interesting views in different historical publications concerning the nature and development of Palestrina's style. His theory, which has by degrees received a kind of tacit acknowledgement, is that Palestrina music represents the last stage in a process of vocalization that began with Okeghem's generation. As he laconically expresses it in one place: "Das zunächst aus dem begleitenden Vokalstil des 15. Jahrhunderts in die a-cappella-Vokalmusik der Schule Okeghems (Josquin des Pres, Pierre de la Rue usw.) übergegangene instrumentale Figurenwerk wird allmählich ausgeschieden, wodurch der gereinigte Kirchenstil der Palestrinaepoche entsteht."[1]

Unfortunately Riemann has not here or elsewhere in his works given any proofs of the correctness of his assertions. Upon the basis of researches connected with the present treatise, I am forced to doubt whether on the whole it is possible to verify his statements. Apparently Hugo Riemann's opinion is that the history of the development of Palestrina's style is identical with a gradual transition from an instrumental to a vocal mode of writing, which found its musico-tech-

---

[1] "Grundriss der Musikwissenschaft", 3. impression, 1919, p. 143. That Riemann by the elimination of the "instrumental figures" really means something else, (not quite clearly explained in the "Handbuch der Musikgeschichte", cf. Bd. II, 1, 1907, p. 318 and 419 sqq.), than a limitation of the melismatas which he thinks is encountered in Palestrina in contradistinction to the earlier Netherlanders, is evident from the "Kleines Handbuch der Musikgeschichte", (1907), in which he writes (2nd. impression, p. 98): "Das erste bedeutsame Ergebnis dieses Abklärungsprozesses ist der sogenannte P a l e s t r i n a s t i l, der daher einerseits als eine Einschränkung des Reichtums der Melodik der Zeit Josquins zugunsten harmonischer Klarheit und anderseits als letzte Durchführung des Prozesses der strengen V o k a l i s i e r u n g d e s K i r c h e n s t i l s durch Ausscheidung des dem Instrumentalstile entstammenden Figurenwerks bezeichnet werden muss."

nical expression, during the process of vocalization, in gradually eliminating the ornaments and figures borrowed from instrumental sources. This, however, is a thoroughly untenable assumption. The constant recurrence of the almost refrain-like sentence, "this phrase was used consonantly and dissonantly by the early Netherland composers, while Palestrina only employed it consonantly", will be remembered from the inquiry into ornamental dissonance in this treatise.

To the example already given is added here a last, characteristic one—an ornament which may be traced back at any rate to the First Netherland School:

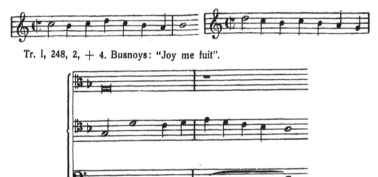

Tr. I, 248, 2, + 4. Busnoys: "Joy me fuit".

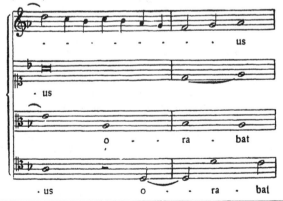

and which held its own during the entire Netherland epoch up to the time of Palestrina style:

P. V, 54, 4. 1.[1]) Motet: Beatus Laurentius.

---

[1] Compare also: P. I, 20, 3, 3; 23, 1, 1; 32, 3, + 2; 73, 2, + 2; 85, 3, + 3; 123, 2, 4; 123, 3, 2. P. II, 28, 1, 3. P. III, 18, 3, + 3; 46, 2, + 2; 60, 1, + 4; 78, 3, 4; 120, 2, 1.

In contrast to its treatment in Palestrina music, (where it can only be used with dissonance upon the 2nd, 4th and 6th crotchets, or eventually as a relatively accented passing dissonance upon the 5th crotchet), it is not very unusual to see it employed by the Netherlanders as dissonance upon the top note (3rd crotchet):

Obr. I, 218, 2, 2. Missa: Salve diva parens. (Cf. Obr. I. 190, 2, 3. Okeghem.)

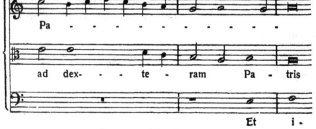

Josquin des Prés. Missa: Ad fugam, Credo, bar 9.

P. IV, 3, 1, + 3; 36, 2, + 2; 81, 1, 4; 166, 2, + 3. P. V, 26, 3, + 1; 54, 4, 1; 96, 2, 3; 107, 2, 1; 118, 3, 3; 120, 3, 3; 144, 3, 4; 151, 2, + 3. P. VIII, 9, 1, 3; 15, 2, + 2; 38, 4, + 2; 78, 2, 1; 102, 1, + 1; 114, 4, + 3; 132, 2, + 1; 147, 3, + 2; 179, 4, 1. P. IX, 4, 2, + 2; 58, 3, + 1; 64, 2, 2; 84, 1, + 2; 134, 1, + 2; 186, 3, 1. P. X, 22, 4, 1; 47, 1, 3; 119, 3, 2. P. XI, 4, 2, 4; 12, 2, + 2; 14, 1, + 2; 30, 5, 2; 41, 1, + 3; 73, 3, 3; 98, 2, + 2; 121, 3, 4. P. XII, 9, 1, + 3; 60, 1, 4; 89, 1, + 1; 129, 3, 3; 129, 5, 1 sqq.; 130, 1, 3 and + 4; 157, 4, 2. P. XIII, 10, 2, + 3; 27, 3, 2; 42, 1, 3; 55, 2, + 4 and + 3; 107, 2, 4. P. XIV, 12, 3, 4; 37, 4, + 4; 67, 3, 1; 68, 3, + 3; 77, 2, 1; 94, 1, 1; 108, 3, 2; 112, 1, + 2. P. XV, 33, 1; 1; 33, 2, 3; 35, 4, + 2; 38, 2, + 2; 56, 2, + 1; 58, 1, 1; 59, 1, + 3; 67, 2, 1; 80, 1, + 2; 112, 2, + 3; 143, 1, 5. P. XVI, 1, 1, + 2; 2, 4, + 3; 14, 4, 2; 38, 5, + 3; 43, 3, 1; 70, 2, 3; 105, 3, + 2; 106, 1, 3; 108, 3, 2. P. XVII, 12,

Indeed these ornaments are really, for the most part, the same with Okeghem as with Palestrina, with Josquin as with Victoria.[1] Certain "perihelitic" ornaments, to be sure, were gradually withdrawn, (as remarked in the foregoing pages), so that some of the melodic phrases—much used in the "Ars nova" period—became more and more rare in the course of the 15th and 16th centuries, and in Palestrina's time had almost entirely passed out of use.

Certainly it is not always easy to decide when an ornament is to be regarded as instrumental, and when vocal. The embellishments just mentioned as having been gradually discarded were all legitimate in plainsong (the purely vocal nature of which no one has ever doubted):

4, 3 and 4; 20, 1, + 2; 25, 4, 1; 44, 1, + 3; 44, 2, + 4; 49, 2, + 1; 56, 3, 3 and + 3; 57, 1, 2 and + 2; 57, 2, 3; 86, 3, 4; 93, 1, + 3; 94, 2, + 3; 105, 1, 2; 139, 3, 2. P. XVIII, 12, 2, + 3; 17, 1, + 3; 18, 4, + 1; 23, 1, 1; 31, 2, + 3; 32, 5, + 3; 33, 1, 2; 34, 4, + 1; 45, 3, 3; 80, 1, 4; 94, 1, + 2; 105, 1, + 3; 132, 4, + 1; 140, 3, + 4. P. XIX, 6, 4, + 3; 54, 3, + 3; 91, 2, 3. P. XX, 2, 3. + 1; 19, 3, 3; 26, 1, + 1; 32, 1, + 4; 83, 2, 2; 93, 2, + 3; 113, 3, + 3. P. XXI, 4, 2, 2; 7, 2, 2; 22, 1, + 4; 33, 3, + 3; 68, 1, + 4; 102, 2, + 3; 132, 3, + 1. P. XXII, 11, 2, + 2; 20, 3, + 2; 34, 4, 4; 103, 3, 1; 145, 3, 1. P. XXIII, 7, 3, 1; 48, 2, + 2; 92, 4, + 2; 96, 2, 1; 100, 1, 2; 139, 2, + 3; 143, 1, + 2 P. XXIV, 14, 4, 2; 27, 1, + 3; 37, 1, + 3; 39, 1, + 2; 128, 3, 4; 131, 2, + 1. P. XXV, 75, 3, + 2; 170, 1, 4. P. XXVII, 32, 3, 4; 64, 4, 1; 70, 2, + 1. P. XXIX, 50, 1, 3. P. XXXII, 147, 3, + 3.

[1] Unfortunately it is difficult to know exactly what Riemann really means by "instrumentalism"; however, it is true that if any phrase deserve this designation, it must certainly be the one just quoted. It is only necessary to glance cursorily at the evidently instrumental music of the 15th and 16th centuries to be convinced that this phrase was present in a much greater number of instances than in the contemporary vocal or (as Riemann thinks) partially instrumental musical art of the 15th century. From a host of examples, I have chosen the following:

Conrad Paumann (ca. 1410-1473): "Fundamentum organisandi", Jahrbücher für musikalische Wissenschaft, published by Friedrich Chrysander. II. Vol. Leipzig 1868, p. 211.

La Rote de Rode (Attaignant: 18 basses dances, 1529), Lute-Tablature. Cf. Tappert: Sang und Klang aus alter Zeit.

Also a phrase such as:

which on account of the leap from the accented first crotchet was not used in Palestrina's style, as repeatedly stated, belonged to the

favourite ornaments of the plainsong: [5] ; its elimination had,

therefore, nothing to do with the vocalization of the composition, but was a question of accent, as already noted. To summarize, this melodic evolution was of a musico-intellectual order, which in its inwardness far surpasses the constellation "vocal-instrumental", of which the style-formative potency has recently been much overrated, especially where it concerns the older music.

As previously stated, essentially the same ornaments were used in the early polyphonic as in Palestrinian music. The difference lies main- ly in the ever increasing care exercised in their employment, so that

---

[1] Consult the Graduale romanum (Vaticana), p. 4, line 6.

[2] l. c. p. 2, line 4.

[3] l. c. p. 355, line 9-356.

[4] l. c. p. 24, line 8.

[5] l. c. p. [48], line 6. According to the traditional way of executing the cantus planus, such a figure should probably be performed approximately in the tempo of crotchet movement in Palestrina music. Refer to Johner: "Neue Schule des Choral- gesanges". 5th. impression, 1921, p. 127*.

they should only be used in connections which would not give rise to freely treated, conspicuous dissonances. Whether the mass and motet music of the early Netherlanders is intended to be performed with or without instruments, (which at this date cannot be ascertained), the one fact which is at least certain is, that this relation had but little influence upon the development of style with respect to ornamentation. The feature which represents the real essence of the evolution of style is *the dissonance.* In the 15th and 16th centuries, when its faculty of expression was not yet fully appreciated, it signified principally a point of friction between the vertical and horizontal conceptions of music.[1]

The mighty organization of the harmonic elements in the 16th century forced the linear interests over into a defensive position, compelling them, (particularly in conflicting situations), to assume their most impressive and convincing form in order to be able to assert themselves sufficiently in the face of the vertical expansion of power. The triad was so intensively heard, that only the most decided and convincing motives on the part of the linear development excused its negligence—in brief: melodic concentration, conjunct movement. The fundamental law of Palestrina's style, the strict adherence to the rules concerning the conjunct introduction and continuation of the dissonance, depends upon this circumstance.

It is plain that the stronger the tension grows between the Dimensions, the severer the requirements become regarding the conjunct treatment of the dissonance. Therefore we find a steady increase in the rigour of this demand until Palestrina's era, where—in spite of some isolated archaisms—it may be said to have triumphed completely. Palestrina's style must be defined, by reason of its inmost factors, as, practically, a state of perfect equipoise in the two Dimensions—where the innermost ideal of the vertical is "the full triad placed in the position of greatest sonorous beauty", and where the horizontal ideal is

---

[1] Of course this applies especially to the most commonly used dissonances of the epoch—the passing and ornamental dissonance. But in the syncope dissonance, (which is mainly vertical in motive), there is also an unmistakably horizontal element,—the impulse to conduct the voices in a rhythmically independent manner, instead of in similar motion.

"conjunct, diatonic progression". The criterion of the state of equipoise is the strictly conjunct treatment of dissonance.

In the history of dissonance treatment, the style of Palestrina signifies the moment when the full perception of the dissonance as a musical phenomenon and simultaneously the complete mastery of it were attained. With this accomplishment, the way was open for the new, great epoch of art, "la seconda prattica", which is based upon the intensely conscious and systematic employment of dissonance as a factor of expression.

Appendix

Concerning the treatment of perfect consonances in Palestrina

The Roman musician Antimo Liberati, writing in 1684, says about Palestrina that either he had little inclination or else little time to found a school, and so he confined himself to holding the somewhat freer relation of a teacher in his friend Giovanni Maria Nanino's school, where he was often present and said the decisive word in all musical matters.[1]

Though Liberati's account must very likely be considered somewhat in the light of a legend, we know with certainty that Palestrina had some personal pupils, for instance musicians of importance such as G. A. Dragoni and Annibale Stabile who have both in dedications in their works called themselves pupils of him, and Francesco Soriano whom Pierluigi himself mentions as his pupil in a letter to the Duke of Mantua. But as to how Pierluigi taught, what method he used, we know little. The only thing which can enlighten us here, though indeed very imperfectly, is the important letter which Pierluigi wrote in Rome on March 3. 1570 to Guglielmo Gonzaga, the above-mentioned Duke of Mantua, and which seems to be part of a regular correspondence course in composition. This letter is printed in extenso in Bertolotti's "La Musica in Mantova" and is mentioned by Haberl in his valuable essay "Das Archiv der Gonzaga in Mantua" (Kirchenmusikalisches Jahrbuch 1886, p. 35).

In this letter Palestrina makes the remark, highly interesting for

---

[1] Lettera scritta dal ... in riposta ad una del Sig. Ovidio Persapegi. Roma 1685. Cf. Fr. X. Haberl, "Giovanni Maria Nanino", Kirchenmusikalisches Jahrbuch 1891, p. 88.

his period, that so as to be better able to form a judgment of a motet
sent to him by the Duke, he has scored it. He then praises the composition for its ingeniousness and its expressive character, (its sensitive relation to the words, which, altogether, was demonstratively
stressed in that age), further he considers it a less happy feature that
the imitative manner of carrying through the themes involves too
many unisons (the harmonic saturation of the setting was one of
the principal achievements of Palestrina's style, which compared
with the earlier polyphony has strikingly few "thin" effects to show),
finally he criticises the too complicated interweaving of the imitating
voices, owing to which the text does not come out distinctly enough
—a criticism which, coming from the master of the Marcellus mass,
cannot surprise us. All this is quite clear, only one passage in the
letter is not directly understandable, that in which the interval treatment is dealt with in more detail. The reason is presumably a slight
mistake in the translation made by Haberl. For in the passage in
question it says in the Italian original: "Ho segnati alcuni luoghi, che
mi par che quando si puo far di meno soni meglio l'Harmonia, com'e
sesta et unisono mouendosi ambe le parti et sesta et quinta ascendendo
et discendendo".

Haberl translates the beginning of this sentence as follows: "Some
few places I have noted in which, it seems to me, the harmony would
gain by restrictions". He must have overlooked, however, that "far
di meno" has the special sense of "giving up something", just as
"soni" is not the plural of "suono" but the present subjunctive of
"sonare", so that the translation must in consequence run thus: "I have
noted some places of which I think that, if they could be given up,
the harmony would sound better." Only in this form will the meaning
be clear, namely that Palestrina considers the movements from the
sixth to unison and from the sixth to the fifth unsuitable. Haberl's interpretation of the last remark concerning the sixth and the fifth, namely
that it seems to allude to the case when the sixth in cadences has to
be a major one, surely does not hold good; for here the reference
is no doubt to the doctrine of the harmonic progressions organised
with such wonderful fineness and ingenuity in the cinquecento. This
doctrine which was especially codified by Zarlino in his "l'Istitutioni
harmoniche" (1558), besides the question of the dissonance, also deals

very thoroughly with the progression from one species of consonance into the other (how e.g. one may proceed from a perfect to an imperfect consonance or to another perfect one, or the reverse). Here especially the rule of the similar motion to a perfect consonance is important, that is to say, in more modern language, of the treatment of the "hidden" consecutives. It would no doubt take us too far to enter into the details of this very complicated doctrine apparently formulated in an unnecessarily florid and elaborate way by the theorists. Let us merely note that it seems to be a chief rule that one may move in similar motion to a perfect consonance if only one of the two voices moves by steps. This mostly applies too when the movement is only for two voices, and so in Palestrina's compositions we for instance encounter (though indeed not very often) passages like the following in the motet "Haec dies" (P. V, 168, 1 + 2):

or in the litany (P. XXVI, 15, 3, 1):

or in the Pleni of the four-part mass "Sanctorum meritis" (P. XVI, 38, 4, 2):

It should be noted, however, that most cases of this kind occur in connection with an imitative carrying out of the themes; on the other hand, it is also noteworthy that passages in which both voices move disjunctly, even where it might be excused by imitation, do not seem to occur in Palestrina.

When several voices take part, these rules are indeed applied with greater freedom, but even in two-part writing, two typical exceptions may always be encountered. One is the leap from the third to the fifth by which the lower voice ascends a fifth and the upper voice descends a third. Already Vicentino mentions this practice (in "L'antica musica ridotta alla moderna prattica" 1557, f. 41 v.) as one of those allowed with two parts which, consequently, belongs to the most legitimate of these kinds of phrases, and Zarlino (Opere 1589, Vol. I, p. 228) characterises it expressly as "mouimento sopportabile". As a matter of fact, we meet with this effect relatively often even in two-part writing in Palestrina, e.g. in the Agnus of the "Missa prima" (P. XIII, 83, 1, 4):

or from the motet "Magnus sanctus Paulus" (P. V, 46, 1, 4):

The other exception is the somewhat curious one to a modern audience (when viewed against the background of the aforementioned liberty), that even where one of the voices moves conjunctly it was not allowable with only two parts to go from the sixth to the fifth, the following progression being thus prohibited.[1]

It is indeed not easy to understand the reason for this; perhaps, however, Artusi is right when in his "L'arte del contraponto" (1598) he explains it by the fact that this phrase has too much similarity to consecutive fifths.[2] As far as I know, such examples do not occur in Palestrina's works—that is to say, in two-part writing, for already Vicentino (a. a. O. f. 41 r.) includes it among the phrases allowed with four parts, a contention supported by practical examples from Palestrina such as the following, e.g. from the four-part motet "Salvator mundi" (P. V, 69, 1, 3):

---

[1] Zarlino, Opere I, p. 227: "Ne anco torna bene il por la Sesta auanti la Quinta, quando le parti ascendono o discendono insieme; ancora che l'una si muoui per grado, & l'altra per salto."

[2] P. 34: "per che tiene questo moto della natura delle due quinte."

and from the four-part motet "Dum aurora" (P. V, 78, 1, 2):

Even though the compositions of the Duke of Mantua which Palestrina had before him have probably long ago perished and as a
consequence we cannot be quite certain in our identification of the
musical technical details criticised by Palestrina, we shall hardly be
far wrong if we assume that the phrase in the letter about the sixth
and the fifth in ascending and descending movements is motived by
the above-mentioned dislike of the 16th century theorists and practical
mucisians for the direct progression from the sixth to the fifth in two-
part writing (similar motion). In the same way Palestrina's dislike of
the sixth and unison when the two parts move at the same time is easy
to understand viewed against the background of the musical theory
of his time. For here we can only be concerned with contrary or similar
motion. As regards the contrary motion it is altogether somewhat
unusual in Palestrina that two voices move towards unison at the
same time; as a rule one is stationary while the other moves, and ac-
cordingly situations such as

are rarely or never to be found in Palestrina with two parts. But in
similar motion the case, if possible, becomes even less practicable, for

here is also added the feature that both voices move disjunctly towards perfect consonance:

whereby the chief rule referred to above the treatment of hidden
perfect consonances is transgressed. We may probably assume, therefore, that the passage which Palestrina corrected in the Duke's composition belonged to one of the above-mentioned groups, and so the
musical contents of the letter seem clear throughout.

Table of References

A CATALOG OF SELECTED
DOVER BOOKS
IN ALL FIELDS OF INTEREST

A CATALOG OF SELECTED DOVER
BOOKS IN ALL FIELDS OF INTEREST

100 BEST-LOVED POEMS, Edited by Philip Smith. "The Passionate Shepherd to His Love," "Shall I compare thee to a summer's day?" "Death, be not proud," "The Raven," "The Road Not Taken," plus works by Blake, Wordsworth, Byron, Shelley, Keats, many others. 96pp. 5 3/16 x 8 1/4. 0-486-28553-7

100 SMALL HOUSES OF THE THIRTIES, Brown-Blodgett Company. Exterior photographs and floor plans for 100 charming structures. Illustrations of models accompanied by descriptions of interiors, color schemes, closet space, and other amenities. 200 illustrations. 112pp. 8 3/8 x 11. 0-486-44131-8

1000 TURN-OF-THE-CENTURY HOUSES: With Illustrations and Floor Plans, Herbert C. Chivers. Reproduced from a rare edition, this showcase of homes ranges from cottages and bungalows to sprawling mansions. Each house is meticulously illustrated and accompanied by complete floor plans. 256pp. 9 3/8 x 12 1/4.
0-486-45596-3

101 GREAT AMERICAN POEMS, Edited by The American Poetry & Literacy Project. Rich treasury of verse from the 19th and 20th centuries includes works by Edgar Allan Poe, Robert Frost, Walt Whitman, Langston Hughes, Emily Dickinson, T. S. Eliot, other notables. 96pp. 5 3/16 x 8 1/4. 0-486-40158-8

101 GREAT SAMURAI PRINTS, Utagawa Kuniyoshi. Kuniyoshi was a master of the warrior woodblock print — and these 18th-century illustrations represent the pinnacle of his craft. Full-color portraits of renowned Japanese samurais pulse with movement, passion, and remarkably fine detail. 112pp. 8 3/8 x 11. 0-486-46523-3

ABC OF BALLET, Janet Grosser. Clearly worded, abundantly illustrated little guide defines basic ballet-related terms: arabesque, battement, pas de chat, relevé, sissonne, many others. Pronunciation guide included. Excellent primer. 48pp. 4 3/16 x 5 3/4.
0-486-40871-X

ACCESSORIES OF DRESS: An Illustrated Encyclopedia, Katherine Lester and Bess Viola Oerke. Illustrations of hats, veils, wigs, cravats, shawls, shoes, gloves, and other accessories enhance an engaging commentary that reveals the humor and charm of the many-sided story of accessorized apparel. 644 figures and 59 plates. 608pp. 6 1/8 x 9 1/4.
0-486-43378-1

ADVENTURES OF HUCKLEBERRY FINN, Mark Twain. Join Huck and Jim as their boyhood adventures along the Mississippi River lead them into a world of excitement, danger, and self-discovery. Humorous narrative, lyrical descriptions of the Mississippi valley, and memorable characters. 224pp. 5 3/16 x 8 1/4. 0-486-28061-6

ALICE STARMORE'S BOOK OF FAIR ISLE KNITTING, Alice Starmore. A noted designer from the region of Scotland's Fair Isle explores the history and techniques of this distinctive, stranded-color knitting style and provides copious illustrated instructions for 14 original knitwear designs. 208pp. 8 3/8 x 10 7/8. 0-486-47218-3

ALICE'S ADVENTURES IN WONDERLAND, Lewis Carroll. Beloved classic about a little girl lost in a topsy-turvy land and her encounters with the White Rabbit, March Hare, Mad Hatter, Cheshire Cat, and other delightfully improbable characters. 42 illustrations by Sir John Tenniel. 96pp. 5³⁄₁₆ x 8¼. 0-486-27543-4

AMERICA'S LIGHTHOUSES: An Illustrated History, Francis Ross Holland. Profusely illustrated fact-filled survey of American lighthouses since 1716. Over 200 stations — East, Gulf, and West coasts, Great Lakes, Hawaii, Alaska, Puerto Rico, the Virgin Islands, and the Mississippi and St. Lawrence Rivers. 240pp. 8 x 10¾. 0-486-25576-X

AN ENCYCLOPEDIA OF THE VIOLIN, Alberto Bachmann. Translated by Frederick H. Martens. Introduction by Eugene Ysaye. First published in 1925, this renowned reference remains unsurpassed as a source of essential information, from construction and evolution to repertoire and technique. Includes a glossary and 73 illustrations. 496pp. 6½ x 9¼. 0-486-46618-3

ANIMALS: 1,419 Copyright-Free Illustrations of Mammals, Birds, Fish, Insects, etc., Selected by Jim Harter. Selected for its visual impact and ease of use, this outstanding collection of wood engravings presents over 1,000 species of animals in extremely lifelike poses. Includes mammals, birds, reptiles, amphibians, fish, insects, and other invertebrates. 284pp. 9 x 12. 0-486-23766-4

THE ANNALS, Tacitus. Translated by Alfred John Church and William Jackson Brodribb. This vital chronicle of Imperial Rome, written by the era's great historian, spans A.D. 14-68 and paints incisive psychological portraits of major figures, from Tiberius to Nero. 416pp. 5³⁄₁₆ x 8¼. 0-486-45236-0

ANTIGONE, Sophocles. Filled with passionate speeches and sensitive probing of moral and philosophical issues, this powerful and often-performed Greek drama reveals the grim fate that befalls the children of Oedipus. Footnotes. 64pp. 5³⁄₁₆ x 8 ¼. 0-486-27804-2

ART DECO DECORATIVE PATTERNS IN FULL COLOR, Christian Stoll. Reprinted from a rare 1910 portfolio, 160 sensuous and exotic images depict a breathtaking array of florals, geometrics, and abstracts — all elegant in their stark simplicity. 64pp. 8⅜ x 11. 0-486-44862-2

THE ARTHUR RACKHAM TREASURY: 86 Full-Color Illustrations, Arthur Rackham. Selected and Edited by Jeff A. Menges. A stunning treasury of 86 full-page plates span the famed English artist's career, from *Rip Van Winkle* (1905) to masterworks such as *Undine, A Midsummer Night's Dream,* and *Wind in the Willows* (1939). 96pp. 8⅜ x 11. 0-486-44685-9

THE AUTHENTIC GILBERT & SULLIVAN SONGBOOK, W. S. Gilbert and A. S. Sullivan. The most comprehensive collection available, this songbook includes selections from every one of Gilbert and Sullivan's light operas. Ninety-two numbers are presented uncut and unedited, and in their original keys. 410pp. 9 x 12. 0-486-23482-7

THE AWAKENING, Kate Chopin. First published in 1899, this controversial novel of a New Orleans wife's search for love outside a stifling marriage shocked readers. Today, it remains a first-rate narrative with superb characterization. New introductory Note. 128pp. 5³⁄₁₆ x 8¼. 0-486-27786-0

BASIC DRAWING, Louis Priscilla. Beginning with perspective, this commonsense manual progresses to the figure in movement, light and shade, anatomy, drapery, composition, trees and landscape, and outdoor sketching. Black-and-white illustrations throughout. 128pp. 8⅜ x 11. 0-486-45815-6

Browse over 9,000 books at www.doverpublications.com

THE BATTLES THAT CHANGED HISTORY, Fletcher Pratt. Historian profiles 16 crucial conflicts, ancient to modern, that changed the course of Western civilization. Gripping accounts of battles led by Alexander the Great, Joan of Arc, Ulysses S. Grant, other commanders. 27 maps. 352pp. 5⅜ x 8½. 0-486-41129-X

BEETHOVEN'S LETTERS, Ludwig van Beethoven. Edited by Dr. A. C. Kalischer. Features 457 letters to fellow musicians, friends, greats, patrons, and literary men. Reveals musical thoughts, quirks of personality, insights, and daily events. Includes 15 plates. 410pp. 5⅜ x 8½. 0-486-22769-3

BERNICE BOBS HER HAIR AND OTHER STORIES, F. Scott Fitzgerald. This brilliant anthology includes 6 of Fitzgerald's most popular stories: "The Diamond as Big as the Ritz," the title tale, "The Offshore Pirate," "The Ice Palace," "The Jelly Bean," and "May Day." 176pp. 5⅜ x 8½. 0-486-47049-0

BESLER'S BOOK OF FLOWERS AND PLANTS: 73 Full-Color Plates from Hortus Eystettensis, 1613, Basilius Besler. Here is a selection of magnificent plates from the *Hortus Eystettensis,* which vividly illustrated and identified the plants, flowers, and trees that thrived in the legendary German garden at Eichstätt. 80pp. 8⅜ x 11.
0-486-46005-3

THE BOOK OF KELLS, Edited by Blanche Cirker. Painstakingly reproduced from a rare facsimile edition, this volume contains full-page decorations, portraits, illustrations, plus a sampling of textual leaves with exquisite calligraphy and ornamentation. 32 full-color illustrations. 32pp. 9⅜ x 12¼. 0-486-24345-1

THE BOOK OF THE CROSSBOW: With an Additional Section on Catapults and Other Siege Engines, Ralph Payne-Gallwey. Fascinating study traces history and use of crossbow as military and sporting weapon, from Middle Ages to modern times. Also covers related weapons: balistas, catapults, Turkish bows, more. Over 240 illustrations. 400pp. 7¼ x 10⅛. 0-486-28720-3

THE BUNGALOW BOOK: Floor Plans and Photos of 112 Houses, 1910, Henry L. Wilson. Here are 112 of the most popular and economic blueprints of the early 20th century — plus an illustration or photograph of each completed house. A wonderful time capsule that still offers a wealth of valuable insights. 160pp. 8⅜ x 11.
0-486-45104-6

THE CALL OF THE WILD, Jack London. A classic novel of adventure, drawn from London's own experiences as a Klondike adventurer, relating the story of a heroic dog caught in the brutal life of the Alaska Gold Rush. Note. 64pp. 5³⁄₁₆ x 8¼.
0-486-26472-6

CANDIDE, Voltaire. Edited by Francois-Marie Arouet. One of the world's great satires since its first publication in 1759. Witty, caustic skewering of romance, science, philosophy, religion, government — nearly all human ideals and institutions. 112pp. 5³⁄₁₆ x 8¼. 0-486-26689-3

CELEBRATED IN THEIR TIME: Photographic Portraits from the George Grantham Bain Collection, Edited by Amy Pastan. With an Introduction by Michael Carlebach. Remarkable portrait gallery features 112 rare images of Albert Einstein, Charlie Chaplin, the Wright Brothers, Henry Ford, and other luminaries from the worlds of politics, art, entertainment, and industry. 128pp. 8⅜ x 11. 0-486-46754-6

CHARIOTS FOR APOLLO: The NASA History of Manned Lunar Spacecraft to 1969, Courtney G. Brooks, James M. Grimwood, and Loyd S. Swenson, Jr. This illustrated history by a trio of experts is the definitive reference on the Apollo spacecraft and lunar modules. It traces the vehicles' design, development, and operation in space. More than 100 photographs and illustrations. 576pp. 6¾ x 9¼. 0-486-46756-2

Browse over 9,000 books at www.doverpublications.com

A CHRISTMAS CAROL, Charles Dickens. This engrossing tale relates Ebenezer Scrooge's ghostly journeys through Christmases past, present, and future and his ultimate transformation from a harsh and grasping old miser to a charitable and compassionate human being. 80pp. 5⅜₆ x 8¼. 0-486-26865-9

COMMON SENSE, Thomas Paine. First published in January of 1776, this highly influential landmark document clearly and persuasively argued for American separation from Great Britain and paved the way for the Declaration of Independence. 64pp. 5⅜₆ x 8¼. 0-486-29602-4

THE COMPLETE SHORT STORIES OF OSCAR WILDE, Oscar Wilde. Complete texts of "The Happy Prince and Other Tales," "A House of Pomegranates," "Lord Arthur Savile's Crime and Other Stories," "Poems in Prose," and "The Portrait of Mr. W. H." 208pp. 5⅜₆ x 8¼. 0-486-45216-6

COMPLETE SONNETS, William Shakespeare. Over 150 exquisite poems deal with love, friendship, the tyranny of time, beauty's evanescence, death, and other themes in language of remarkable power, precision, and beauty. Glossary of archaic terms. 80pp. 5⅜₆ x 8¼. 0-486-26686-9

THE COUNT OF MONTE CRISTO: Abridged Edition, Alexandre Dumas. Falsely accused of treason, Edmond Dantès is imprisoned in the bleak Chateau d'If. After a hair-raising escape, he launches an elaborate plot to extract a bitter revenge against those who betrayed him. 448pp. 5⅜₆ x 8¼. 0-486-45643-9

CRAFTSMAN BUNGALOWS: Designs from the Pacific Northwest, Yoho & Merritt. This reprint of a rare catalog, showcasing the charming simplicity and cozy style of Craftsman bungalows, is filled with photos of completed homes, plus floor plans and estimated costs. An indispensable resource for architects, historians, and illustrators. 112pp. 10 x 7. 0-486-46875-5

CRAFTSMAN BUNGALOWS: 59 Homes from "The Craftsman," Edited by Gustav Stickley. Best and most attractive designs from Arts and Crafts Movement publication — 1903–1916 — includes sketches, photographs of homes, floor plans, descriptive text. 128pp. 8¼ x 11. 0-486-25829-7

CRIME AND PUNISHMENT, Fyodor Dostoyevsky. Translated by Constance Garnett. Supreme masterpiece tells the story of Raskolnikov, a student tormented by his own thoughts after he murders an old woman. Overwhelmed by guilt and terror, he confesses and goes to prison. 480pp. 5⅜₆ x 8¼. 0-486-41587-2

THE DECLARATION OF INDEPENDENCE AND OTHER GREAT DOCUMENTS OF AMERICAN HISTORY: 1775-1865, Edited by John Grafton. Thirteen compelling and influential documents: Henry's "Give Me Liberty or Give Me Death," Declaration of Independence, The Constitution, Washington's First Inaugural Address, The Monroe Doctrine, The Emancipation Proclamation, Gettysburg Address, more. 64pp. 5⅜₆ x 8¼. 0-486-41124-9

THE DESERT AND THE SOWN: Travels in Palestine and Syria, Gertrude Bell. "The female Lawrence of Arabia," Gertrude Bell wrote captivating, perceptive accounts of her travels in the Middle East. This intriguing narrative, accompanied by 160 photos, traces her 1905 sojourn in Lebanon, Syria, and Palestine. 368pp. 5⅜ x 8½. 0-486-46876-3

A DOLL'S HOUSE, Henrik Ibsen. Ibsen's best-known play displays his genius for realistic prose drama. An expression of women's rights, the play climaxes when the central character, Nora, rejects a smothering marriage and life in "a doll's house." 80pp. 5⅜₆ x 8¼. 0-486-27062-9

DOOMED SHIPS: Great Ocean Liner Disasters, William H. Miller, Jr. Nearly 200 photographs, many from private collections, highlight tales of some of the vessels whose pleasure cruises ended in catastrophe: the *Morro Castle, Normandie, Andrea Doria, Europa,* and many others. 128pp. 8⅞ x 11¾.   0-486-45366-9

THE DORÉ BIBLE ILLUSTRATIONS, Gustave Doré. Detailed plates from the Bible: the Creation scenes, Adam and Eve, horrifying visions of the Flood, the battle sequences with their monumental crowds, depictions of the life of Jesus, 241 plates in all. 241pp. 9 x 12.   0-486-23004-X

DRAWING DRAPERY FROM HEAD TO TOE, Cliff Young. Expert guidance on how to draw shirts, pants, skirts, gloves, hats, and coats on the human figure, including folds in relation to the body, pull and crush, action folds, creases, more. Over 200 drawings. 48pp. 8¼ x 11.   0-486-45591-2

DUBLINERS, James Joyce. A fine and accessible introduction to the work of one of the 20th century's most influential writers, this collection features 15 tales, including a masterpiece of the short-story genre, "The Dead." 160pp. 5³⁄₁₆ x 8¼.

0-486-26870-5

EASY-TO-MAKE POP-UPS, Joan Irvine. Illustrated by Barbara Reid. Dozens of wonderful ideas for three-dimensional paper fun — from holiday greeting cards with moving parts to a pop-up menagerie. Easy-to-follow, illustrated instructions for more than 30 projects. 299 black-and-white illustrations. 96pp. 8⅜ x 11.

0-486-44622-0

EASY-TO-MAKE STORYBOOK DOLLS: A "Novel" Approach to Cloth Dollmaking, Sherralyn St. Clair. Favorite fictional characters come alive in this unique beginner's dollmaking guide. Includes patterns for Pollyanna, Dorothy from *The Wonderful Wizard of Oz,* Mary of *The Secret Garden,* plus easy-to-follow instructions, 263 black-and-white illustrations, and an 8-page color insert. 112pp. 8¼ x 11.   0-486-47360-0

EINSTEIN'S ESSAYS IN SCIENCE, Albert Einstein. Speeches and essays in accessible, everyday language profile influential physicists such as Niels Bohr and Isaac Newton. They also explore areas of physics to which the author made major contributions. 128pp. 5 x 8.   0-486-47011-3

EL DORADO: Further Adventures of the Scarlet Pimpernel, Baroness Orczy. A popular sequel to *The Scarlet Pimpernel,* this suspenseful story recounts the Pimpernel's attempts to rescue the Dauphin from imprisonment during the French Revolution. An irresistible blend of intrigue, period detail, and vibrant characterizations. 352pp. 5³⁄₁₆ x 8¼.   0-486-44026-5

ELEGANT SMALL HOMES OF THE TWENTIES: 99 Designs from a Competition, Chicago Tribune. Nearly 100 designs for five- and six-room houses feature New England and Southern colonials, Normandy cottages, stately Italianate dwellings, and other fascinating snapshots of American domestic architecture of the 1920s. 112pp. 9 x 12.   0-486-46910-7

THE ELEMENTS OF STYLE: The Original Edition, William Strunk, Jr. This is the book that generations of writers have relied upon for timeless advice on grammar, diction, syntax, and other essentials. In concise terms, it identifies the principal requirements of proper style and common errors. 64pp. 5⅜ x 8¼.   0-486-44798-7

THE ELUSIVE PIMPERNEL, Baroness Orczy. Robespierre's revolutionaries find their wicked schemes thwarted by the heroic Pimpernel — Sir Percival Blakeney. In this thrilling sequel, Chauvelin devises a plot to eliminate the Pimpernel and his wife. 272pp. 5³⁄₁₆ x 8¼.   0-486-45464-9

AN ENCYCLOPEDIA OF BATTLES: Accounts of Over 1,560 Battles from 1479 B.C. to the Present, David Eggenberger. Essential details of every major battle in recorded history from the first battle of Megiddo in 1479 B.C. to Grenada in 1984. List of battle maps. 99 illustrations. 544pp. 6½ x 9¼. 0-486-24913-1

ENCYCLOPEDIA OF EMBROIDERY STITCHES, INCLUDING CREWEL, Marion Nichols. Precise explanations and instructions, clearly illustrated, on how to work chain, back, cross, knotted, woven stitches, and many more — 178 in all, including Cable Outline, Whipped Satin, and Eyelet Buttonhole. Over 1400 illustrations. 219pp. 8⅜ x 11¼. 0-486-22929-7

ENTER JEEVES: 15 Early Stories, P. G. Wodehouse. Splendid collection contains first 8 stories featuring Bertie Wooster, the deliciously dim aristocrat and Jeeves, his brainy, imperturbable manservant. Also, the complete Reggie Pepper (Bertie's prototype) series. 288pp. 5⅜ x 8½. 0-486-29717-9

ERIC SLOANE'S AMERICA: Paintings in Oil, Michael Wigley. With a Foreword by Mimi Sloane. Eric Sloane's evocative oils of America's landscape and material culture shimmer with immense historical and nostalgic appeal. This original hardcover collection gathers nearly a hundred of his finest paintings, with subjects ranging from New England to the American Southwest. 128pp. 10⅝ x 9.
0-486-46525-X

ETHAN FROME, Edith Wharton. Classic story of wasted lives, set against a bleak New England background. Superbly delineated characters in a hauntingly grim tale of thwarted love. Considered by many to be Wharton's masterpiece. 96pp. 5³⁄₁₆ x 8 ¼. 0-486-26690-7

THE EVERLASTING MAN, G. K. Chesterton. Chesterton's view of Christianity — as a blend of philosophy and mythology, satisfying intellect and spirit — applies to his brilliant book, which appeals to readers' heads as well as their hearts. 288pp. 5⅜ x 8½. 0-486-46036-3

THE FIELD AND FOREST HANDY BOOK, Daniel Beard. Written by a co-founder of the Boy Scouts, this appealing guide offers illustrated instructions for building kites, birdhouses, boats, igloos, and other fun projects, plus numerous helpful tips for campers. 448pp. 5³⁄₁₆ x 8¼. 0-486-46191-2

FINDING YOUR WAY WITHOUT MAP OR COMPASS, Harold Gatty. Useful, instructive manual shows would-be explorers, hikers, bikers, scouts, sailors, and survivalists how to find their way outdoors by observing animals, weather patterns, shifting sands, and other elements of nature. 288pp. 5⅜ x 8½. 0-486-40613-X

FIRST FRENCH READER: A Beginner's Dual-Language Book, Edited and Translated by Stanley Appelbaum. This anthology introduces 50 legendary writers — Voltaire, Balzac, Baudelaire, Proust, more — through passages from *The Red and the Black, Les Misérables, Madame Bovary,* and other classics. Original French text plus English translation on facing pages. 240pp. 5⅜ x 8½. 0-486-46178-5

FIRST GERMAN READER: A Beginner's Dual-Language Book, Edited by Harry Steinhauer. Specially chosen for their power to evoke German life and culture, these short, simple readings include poems, stories, essays, and anecdotes by Goethe, Hesse, Heine, Schiller, and others. 224pp. 5⅜ x 8½. 0-486-46179-3

FIRST SPANISH READER: A Beginner's Dual-Language Book, Angel Flores. Delightful stories, other material based on works of Don Juan Manuel, Luis Taboada, Ricardo Palma, other noted writers. Complete faithful English translations on facing pages. Exercises. 176pp. 5⅜ x 8½. 0-486-25810-6

FIVE ACRES AND INDEPENDENCE, Maurice G. Kains. Great back-to-the-land classic explains basics of self-sufficient farming. The one book to get. 95 illustrations. 397pp. 5⅜ x 8½. 0-486-20974-1

FLAGG'S SMALL HOUSES: Their Economic Design and Construction, 1922, Ernest Flagg. Although most famous for his skyscrapers, Flagg was also a proponent of the well-designed single-family dwelling. His classic treatise features innovations that save space, materials, and cost. 526 illustrations. 160pp. 9⅜ x 12¼. 0-486-45197-6

FLATLAND: A Romance of Many Dimensions, Edwin A. Abbott. Classic of science (and mathematical) fiction — charmingly illustrated by the author — describes the adventures of A. Square, a resident of Flatland, in Spaceland (three dimensions), Lineland (one dimension), and Pointland (no dimensions). 96pp. 5³⁄₁₆ x 8¼. 0-486-27263-X

FRANKENSTEIN, Mary Shelley. The story of Victor Frankenstein's monstrous creation and the havoc it caused has enthralled generations of readers and inspired countless writers of horror and suspense. With the author's own 1831 introduction. 176pp. 5³⁄₁₆ x 8¼. 0-486-28211-2

THE GARGOYLE BOOK: 572 Examples from Gothic Architecture, Lester Burbank Bridaham. Dispelling the conventional wisdom that French Gothic architectural flourishes were born of despair or gloom, Bridaham reveals the whimsical nature of these creations and the ingenious artisans who made them. 572 illustrations. 224pp. 8⅜ x 11. 0-486-44754-5

THE GIFT OF THE MAGI AND OTHER SHORT STORIES, O. Henry. Sixteen captivating stories by one of America's most popular storytellers. Included are such classics as "The Gift of the Magi," "The Last Leaf," and "The Ransom of Red Chief." Publisher's Note. 96pp. 5³⁄₁₆ x 8¼. 0-486-27061-0

THE GOETHE TREASURY: Selected Prose and Poetry, Johann Wolfgang von Goethe. Edited, Selected, and with an Introduction by Thomas Mann. In addition to his lyric poetry, Goethe wrote travel sketches, autobiographical studies, essays, letters, and proverbs in rhyme and prose. This collection presents outstanding examples from each genre. 368pp. 5⅜ x 8½. 0-486-44780-4

GREAT EXPECTATIONS, Charles Dickens. Orphaned Pip is apprenticed to the dirty work of the forge but dreams of becoming a gentleman — and one day finds himself in possession of "great expectations." Dickens' finest novel. 400pp. 5³⁄₁₆ x 8¼. 0-486-41586-4

GREAT WRITERS ON THE ART OF FICTION: From Mark Twain to Joyce Carol Oates, Edited by James Daley. An indispensable source of advice and inspiration, this anthology features essays by Henry James, Kate Chopin, Willa Cather, Sinclair Lewis, Jack London, Raymond Chandler, Raymond Carver, Eudora Welty, and Kurt Vonnegut, Jr. 192pp. 5⅜ x 8½. 0-486-45128-3

HAMLET, William Shakespeare. The quintessential Shakespearean tragedy, whose highly charged confrontations and anguished soliloquies probe depths of human feeling rarely sounded in any art. Reprinted from an authoritative British edition complete with illuminating footnotes. 128pp. 5³⁄₁₆ x 8¼. 0-486-27278-8

THE HAUNTED HOUSE, Charles Dickens. A Yuletide gathering in an eerie country retreat provides the backdrop for Dickens and his friends — including Elizabeth Gaskell and Wilkie Collins — who take turns spinning supernatural yarns. 144pp. 5⅜ x 8½. 0-486-46309-5

HEART OF DARKNESS, Joseph Conrad. Dark allegory of a journey up the Congo River and the narrator's encounter with the mysterious Mr. Kurtz. Masterly blend of adventure, character study, psychological penetration. For many, Conrad's finest, most enigmatic story. 80pp. 5³⁄₁₆ x 8¼. 0-486-26464-5

HENSON AT THE NORTH POLE, Matthew A. Henson. This thrilling memoir by the heroic African-American who was Peary's companion through two decades of Arctic exploration recounts a tale of danger, courage, and determination. "Fascinating and exciting." — *Commonweal.* 128pp. 5⅜ x 8½. 0-486-45472-X

HISTORIC COSTUMES AND HOW TO MAKE THEM, Mary Fernald and E. Shenton. Practical, informative guidebook shows how to create everything from short tunics worn by Saxon men in the fifth century to a lady's bustle dress of the late 1800s. 81 illustrations. 176pp. 5⅜ x 8½. 0-486-44906-8

THE HOUND OF THE BASKERVILLES, Arthur Conan Doyle. A deadly curse in the form of a legendary ferocious beast continues to claim its victims from the Baskerville family until Holmes and Watson intervene. Often called the best detective story ever written. 128pp. 5³⁄₁₆ x 8¼. 0-486-28214-7

THE HOUSE BEHIND THE CEDARS, Charles W. Chesnutt. Originally published in 1900, this groundbreaking novel by a distinguished African-American author recounts the drama of a brother and sister who "pass for white" during the dangerous days of Reconstruction. 208pp. 5⅜ x 8½. 0-486-46144-0

THE HUMAN FIGURE IN MOTION, Eadweard Muybridge. The 4,789 photographs in this definitive selection show the human figure — models almost all undraped — engaged in over 160 different types of action: running, climbing stairs, etc. 390pp. 7⅞ x 10⅝. 0-486-20204-6

THE IMPORTANCE OF BEING EARNEST, Oscar Wilde. Wilde's witty and buoyant comedy of manners, filled with some of literature's most famous epigrams, reprinted from an authoritative British edition. Considered Wilde's most perfect work. 64pp. 5³⁄₁₆ x 8¼. 0-486-26478-5

THE INFERNO, Dante Alighieri. Translated and with notes by Henry Wadsworth Longfellow. The first stop on Dante's famous journey from Hell to Purgatory to Paradise, this 14th-century allegorical poem blends vivid and shocking imagery with graceful lyricism. Translated by the beloved 19th-century poet, Henry Wadsworth Longfellow. 256pp. 5³⁄₁₆ x 8¼. 0-486-44288-8

JANE EYRE, Charlotte Brontë. Written in 1847, *Jane Eyre* tells the tale of an orphan girl's progress from the custody of cruel relatives to an oppressive boarding school and its culmination in a troubled career as a governess. 448pp. 5³⁄₁₆ x 8¼. 0-486-42449-9

JAPANESE WOODBLOCK FLOWER PRINTS, Tanigami Kônan. Extraordinary collection of Japanese woodblock prints by a well-known artist features 120 plates in brilliant color. Realistic images from a rare edition include daffodils, tulips, and other familiar and unusual flowers. 128pp. 11 x 8¼. 0-486-46442-3

JEWELRY MAKING AND DESIGN, Augustus F. Rose and Antonio Cirino. Professional secrets of jewelry making are revealed in a thorough, practical guide. Over 200 illustrations. 306pp. 5⅜ x 8½. 0-486-21750-7

JULIUS CAESAR, William Shakespeare. Great tragedy based on Plutarch's account of the lives of Brutus, Julius Caesar and Mark Antony. Evil plotting, ringing oratory, high tragedy with Shakespeare's incomparable insight, dramatic power. Explanatory footnotes. 96pp. 5³⁄₁₆ x 8¼. 0-486-26876-4

THE JUNGLE, Upton Sinclair. 1906 bestseller shockingly reveals intolerable labor practices and working conditions in the Chicago stockyards as it tells the grim story of a Slavic family that emigrates to America full of optimism but soon faces despair. 320pp. 5$\frac{3}{16}$ x 8¼. 0-486-41923-1

THE KINGDOM OF GOD IS WITHIN YOU, Leo Tolstoy. The soul-searching book that inspired Gandhi to embrace the concept of passive resistance, Tolstoy's 1894 polemic clearly outlines a radical, well-reasoned revision of traditional Christian thinking. 352pp. 5$\frac{3}{16}$ x 8¼. 0-486-45138-0

THE LADY OR THE TIGER?: and Other Logic Puzzles, Raymond M. Smullyan. Created by a renowned puzzle master, these whimsically themed challenges involve paradoxes about probability, time, and change; metapuzzles; and self-referentiality. Nineteen chapters advance in difficulty from relatively simple to highly complex. 1982 edition. 240pp. 5⅜ x 8½. 0-486-47027-X

LEAVES OF GRASS: The Original 1855 Edition, Walt Whitman. Whitman's immortal collection includes some of the greatest poems of modern times, including his masterpiece, "Song of Myself." Shattering standard conventions, it stands as an unabashed celebration of body and nature. 128pp. 5$\frac{3}{16}$ x 8¼. 0-486-45676-5

LES MISÉRABLES, Victor Hugo. Translated by Charles E. Wilbour. Abridged by James K. Robinson. A convict's heroic struggle for justice and redemption plays out against a fiery backdrop of the Napoleonic wars. This edition features the excellent original translation and a sensitive abridgment. 304pp. 6⅛ x 9¼. 0-486-45789-3

LILITH: A Romance, George MacDonald. In this novel by the father of fantasy literature, a man travels through time to meet Adam and Eve and to explore humanity's fall from grace and ultimate redemption. 240pp. 5⅜ x 8½. 0-486-46818-6

THE LOST LANGUAGE OF SYMBOLISM, Harold Bayley. This remarkable book reveals the hidden meaning behind familiar images and words, from the origins of Santa Claus to the fleur-de-lys, drawing from mythology, folklore, religious texts, and fairy tales. 1,418 illustrations. 784pp. 5⅜ x 8½. 0-486-44787-1

MACBETH, William Shakespeare. A Scottish nobleman murders the king in order to succeed to the throne. Tortured by his conscience and fearful of discovery, he becomes tangled in a web of treachery and deceit that ultimately spells his doom. 96pp. 5$\frac{3}{16}$ x 8¼. 0-486-27802-6

MAKING AUTHENTIC CRAFTSMAN FURNITURE: Instructions and Plans for 62 Projects, Gustav Stickley. Make authentic reproductions of handsome, functional, durable furniture: tables, chairs, wall cabinets, desks, a hall tree, and more. Construction plans with drawings, schematics, dimensions, and lumber specs reprinted from 1900s *The Craftsman* magazine. 128pp. 8⅛ x 11. 0-486-25000-8

MATHEMATICS FOR THE NONMATHEMATICIAN, Morris Kline. Erudite and entertaining overview follows development of mathematics from ancient Greeks to present. Topics include logic and mathematics, the fundamental concept, differential calculus, probability theory, much more. Exercises and problems. 641pp. 5⅜ x 8½. 0-486-24823-2

MEMOIRS OF AN ARABIAN PRINCESS FROM ZANZIBAR, Emily Ruete. This 19th-century autobiography offers a rare inside look at the society surrounding a sultan's palace. A real-life princess in exile recalls her vanished world of harems, slave trading, and court intrigues. 288pp. 5⅜ x 8½. 0-486-47121-7

THE METAMORPHOSIS AND OTHER STORIES, Franz Kafka. Excellent new English translations of title story (considered by many critics Kafka's most perfect work), plus "The Judgment," "In the Penal Colony," "A Country Doctor," and "A Report to an Academy." Note. 96pp. 5¾₆ x 8¼. 0-486-29030-1

MICROSCOPIC ART FORMS FROM THE PLANT WORLD, R. Anheisser. From undulating curves to complex geometrics, a world of fascinating images abound in this classic, illustrated survey of microscopic plants. Features 400 detailed illustrations of nature's minute but magnificent handiwork. The accompanying CD-ROM includes all of the images in the book. 128pp. 9 x 9. 0-486-46013-4

A MIDSUMMER NIGHT'S DREAM, William Shakespeare. Among the most popular of Shakespeare's comedies, this enchanting play humorously celebrates the vagaries of love as it focuses upon the intertwined romances of several pairs of lovers. Explanatory footnotes. 80pp. 5¾₆ x 8¼. 0-486-27067-X

THE MONEY CHANGERS, Upton Sinclair. Originally published in 1908, this cautionary novel from the author of *The Jungle* explores corruption within the American system as a group of power brokers joins forces for personal gain, triggering a crash on Wall Street. 192pp. 5⅜ x 8½. 0-486-46917-4

THE MOST POPULAR HOMES OF THE TWENTIES, William A. Radford. With a New Introduction by Daniel D. Reiff. Based on a rare 1925 catalog, this architectural showcase features floor plans, construction details, and photos of 26 homes, plus articles on entrances, porches, garages, and more. 250 illustrations, 21 color plates. 176pp. 8⅜ x 11. 0-486-47028-8

MY 66 YEARS IN THE BIG LEAGUES, Connie Mack. With a New Introduction by Rich Westcott. A Founding Father of modern baseball, Mack holds the record for most wins — and losses — by a major league manager. Enhanced by 70 photographs, his warmhearted autobiography is populated by many legends of the game. 288pp. 5⅜ x 8½. 0-486-47184-5

NARRATIVE OF THE LIFE OF FREDERICK DOUGLASS, Frederick Douglass. Douglass's graphic depictions of slavery, harrowing escape to freedom, and life as a newspaper editor, eloquent orator, and impassioned abolitionist. 96pp. 5¾₆ x 8¼. 0-486-28499-9

THE NIGHTLESS CITY: Geisha and Courtesan Life in Old Tokyo, J. E. de Becker. This unsurpassed study from 100 years ago ventured into Tokyo's red-light district to survey geisha and courtesan life and offer meticulous descriptions of training, dress, social hierarchy, and erotic practices. 49 black-and-white illustrations; 2 maps. 496pp. 5⅜ x 8½. 0-486-45563-7

THE ODYSSEY, Homer. Excellent prose translation of ancient epic recounts adventures of the homeward-bound Odysseus. Fantastic cast of gods, giants, cannibals, sirens, other supernatural creatures — true classic of Western literature. 256pp. 5¾₆ x 8¼. 0-486-40654-7

OEDIPUS REX, Sophocles. Landmark of Western drama concerns the catastrophe that ensues when King Oedipus discovers he has inadvertently killed his father and married his mother. Masterly construction, dramatic irony. Explanatory footnotes. 64pp. 5¾₆ x 8¼. 0-486-26877-2

ONCE UPON A TIME: The Way America Was, Eric Sloane. Nostalgic text and drawings brim with gentle philosophies and descriptions of how we used to live — self-sufficiently — on the land, in homes, and among the things built by hand. 44 line illustrations. 64pp. 8⅜ x 11. 0-486-44411-2

ONE OF OURS, Willa Cather. The Pulitzer Prize–winning novel about a young Nebraskan looking for something to believe in. Alienated from his parents, rejected by his wife, he finds his destiny on the bloody battlefields of World War I. 352pp. 5³⁄₁₆ x 8¼.   0-486-45599-8

ORIGAMI YOU CAN USE: 27 Practical Projects, Rick Beech. Origami models can be more than decorative, and this unique volume shows how! The 27 practical projects include a CD case, frame, napkin ring, and dish. Easy instructions feature 400 two-color illustrations. 96pp. 8¼ x 11.   0-486-47057-1

OTHELLO, William Shakespeare. Towering tragedy tells the story of a Moorish general who earns the enmity of his ensign Iago when he passes him over for a promotion. Masterly portrait of an archvillain. Explanatory footnotes. 112pp. 5³⁄₁₆ x 8¼.
                                                                                                                              0-486-29097-2

PARADISE LOST, John Milton. Notes by John A. Himes. First published in 1667, *Paradise Lost* ranks among the greatest of English literature's epic poems. It's a sublime retelling of Adam and Eve's fall from grace and expulsion from Eden. Notes by John A. Himes. 480pp. 5³⁄₁₆ x 8¼.   0-486-44287-X

PASSING, Nella Larsen. Married to a successful physician and prominently ensconced in society, Irene Redfield leads a charmed existence — until a chance encounter with a childhood friend who has been "passing for white." 112pp. 5⅜ x 8½. 0-486-43713-2

PERSPECTIVE DRAWING FOR BEGINNERS, Len A. Doust. Doust carefully explains the roles of lines, boxes, and circles, and shows how visualizing shapes and forms can be used in accurate depictions of perspective. One of the most concise introductions available. 33 illustrations. 64pp. 5⅜ x 8½.   0-486-45149-6

PERSPECTIVE MADE EASY, Ernest R. Norling. Perspective is easy; yet, surprisingly few artists know the simple rules that make it so. Remedy that situation with this simple, step-by-step book, the first devoted entirely to the topic. 256 illustrations. 224pp. 5⅜ x 8½.   0-486-40473-0

THE PICTURE OF DORIAN GRAY, Oscar Wilde. Celebrated novel involves a handsome young Londoner who sinks into a life of depravity. His body retains perfect youth and vigor while his recent portrait reflects the ravages of his crime and sensuality. 176pp. 5³⁄₁₆ x 8¼.   0-486-27807-7

PRIDE AND PREJUDICE, Jane Austen. One of the most universally loved and admired English novels, an effervescent tale of rural romance transformed by Jane Austen's art into a witty, shrewdly observed satire of English country life. 272pp. 5³⁄₁₆ x 8¼.
                                                                                                                              0-486-28473-5

THE PRINCE, Niccolò Machiavelli. Classic, Renaissance-era guide to acquiring and maintaining political power. Today, nearly 500 years after it was written, this calculating prescription for autocratic rule continues to be much read and studied. 80pp. 5³⁄₁₆ x 8¼.   0-486-27274-5

QUICK SKETCHING, Carl Cheek. A perfect introduction to the technique of "quick sketching." Drawing upon an artist's immediate emotional responses, this is an extremely effective means of capturing the essential form and features of a subject. More than 100 black-and-white illustrations throughout. 48pp. 11 x 8¼.
                                                                                                                              0-486-46608-6

RANCH LIFE AND THE HUNTING TRAIL, Theodore Roosevelt. Illustrated by Frederic Remington. Beautifully illustrated by Remington, Roosevelt's celebration of the Old West recounts his adventures in the Dakota Badlands of the 1880s, from round-ups to Indian encounters to hunting bighorn sheep. 208pp. 6¼ x 9¼.   0-486-47340-6

Browse over 9,000 books at www.doverpublications.com

THE RED BADGE OF COURAGE, Stephen Crane. Amid the nightmarish chaos of a Civil War battle, a young soldier discovers courage, humility, and, perhaps, wisdom. Uncanny re-creation of actual combat. Enduring landmark of American fiction. 112pp. 5³⁄₁₆ x 8¼. 0-486-26465-3

RELATIVITY SIMPLY EXPLAINED, Martin Gardner. One of the subject's clearest, most entertaining introductions offers lucid explanations of special and general theories of relativity, gravity, and spacetime, models of the universe, and more. 100 illustrations. 224pp. 5⅜ x 8½. 0-486-29315-7

REMBRANDT DRAWINGS: 116 Masterpieces in Original Color, Rembrandt van Rijn. This deluxe hardcover edition features drawings from throughout the Dutch master's prolific career. Informative captions accompany these beautifully reproduced landscapes, biblical vignettes, figure studies, animal sketches, and portraits. 128pp. 8⅜ x 11. 0-486-46149-1

THE ROAD NOT TAKEN AND OTHER POEMS, Robert Frost. A treasury of Frost's most expressive verse. In addition to the title poem: "An Old Man's Winter Night," "In the Home Stretch," "Meeting and Passing," "Putting in the Seed," many more. All complete and unabridged. 64pp. 5³⁄₁₆ x 8¼. 0-486-27550-7

ROMEO AND JULIET, William Shakespeare. Tragic tale of star-crossed lovers, feuding families and timeless passion contains some of Shakespeare's most beautiful and lyrical love poetry. Complete, unabridged text with explanatory footnotes. 96pp. 5³⁄₁₆ x 8¼. 0-486-27557-4

SANDITON AND THE WATSONS: Austen's Unfinished Novels, Jane Austen. Two tantalizing incomplete stories revisit Austen's customary milieu of courtship and venture into new territory, amid guests at a seaside resort. Both are worth reading for pleasure and study. 112pp. 5⅜ x 8½. 0-486-45793-1

THE SCARLET LETTER, Nathaniel Hawthorne. With stark power and emotional depth, Hawthorne's masterpiece explores sin, guilt, and redemption in a story of adultery in the early days of the Massachusetts Colony. 192pp. 5³⁄₁₆ x 8¼.
0-486-28048-9

THE SEASONS OF AMERICA PAST, Eric Sloane. Seventy-five illustrations depict cider mills and presses, sleds, pumps, stump-pulling equipment, plows, and other elements of America's rural heritage. A section of old recipes and household hints adds additional color. 160pp. 8⅜ x 11. 0-486-44220-9

SELECTED CANTERBURY TALES, Geoffrey Chaucer. Delightful collection includes the General Prologue plus three of the most popular tales: "The Knight's Tale," "The Miller's Prologue and Tale," and "The Wife of Bath's Prologue and Tale." In modern English. 144pp. 5³⁄₁₆ x 8¼. 0-486-28241-4

SELECTED POEMS, Emily Dickinson. Over 100 best-known, best-loved poems by one of America's foremost poets, reprinted from authoritative early editions. No comparable edition at this price. Index of first lines. 64pp. 5³⁄₁₆ x 8¼. 0-486-26466-1

SIDDHARTHA, Hermann Hesse. Classic novel that has inspired generations of seekers. Blending Eastern mysticism and psychoanalysis, Hesse presents a strikingly original view of man and culture and the arduous process of self-discovery, reconciliation, harmony, and peace. 112pp. 5³⁄₁₆ x 8¼. 0-486-40653-9

SKETCHING OUTDOORS, Leonard Richmond. This guide offers beginners step-by-step demonstrations of how to depict clouds, trees, buildings, and other outdoor sights. Explanations of a variety of techniques include shading and constructional drawing. 48pp. 11 x 8¼. 0-486-46922-0

SMALL HOUSES OF THE FORTIES: With Illustrations and Floor Plans, Harold E. Group. 56 floor plans and elevations of houses that originally cost less than $15,000 to build. Recommended by financial institutions of the era, they range from Colonials to Cape Cods. 144pp. 8⅜ x 11. 0-486-45598-X

SOME CHINESE GHOSTS, Lafcadio Hearn. Rooted in ancient Chinese legends, these richly atmospheric supernatural tales are recounted by an expert in Oriental lore. Their originality, power, and literary charm will captivate readers of all ages. 96pp. 5⅜ x 8½. 0-486-46306-0

SONGS FOR THE OPEN ROAD: Poems of Travel and Adventure, Edited by The American Poetry & Literacy Project. More than 80 poems by 50 American and British masters celebrate real and metaphorical journeys. Poems by Whitman, Byron, Millay, Sandburg, Langston Hughes, Emily Dickinson, Robert Frost, Shelley, Tennyson, Yeats, many others. Note. 80pp. 5³⁄₁₆ x 8¼. 0-486-40646-6

SPOON RIVER ANTHOLOGY, Edgar Lee Masters. An American poetry classic, in which former citizens of a mythical midwestern town speak touchingly from the grave of the thwarted hopes and dreams of their lives. 144pp. 5³⁄₁₆ x 8¼.
0-486-27275-3

STAR LORE: Myths, Legends, and Facts, William Tyler Olcott. Captivating retellings of the origins and histories of ancient star groups include Pegasus, Ursa Major, Pleiades, signs of the zodiac, and other constellations. "Classic." — *Sky & Telescope*. 58 illustrations. 544pp. 5⅜ x 8½. 0-486-43581-4

THE STRANGE CASE OF DR. JEKYLL AND MR. HYDE, Robert Louis Stevenson. This intriguing novel, both fantasy thriller and moral allegory, depicts the struggle of two opposing personalities — one essentially good, the other evil — for the soul of one man. 64pp. 5³⁄₁₆ x 8¼. 0-486-26688-5

SURVIVAL HANDBOOK: The Official U.S. Army Guide, Department of the Army. This special edition of the Army field manual is geared toward civilians. An essential companion for campers and all lovers of the outdoors, it constitutes the most authoritative wilderness guide. 288pp. 5³⁄₁₆ x 8¼. 0-486-46184-X

A TALE OF TWO CITIES, Charles Dickens. Against the backdrop of the French Revolution, Dickens unfolds his masterpiece of drama, adventure, and romance about a man falsely accused of treason. Excitement and derring-do in the shadow of the guillotine. 304pp. 5³⁄₁₆ x 8¼. 0-486-40651-2

TEN PLAYS, Anton Chekhov. *The Sea Gull, Uncle Vanya, The Three Sisters, The Cherry Orchard,* and *Ivanov,* plus 5 one-act comedies: *The Anniversary, An Unwilling Martyr, The Wedding, The Bear,* and *The Proposal.* 336pp. 5³⁄₁₆ x 8¼. 0-486-46560-8

THE FLYING INN, G. K. Chesterton. Hilarious romp in which pub owner Humphrey Hump and friend take to the road in a donkey cart filled with rum and cheese, inveighing against Prohibition and other "oppressive forms of modernity." 320pp. 5⅜ x 8½. 0-486-41910-X

THIRTY YEARS THAT SHOOK PHYSICS: The Story of Quantum Theory, George Gamow. Lucid, accessible introduction to the influential theory of energy and matter features careful explanations of Dirac's anti-particles, Bohr's model of the atom, and much more. Numerous drawings. 1966 edition. 240pp. 5⅜ x 8½. 0-486-24895-X

TREASURE ISLAND, Robert Louis Stevenson. Classic adventure story of a perilous sea journey, a mutiny led by the infamous Long John Silver, and a lethal scramble for buried treasure — seen through the eyes of cabin boy Jim Hawkins. 160pp. 5³⁄₁₆ x 8¼.
0-486-27559-0

THE TRIAL, Franz Kafka. Translated by David Wyllie. From its gripping first sentence onward, this novel exemplifies the term "Kafkaesque." Its darkly humorous narrative recounts a bank clerk's entrapment in a bureaucratic maze, based on an undisclosed charge. 176pp. 5³⁄₁₆ x 8¼. 0-486-47061-X

THE TURN OF THE SCREW, Henry James. Gripping ghost story by great novelist depicts the sinister transformation of 2 innocent children into flagrant liars and hypocrites. An elegantly told tale of unspoken horror and psychological terror. 96pp. 5³⁄₁₆ x 8¼. 0-486-26684-2

UP FROM SLAVERY, Booker T. Washington. Washington (1856-1915) rose to become the most influential spokesman for African-Americans of his day. In this eloquently written book, he describes events in a remarkable life that began in bondage and culminated in worldwide recognition. 160pp. 5³⁄₁₆ x 8¼. 0-486-28738-6

VICTORIAN HOUSE DESIGNS IN AUTHENTIC FULL COLOR: 75 Plates from the "Scientific American – Architects and Builders Edition," 1885-1894, Edited by Blanche Cirker. Exquisitely detailed, exceptionally handsome designs for an enormous variety of attractive city dwellings, spacious suburban and country homes, charming "cottages" and other structures — all accompanied by perspective views and floor plans. 80pp. 9¼ x 12¼. 0-486-29438-2

VILLETTE, Charlotte Brontë. Acclaimed by Virginia Woolf as "Brontë's finest novel," this moving psychological study features a remarkably modern heroine who abandons her native England for a new life as a schoolteacher in Belgium. 480pp. 5³⁄₁₆ x 8¼. 0-486-45557-2

THE VOYAGE OUT, Virginia Woolf. A moving depiction of the thrills and confusion of youth, Woolf's acclaimed first novel traces a shipboard journey to South America for a captivating exploration of a woman's growing self-awareness. 288pp. 5³⁄₁₆ x 8¼. 0-486-45005-8

WALDEN; OR, LIFE IN THE WOODS, Henry David Thoreau. Accounts of Thoreau's daily life on the shores of Walden Pond outside Concord, Massachusetts, are interwoven with musings on the virtues of self-reliance and individual freedom, on society, government, and other topics. 224pp. 5³⁄₁₆ x 8¼. 0-486-28495-6

WILD PILGRIMAGE: A Novel in Woodcuts, Lynd Ward. Through startling engravings shaded in black and red, Ward wordlessly tells the story of a man trapped in an industrial world, struggling between the grim reality around him and the fantasies his imagination creates. 112pp. 6⅛ x 9¼. 0-486-46583-7

WILLY POGÁNY REDISCOVERED, Willy Pogány. Selected and Edited by Jeff A. Menges. More than 100 color and black-and-white Art Nouveau–style illustrations from fairy tales and adventure stories include scenes from Wagner's "Ring" cycle, *The Rime of the Ancient Mariner, Gulliver's Travels,* and *Faust.* 144pp. 8⅜ x 11. 0-486-47046-6

WOOLLY THOUGHTS: Unlock Your Creative Genius with Modular Knitting, Pat Ashforth and Steve Plummer. Here's the revolutionary way to knit — easy, fun, and foolproof! Beginners and experienced knitters need only master a single stitch to create their own designs with patchwork squares. More than 100 illustrations. 128pp. 6½ x 9¼. 0-486-46084-3

WUTHERING HEIGHTS, Emily Brontë. Somber tale of consuming passions and vengeance — played out amid the lonely English moors — recounts the turbulent and tempestuous love story of Cathy and Heathcliff. Poignant and compelling. 256pp. 5³⁄₁₆ x 8¼. 0-486-29256-8